# Architectu Capitalism

*Architecture and Capitalism* tells a story of the relationship between the economy and architectural design. Eleven historians each discuss in brand new essays the time period they know best, looking at cultural and economic issues, which in light of current financial crises you will find have dealt with diverse but surprisingly familiar issues. Told through case studies, the narrative begins in the mid-nineteenth century and ends with 2011, with introductions by editor Peggy Deamer to pull the main themes together so that you can see how other architects in different times and in different countries have dealt with similar conditions. By focussing on what previous architects experienced, you have the opportunity to avoid repeating the past.

With new essays by Pier Vittorio Aureli, Ellen Dunham-Jones, Keller Easterling, Lauren Kogod, Robert Hewison, Joanna Merwood-Salisbury, Robin Schuldenfrei, Deborah Gans, Simon Sadler, Nathan Rich, and Michael Sorkin.

**Peggy Deamer** is a professor of architecture at Yale University, New Haven, USA.

# Architecture and Capitalism

1845 to the Present

**Peggy Deamer**

Routledge
Taylor & Francis Group

LONDON AND NEW YORK

First published 2014
by Routledge
711 Third Avenue, New York, NY 10017

Simultaneously published in the UK
by Routledge
2 Park Square, Milton Park, Abingdon, Oxon OX14 4RN

*Routledge is an imprint of the Taylor & Francis Group, an informa business*

© 2014 Taylor & Francis

*Library of Congress Cataloging in Publication Data*
Architecture and capitalism : 1845 to the present / [edited by] Peggy Deamer.
pages cm
Includes bibliographical references and index.
1. Architecture and society—History. 2. Architecture—Economic aspects. I. Deamer, Peggy, editor of compilation.
NA2543.S6A6272 2013
720.1'08—dc23
2012046775

ISBN: 978-0-415-53487-1 (hbk)
ISBN: 978-0-415-53488-8 (pbk)
ISBN: 978-0-203-49902-3 (ebk)

Typeset in Joanna and Univers
by Keystroke, Station Road, Codsall, Wolverhampton

Printed and bound in the United States of America on acid-free paper.

Acquisition Editor: Wendy Fuller
Editorial Assistant: Laura Williamson
Production Editor: Jennifer Birtill
Project Assistant to Peggy Deamer: Dariel Cobb

Printed and bound in Great Britain by
TJ International Ltd, Padstow, Cornwall

# Contents

# Contents

# Contributors

**Peggy Deamer** is Professor of Architecture at Yale University. She is also a visiting scholar at Victoria University in Wellington, New Zealand. She has taught at Parsons, Columbia, and Princeton as well as The University of Auckland, Unitec, and Victoria University in New Zealand. She received her BA from Oberlin College, her B.Arch from The Cooper Union and her Ph.D. from Princeton University. She is a principal in the firm of Deamer, Studio. She is author of the *Millennium House* (Monacelli Press, 2004) and co-editor of *Rereading Perspecta* (MIT Press, 2009) with Alan Plattus and Robert A. M. Stern. She is also the co-editor, with Phil Bernstein, of *Building in the Future: Recasting Architectural Labor* (Princeton Architectural Press, 2010) and *BIM in Academia* (Yale School of Architecture, 2011).

**Dariel Cobb** is an Assistant Professor of Architecture at the University of Hartford. She received a BA in architecture from UC Berkeley and an M.Arch from Yale where she was also a teaching Fellow in both the School of Architecture and the History of Art Department. Her recent conference publications have focused on ephemeral conceptualizations of space across cultural modes.

**Robert Hewison** has spent a lifetime working on aspects of Ruskin. His first book, *John Ruskin: The Argument of the Eye*, was published by Princeton University Press in 1976; his most recent in this field is *Ruskin on Venice: The Paradise of Cities*, published by Yale University Press in 2010. He was Slade Professor of Fine Art at Oxford and co-curator of the Tate Britain exhibition "Ruskin, Turner and the Pre-Raphaelites" in Ruskin's centenary year, 2000. He has written on the arts for the *Sunday Times* since 1981, is an Associate of the think tank Demos, and a Visiting Professor at the Ruskin research center, Lancaster University. He is writing a study of the cultural policies of the New Labour government, 1997–2010.

**Joanna Merwood-Salisbury** is Associate Professor of Architecture at Parsons The New School for Design in New York City. She is author of *Chicago 1890: The Skyscraper and the Modern City* (University of Chicago Press, 2009) and a co-editor of *After Taste: Expanded Practice in Interior Design* (Princeton Architectural Press, 2011). She has published essays on architecture and design in a number of journals including *The Journal of the Society of Architectural Historians*, *AA Files*, *Grey Room*, *Technology and Culture*, *Design Issues*, and *Lotus International*.

**Lauren Kogod** earned BFA and B.Arch at the Rhode Island School of Design, MS in Architecture at Columbia University, and is Ph.D. candidate in architectural history and theory at Harvard University, writing on reforms in the spatial organization and stylistic representation of middle-class German domestic life, 1890–1918. Kogod most recently was Lecturer in Architectural History and Theory at Yale University.

**Robin Schuldenfrei** is Junior Professor of Art History at Humboldt University, Berlin. Her publications include the edited volume *Atomic Dwelling: Anxiety, Domesticity, and Postwar Architecture* (Routledge, 2012) and with Jeffrey Saletnik, *Bauhaus Construct: Fashioning Identity, Discourse, and Modernism* (Routledge, 2009). Her research focuses on the points of convergence between design, architecture, and interior architecture, with an emphasis on the history and theory of the object, particularly its status in society. She is currently working on a full-length study of luxury and modernism in architecture and design in early twentieth-century Germany.

**Deborah Gans** is the author of *The Le Corbusier Guide*, now in its third edition, as well as numerous articles on Le Corbusier including the introduction to his *Talks With Students*. She is currently Professor in Architecture at Pratt Institute and has taught frequently as a visiting critic at Yale School of Architecture. She is an architect and principal of Gans studio.

**Simon Sadler** is Professor of Architectural and Urban History in the Department of Design at the University of California, Davis. Formerly he taught at the University of Nottingham in the UK; Trinity College, University of Dublin, Ireland; Birmingham City University, UK; and the Open University, UK. His publications include *Archigram: Architecture without Architecture* (MIT Press, 2005); *Non-Plan: Essays on Freedom, Participation and Change in Modern Architecture and Urbanism* (Architectural Press, 2000, co-editor Jonathan Hughes); and *The Situationist City* (MIT Press, 1998). He serves on the editorial board of the *Journal of Architectural Education* and the advisory board of *The Architect's Newspaper* and is a past UC Davis Chancellor's Fellow and Fellow of the Paul Mellon Center for Studies in British Art.

**Pier Vittorio Aureli** is an architect and educator. He teaches at the Architectural Association in London and he is Visiting Professor at Yale School of Architecture. His writing and teaching focus on the relationship between architectural form, political theory, and urban history. He is the author of publications including *The Possibility of an Absolute Architecture* and *The Project of Autonomy: Politics and Architecture Within and Against Capitalism*. Aureli studied at the Istituto di Architettura di Venezia (IUAV), before obtaining his PhD. from the Delft University of Technology. He has taught at the Berlage Institute, Columbia University, the Barcelona Institute of Architecture, and Delft University of Technology. Together with Martino Tattara, Aureli is the co-founder of DOGMA, an office focused on the project of the city.

**Ellen Dunham-Jones** is a Professor of Architecture and Coordinator of the MS Urban Design degree at the Georgia Institute of Technology. Her work seeks to cross-fertilize the worlds of contemporary theory and contemporary development. She is co-author with June Williamson of *Retrofitting Suburbia: Urban Design Solutions for Redesigning Suburbs* (Wiley, 2009/2011) and serves as Chair of the Board of the Congress for the New Urbanism.

**Nathan Rich** is an architect in New York City. He is currently a Project Architect at Steven Holl Architects where he works on both regional and global projects. In 2004–2005 he was a Henry Luce Scholar in Beijing, where he worked on the preservation of China's traditional hutongs. Nathan attended Wesleyan University and the Yale School of Architecture.

**Keller Easterling** is an architect and writer from New York City and a Professor at Yale University. Her book, *Enduring Innocence: Global Architecture and its Political Masquerades* (MIT, 2005) researches familiar spatial products that have landed in difficult or hyperbolic political situations around the world. A previous book, *Organization Space: Landscapes, Highways and Houses in America*, applies network theory to a discussion of American infrastructure and development formats. A forthcoming book, *Extrastatecraft: Global Infrastructure and Political Arts*, examines global infrastructure networks as a medium of polity.

**Michael Sorkin** is Principal of the Michael Sorkin Studio, President of Terreform and of the Institute for Urban Design, Distinguished Professor of Architecture, and Director of the Graduate Program in Urban Design at The City College of New York.

# Timeline

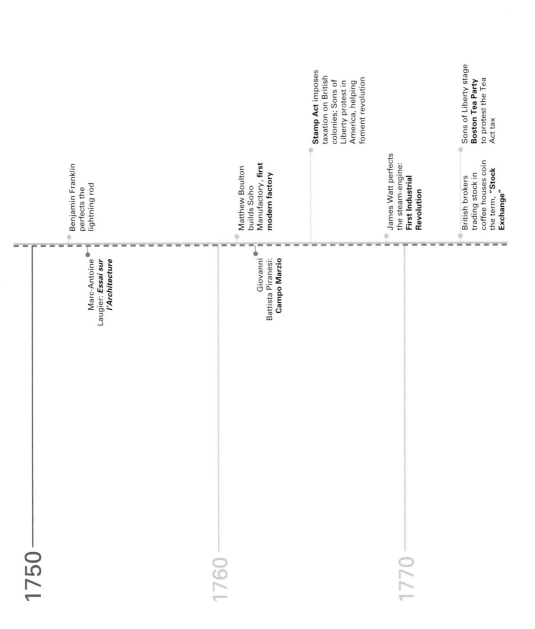

Benjamin Franklin perfects the lightning rod

Marc-Antoine Laugier: *Essai sur l'Architecture*

Matthew Boulton builds Soho Manufactory, **first modern factory**

Giovanni Battista Piranesi: **Campo Marzio**

**Stamp Act** imposes taxation on British colonies; Sons of Liberty protest in America, helping foment revolution

James Watt perfects the steam-engine: **First Industrial Revolution**

British brokers trading stock in coffee houses coin the term, **"Stock Exchange"**

Sons of Liberty stage **Boston Tea Party** to protest the Tea Act tax

1750

1760

1770

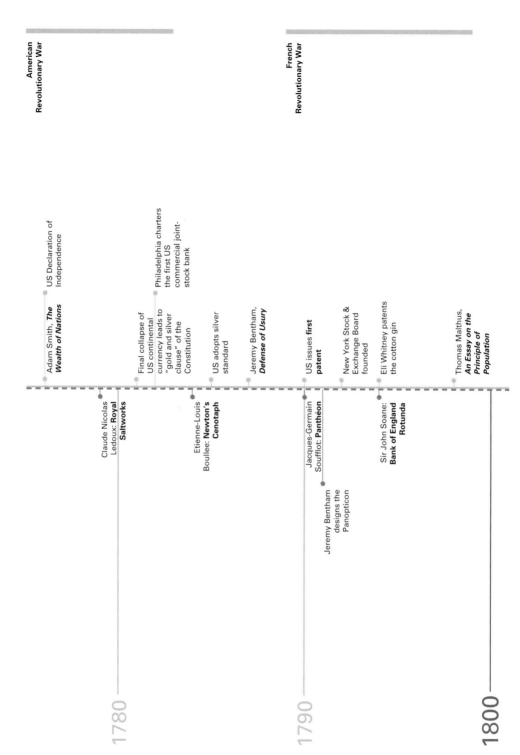

American
Revolutionary War

French
Revolutionary War

Adam Smith, *The Wealth of Nations*

US Declaration of Independence

Final collapse of US continental currency leads to "gold and silver clause" of the Constitution

Philadelphia charters the first US commercial joint-stock bank

US adopts silver standard

Jeremy Bentham, *Defense of Usury*

US issues **first patent**

New York Stock & Exchange Board founded

Eli Whitney patents the cotton gin

Thomas Malthus, *An Essay on the Principle of Population*

Claude Nicolas Ledoux: **Royal Saltworks**

Etienne-Louis Boullee: **Newton's Cenotaph**

Jacques-Germain Soufflot: **Panthéon**

Jeremy Bentham designs the Panopticon

Sir John Soane: **Bank of England Rotunda**

1780

1790

1800

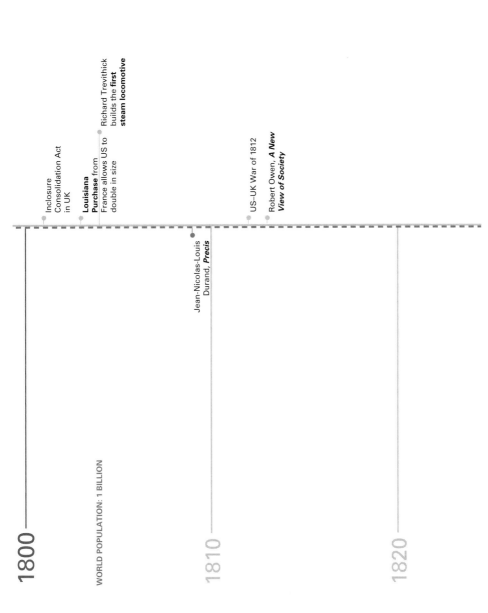

**1800**

WORLD POPULATION: 1 BILLION

Inclosure
Consolidation Act
in UK

**Louisiana
Purchase** from
France allows US to
double in size

Richard Trevithick
builds the **first
steam locomotive**

**1810**

Jean-Nicolas-Louis
Durand, *Precis*

US–UK War of 1812

Robert Owen, *A New
View of Society*

**1820**

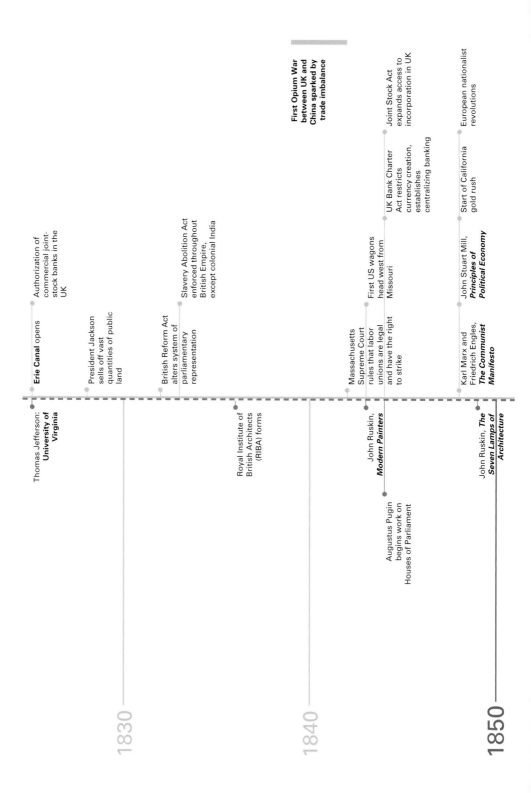

Authorization of commercial joint-stock banks in the UK

**Erie Canal** opens

Thomas Jefferson: **University of Virginia**

President Jackson sells off vast quantities of public land

Slavery Abolition Act enforced throughout British Empire, except colonial India

British Reform Act alters system of parliamentary representation

Royal Institute of British Architects (RIBA) forms

First Opium War between UK and China sparked by trade imbalance

Joint Stock Act expands access to incorporation in UK

UK Bank Charter Act restricts currency creation, establishes centralizing banking

First US wagons head west from Missouri

Massachusetts Supreme Court rules that labor unions are legal and have the right to strike

John Ruskin, *Modern Painters*

Augustus Pugin begins work on Houses of Parliament

Start of California gold rush

European nationalist revolutions

John Stuart Mill, *Principles of Political Economy*

Karl Marx and Friedrich Engles, *The Communist Manifesto*

John Ruskin, *The Seven Lamps of Architecture*

1830

1840

1850

1850

1855

1860

*The Communist Manifesto* translated into English

Gottfried Semper, *Four Elements of Architecture*

John Ruskin, *The Stones of Venice*

Joseph Paxton: **The Crystal Palace**

John Ruskin, *The Nature of Gothic*

American Institute of Architects (AIA) forms

Elisha Otis demonstrates the safety elevator

Henry Bessemer patents Bessemer Process for mass production of steel; **Second Industrial Revolution**

Limited Liability Act allows the public to create LLCs in UK

After Indian Rebellion, UK takes control of India from East India Company

Treaty of Tientsin opens China

**Obstructed trade and refusal to accept Western ambassadors leads to Second Opium War**

John Ruskin, *Unto this Last*, a critique of capitalism

Philip Webb and William Morris: **Red House**

Edward Drake starts the **world's first oil boom** in Pennsylvania

Charles Darwin, *On the Origin of Species*

John Stuart Mill, *On Liberty*

Morrill Tariff Act

US Homestead Act grants land temporarily to farming families

Legal Tender Act allows the US government to issue bonds to the public

**US Civil War**

1865

Thirteenth US Constitutional Amendment abolishes slavery

International Telegraph Union forms

Chicago Union Stockyards built

Karl Marx, *Das Kapital*

**Meiji Restoration** accelerates Japan's industrialization

Alexandre Laplanche: **Magasin au Bon Marché**, world's first department store building

1870

Knights of Labor, first significant US labor union, forms

US completes **Transcontinental Railroad**

**Suez Canal** completed

John D. Rockefeller founds **Standard Oil**

Paris Commune government

Germany unified into a single nation, Second Reich begins

Charles Garnier: **Paris Opera House**

European "Long Depression" follows collapse of demand for silver

British East India Company, founded in 1600, dissolves

Coinage Act moves US to a de-facto gold standard

**Panic of 1873;** credit crisis leads to widespread bank and railroad failure

Christopher Sholes's typewriter is mass-produced by Remington

1875

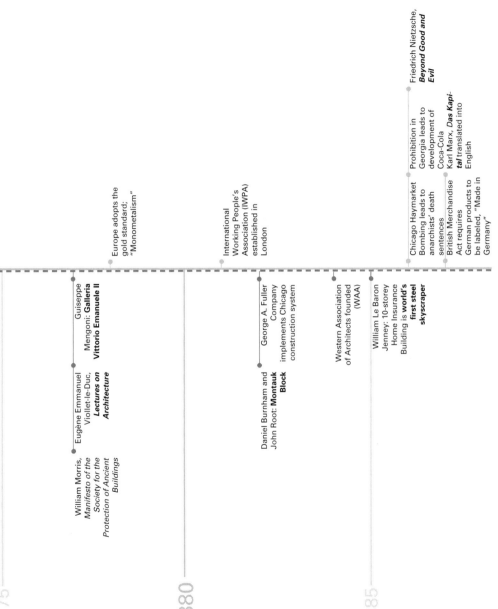

1875

William Morris,
*Manifesto of the
Society for the
Protection of Ancient
Buildings*

Eugène Emmanuel
Viollet-le-Duc,
***Lectures on
Architecture***

Guiseppe
Mengoni: **Galleria
Vittorio Emanuele II**

Europe adopts the
gold standard;
"Monometalism"

1880

Daniel Burnham and
John Root: **Montauk
Block**

George A. Fuller
Company
implements Chicago
construction system

International
Working People's
Association (IWPA)
established in
London

Western Association
of Architects founded
(WAA)

1885

William Le Baron
Jenney: 10-storey
Home Insurance
Building is **world's
first steel
skyscraper**

Chicago Haymarket
Bombing leads to
anarchists' death
sentences

British Merchandise
Act requires
German products to
be labeled, "Made in
Germany"

Prohibition in
Georgia leads to
development of
Coca-Cola

Karl Marx, *Das Kapi-
tal* translated into
English

Friedrich Nietzsche,
***Beyond Good and
Evil***

Gustave Eiffel: **La Tour Eiffel**

Daniel Burnham and John Root: **Monadnock Building**

William Morris, *News from Nowhere*

US passes **Sherman Antitrust Act**

**General Electric** forms

**Panic of 1893** results from a run on gold precipitated by poor railroad financing and bank collapse

World's Columbia Exhibition in Chicago

J.P. Morgan helps bail out the US Federal Reserve

Berlin Trade Exhibit

Start of Klondike gold rush

Ebenezer Howard, **Garden Cities of *To-Morrow***

Sigmund Freud, *The Interpretation of Dreams*

1890

1895

1900

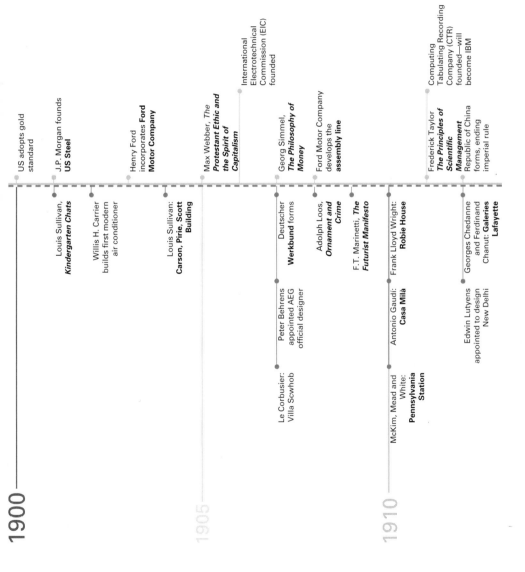

**1900**

US adopts gold standard

J.P. Morgan founds **US Steel**

Louis Sullivan, *Kindergarten Chats*

Willis H. Carrier builds first modern air conditioner

Henry Ford incorporates **Ford Motor Company**

Louis Sullivan: **Carson, Pirie, Scott Building**

Max Webber, *The Protestant Ethic and the Spirit of Capitalism*

**1905**

International Electrotechnical Commission (EIC) founded

Georg Simmel, *The Philosophy of Money*

Peter Behrens appointed AEG official designer

Deutscher **Werkbund** forms

Ford Motor Company develops the **assembly line**

Adolph Loos, *Ornament and Crime*

Le Corbusier: Villa Scwhob

F.T. Marinetti, *The Futurist Manifesto*

**1910**

Antonio Gaudí: **Casa Milà**

Frank Lloyd Wright: **Robie House**

McKim, Mead and White: **Pennsylvania Station**

Frederick Taylor *The Principles of Scientific Management*

Republic of China forms, ending imperial rule

Computing Tabulating Recording Company (CTR) founded—will become IBM

Edwin Lutyens appointed to design New Delhi

Georges Chedanne and Ferdinand Chanut: **Galeries Lafayette**

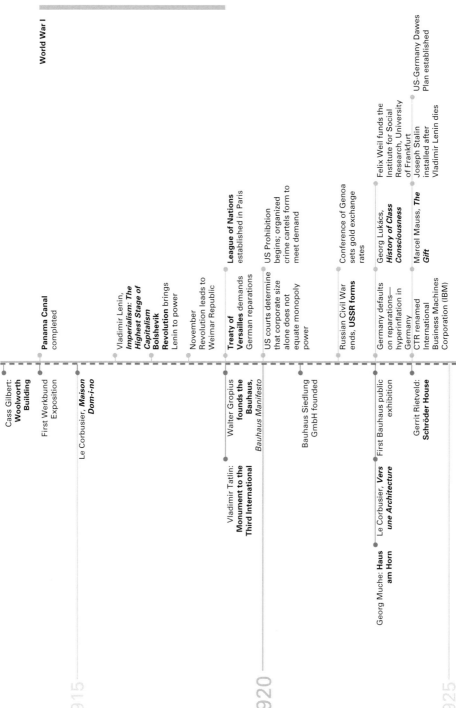

**World War I**

Cass Gilbert: **Woolworth Building**

First Werkbund Exposition

Le Corbusier, ***Maison Dom-i-no***

**Panama Canal** completed

Vladimir Lenin, ***Imperialism: The Highest Stage of Capitalism***

**Bolshevik Revolution** brings Lenin to power

November Revolution leads to Weimar Republic

Vladimir Tatlin: **Monument to the Third International**

Walter Gropius **founds the Bauhaus,** *Bauhaus Manifesto*

**League of Nations** established in Paris

**Treaty of Versailles** demands German reparations

US courts determine that corporate size alone does not equate monopoly power

US Prohibition begins; organized crime cartels form to meet demand

Bauhaus Siedlung GmbH founded

Georg Muche: **Haus am Horn**

Le Corbusier, ***Vers une Architecture***

Russian Civil War ends, **USSR forms**

Conference of Genoa sets gold exchange rates

Georg Lukács, ***History of Class Consciousness***

First Bauhaus public exhibition

Germany defaults on reparations—hyperinflation in Germany

CTR renamed International Business Machines Corporation (IBM)

Felix Weil funds the Institute for Social Research, University of Frankfurt

Marcel Mauss, ***The Gift***

Gerrit Rietveld: **Schröder House**

Joseph Stalin installed after Vladimir Lenin dies

US-Germany Dawes Plan established

1915

1920

1925

# Timeline

**1925**

**1930**

**1935**

WORLD POPULATION: 2 BILLION

Le Corbusier: **Pavillon de l'Esprit Nouveau**

Le Corbusier: **Ville Contemporaine and Plan Voisin**

Walter Gropius: **The Bauhaus School**

Philo Farnsworth demonstrates the television

Ludwig Hilberseimer: **City Plan**

Le Corbusier: **Villa Stein**

Hannes Meyer appointed head of Bauhaus architecture department

Weissenhof Estates built for Werkbund Expo

First Congrès Internationaux d'Architecture Moderne (**CIAM**)

Mies van der Rohe: **Barcelona Pavilion**

R. Buckminster Fuller: **Dymaxion House**

Wall Street crash precipitates US Great Depression

Third CIAM

William Van Alan: **Chrysler Building**

Le Corbusier: **Ville Radieuse**

Soviet Union begins its rise to industrial power

Max Horkheimer becomes director of Institute for Social Research

William Lamb: **Empire State Building**

Le Corbusier: **Villa Savoye**

British Commonwealth of Nations created

UK abandons gold standard so as to devalue the pound

Charles Ramsey and Harold Sleeper, *Architectural Graphic Standards*

Fourth CIAM, *Athens Charter*

MoMA: **International Style**

Walter Gropius: **Törten Estate**

Adolph Hitler comes to power

FDR implements **New Deal**

Albert Speer: **Zeppelinfeld Arena**

US Glass-Steagall Act establishes the **FDIC**, limits bank associations

Le Corbusier: **Plan for Algiers**

Walter Benjamin, *The Work of Art in the Age of Mechanical Reproduction*

Frank Lloyd Wright: **Fallingwater**

Giuseppe Terragni: **Casa del Fascio**

John Maynard Keynes, *The General Theory of Employment, Interest and Money*

Germany achieves complete recovery

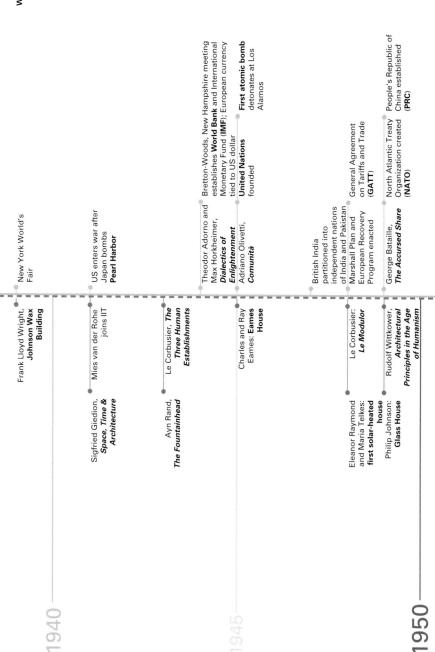

World War II

1940

Frank Lloyd Wright, **Johnson Wax Building**

New York World's Fair

Sigfried Giedion, *Space, Time & Architecture*

Mies van der Rohe joins IIT

US enters war after Japan bombs **Pearl Harbor**

Ayn Rand, *The Fountainhead*

Le Corbusier, *The Three Human Establishments*

1945

Theodor Adorno and Max Horkheimer, *Dialectics of Enlightenment*

Bretton-Woods, New Hampshire meeting establishes **World Bank** and International Monetary Fund (**IMF**); European currency tied to US dollar

Adriano Olivetti, *Comunità*

**United Nations** founded

Charles and Ray Eames: **Eames House**

**First atomic bomb** detonates at Los Alamos

British India partitioned into independent nations of India and Pakistan

Eleanor Raymond and Maria Telkes: **first solar-heated house**

Marshall Plan and European Recovery Program enacted

Le Corbusier: *Le Modulor*

General Agreement on Tariffs and Trade (**GATT**)

Philip Johnson: **Glass House**

George Bataille, *The Accursed Share*

Rudolf Wittkower, *Architectural Principles in the Age of Humanism*

North Atlantic Treaty Organization created (**NATO**)

People's Republic of China established (**PRC**)

1950

**1950**

**US-Korean War**

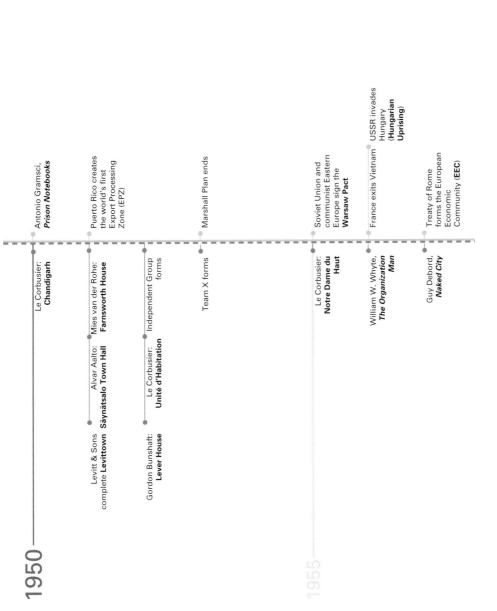

Antonio Gramsci, *Prison Notebooks*

Le Corbusier: **Chandigarh**

Puerto Rico creates the world's first Export Processing Zone (EPZ)

Mies van der Rohe: **Farnsworth House**

Alvar Aalto: **Säynätsalo Town Hall**

Levitt & Sons complete **Levittown**

Marshall Plan ends

Independent Group forms

Le Corbusier: **Unité d'Habitation**

Gordon Bunshaft: **Lever House**

Team X forms

**1955**

Soviet Union and communist Eastern Europe sign the **Warsaw Pact**

Le Corbusier: **Notre Dame du Haut**

France exits Vietnam

William W. Whyte, *The Organization Man*

USSR invades Hungary (**Hungarian Uprising**)

Treaty of Rome forms the European Economic Community (**EEC**)

Guy Debord, *Naked City*

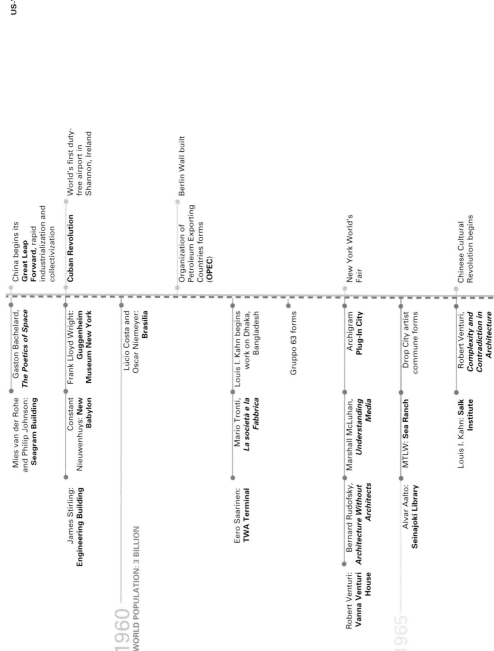

US-Vietnam War

China begins its **Great Leap Forward**, rapid industrialization and collectivization

World's first duty-free airport in Shannon, Ireland

**Cuban Revolution**

Organization of Petroleum Exporting Countries forms **(OPEC)**

Berlin Wall built

New York World's Fair

Chinese Cultural Revolution begins

Gaston Bachelard, *The Poetics of Space*

Mies van der Rohe and Philip Johnson: **Seagram Building**

Frank Lloyd Wright: **Guggenheim Museum New York**

Constant Nieuwenhuys: **New Babylon**

Lúcio Costa and Oscar Niemeyer: **Brasília**

James Stirling: **Engineering Building**

Louis I. Kahn begins work on Dhaka, Bangladesh

Mario Tronti, *La società e la Fabbrica*

Gruppo 63 forms

Archigram **Plug-In City**

Marshall McLuhan, *Understanding Media*

Drop City artist commune forms

Robert Venturi, *Complexity and Contradiction in Architecture*

Eero Saarinen: **TWA Terminal**

Bernard Rudofsky, *Architecture Without Architects*

MTLW: **Sea Ranch**

Louis I. Kahn: **Salk Institute**

Robert Venturi: **Vanna Venturi House**

Alvar Aalto: **Seinajoki Library**

1960
WORLD POPULATION: 3 BILLION

1965

US-Vietnam War

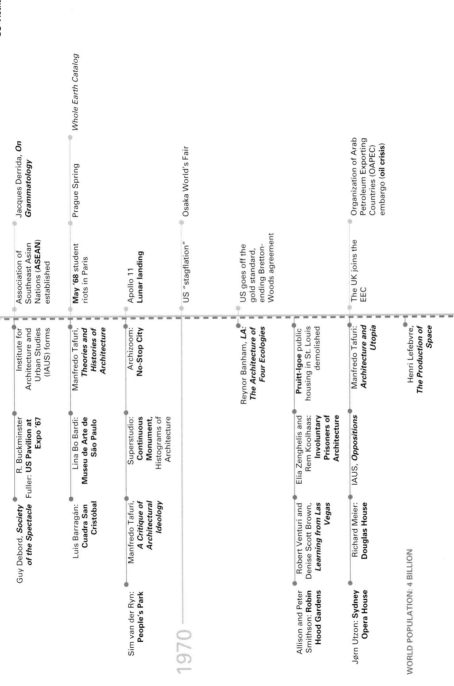

Jacques Derrida, *On Grammatology*

*Whole Earth Catalog*

Prague Spring

Osaka World's Fair

Association of Southeast Asian Nations (**ASEAN**) established

May **'68** student riots in Paris

Apollo 11 **Lunar landing**

US "stagflation"

US goes off the gold standard, ending Bretton-Woods agreement

The UK joins the EEC

Organization of Arab Petroleum Exporting Countries (OAPEC) embargo (**oil crisis**)

Guy Debord, *Society of the Spectacle*

R. Buckminster Fuller: **US Pavilion at Expo '67**

Institute for Architecture and Urban Studies (IAUS) forms

Manfredo Tafuri, *Theories and Histories of Architecture*

Lina Bo Bardi: **Museu de Arte de São Paulo**

Archizoom: **No-Stop City**

Reynor Banham, *LA: The Architecture of Four Ecologies*

**Pruitt-Igoe** public housing in St. Louis demolished

Manfredo Tafuri: *Architecture and Utopia*

Henri Lefebvre, *The Production of Space*

Luis Barragán: **Cuadra San Cristóbal**

Manfredo Tafuri, *A Critique of Architectural Ideology*

Superstudio: **Continuous Monument,** Histograms of Architecture

Robert Venturi and Denise Scott Brown, *Learning from Las Vegas*

Elia Zenghelis and Rem Koolhaas: **Involuntary Prisoners of Architecture**

IAUS, *Oppositions*

Sim van der Ryn: **People's Park**

Allison and Peter Smithson: **Robin Hood Gardens**

Richard Meier: **Douglas House**

Jørn Utzon: **Sydney Opera House**

1970

WORLD POPULATION: 4 BILLION

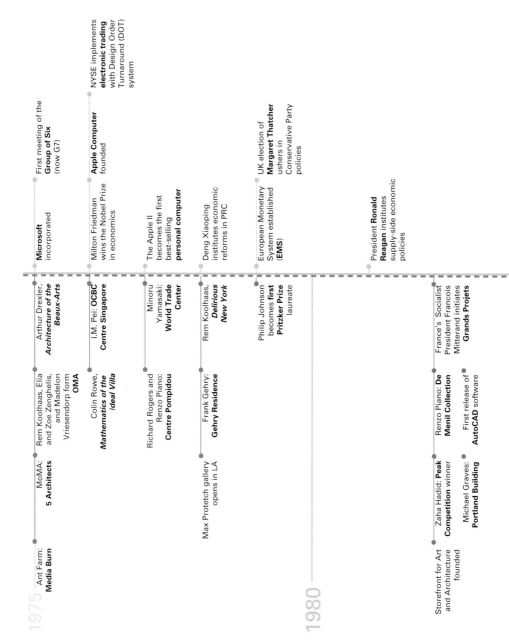

**1975** — Ant Farm: **Media Burn**

First meeting of the **Group of Six** (now G7)

NYSE implements **electronic trading** with Design Order Turnaround (DOT) system

Arthur Drexler, *Architecture of the Beaux-Arts*

MoMA: **5 Architects**

Rem Koolhaas, Elia and Zoe Zenghelis, and Madelon Vriesendorp form **OMA**

**Microsoft** incorporated

**Apple Computer** founded

I.M. Pei: **OCBC Centre Singapore**

Colin Rowe, *Mathematics of the Ideal Villa*

Milton Friedman wins the Nobel Prize in economics

Minoru Yamasaki: **World Trade Center**

Richard Rogers and Renzo Piano: **Centre Pompidou**

The Apple II becomes the first best-selling **personal computer**

Rem Koolhaas, *Delirious New York*

Frank Gehry: **Gehry Residence**

Deng Xiaoping institutes economic reforms in PRC

Philip Johnson becomes **first Pritzker Prize** laureate

Max Protetch gallery opens in LA

European Monetary System established (**EMS**)

UK election of **Margaret Thatcher** ushers in Conservative Party policies

President **Ronald Reagan** institutes supply-side economic policies

France's Socialist President Francois Mitterand initiates **Grands Projets**

Renzo Piano: **De Menil Collection**

First release of **AutoCAD** software

Storefront for Art and Architecture founded

Zaha Hadid: **Peak Competition** winner

Michael Graves: **Portland Building**

**1980**

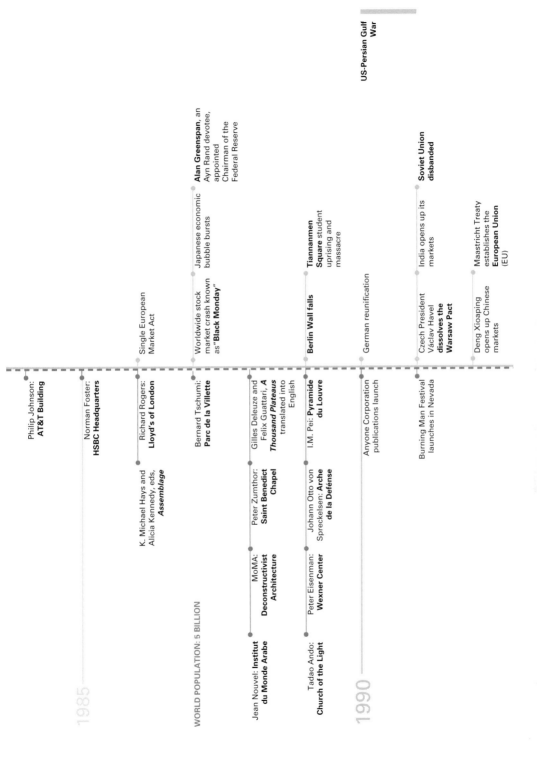

Philip Johnson:
**AT&T Building**

Norman Foster:
**HSBC Headquarters**

K. Michael Hays and
Alicia Kennedy, eds,
***Assemblage***

Richard Rogers:
**Lloyd's of London**

Single European
Market Act

Bernard Tschumi:
**Parc de la Villette**

Worldwide stock
market crash known
as "**Black Monday**"

**Alan Greenspan**, an
Ayn Rand devotee,
appointed
Chairman of the
Federal Reserve

Peter Zumthor:
**Saint Benedict
Chapel**

Gilles Deleuze and
Felix Guattari, **A
*Thousand Plateaus***
translated into
English

Japanese economic
bubble bursts

MoMA:
**Deconstructivist
Architecture**

Johann Otto von
Spreckelsen: **Arche
de la Défense**

I.M. Pei: **Pyramide
du Louvre**

**Tiannanmen
Square** student
uprising and
massacre

WORLD POPULATION: 5 BILLION

Jean Nouvel: **Institut
du Monde Arabe**

Peter Eisenman:
**Wexner Center**

**Berlin Wall falls**

German reunification

Tadao Ando:
**Church of the Light**

Anyone Corporation
publications launch

Czech President
Václav Havel
**dissolves the
Warsaw Pact**

India opens up its
markets

**Soviet Union
disbanded**

Burning Man Festival
launches in Nevada

Deng Xioaping
opens up Chinese
markets

Maastricht Treaty
establishes the
**European Union**
(EU)

**US-Persian Gulf
War**

1985

1990

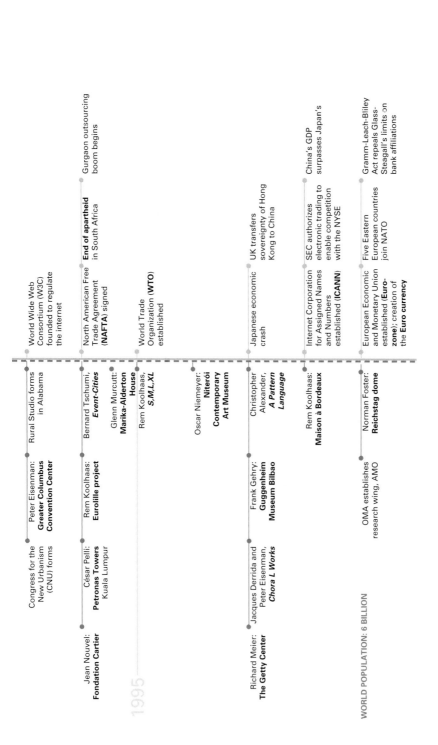

1995

WORLD POPULATION: 6 BILLION

**World events**

- World Wide Web Consortium (W3C) founded to regulate the internet
- North American Free Trade Agreement (NAFTA) signed
- World Trade Organization (WTO) established
- End of apartheid in South Africa
- Gurgaon outsourcing boom begins
- Japanese economic crash
- UK transfers sovereignty of Hong Kong to China
- Internet Corporation for Assigned Names and Numbers established (ICANN)
- SEC authorizes electronic trading to enable competition with the NYSE
- China's GDP surpasses Japan's
- European Economic and Monetary Union established (Eurozone); creation of the Euro currency
- Five Eastern European countries join NATO
- Gramm–Leach–Bliley Act repeals Glass-Steagall's limits on bank affiliations

**Architecture**

- Jean Nouvel: Fondation Cartier
- Congress for the New Urbanism (CNU) forms
- Peter Eisenman: Greater Columbus Convention Center
- Rural Studio forms in Alabama
- César Pelli: Petronas Towers Kuala Lumpur
- Rem Koolhaas: Eurolille project
- Bernard Tschumi, Event-Cities
- Glenn Murcutt: Marika-Alderton House
- Rem Koolhaas, S,M,L,XL
- Oscar Niemeyer: Niterói Contemporary Art Museum
- Richard Meier: The Getty Center
- Jacques Derrida and Peter Eisenman, Chora L Works
- Frank Gehry: Guggenheim Museum Bilbao
- Rem Koolhaas: Maison à Bordeaux
- OMA establishes research wing, AMO
- Norman Foster: Reichstag dome

# 2000

**US-Afghan War**

**US-Iraq War**

Thom Mayne: **Graduate House**

Toyo Ito: **Sendai Mediatheque**

Jacques Herzog and Pierre de Meuron: **Tate Modern**

Norman Foster: **Millennium Dome, Millennium Bridge**

Antonio Negri and Michael Hardt, *Empire*

Dot-com speculative stock bubble bursts

Rem Koolhaas & Harvard GSD, *Harvard Guide to Shopping*

Santiago Calatrava: **Milwaukee Art Museum**

Daniel Libeskind: **Jewish Museum Berlin**

IBM shows that algorithms consistently outperform human stock traders

Jim O'Neill coins the term **BRIC** to refer to the growth economies of Brazil, Russia, India, and China

**9/11**—World Trade Center towers destroyed by terrorist attack

Elizabeth Diller and Ricardo Scofidio: **Blur Building**

Alejandro Zaera Polo and Farshid Moussavi: **Yokohama Port Terminal**

Zaha Hadid: **Contemporary Arts Center**

**Facebook** launches

Kazuyo Seijima and Ryue Nishizawa: **21st Century Museum**

Rem Koolhaas: **Seattle Public Library**

Enlargement of NATO and EU to include seven former Eastern Bloc nations

Autodesk markets **Revit** software

**Kyoto Protocol** on climate change comes into effect

**Twitter** launches

2005

Wang Shu: China **Academy of Art Phase II**

Dow hits historic high above 14,000

Sub-prime housing crisis emerges

Jacques Herzog and
Pierre de Meuron:
**Beijing National
Stadium**

Market crash, Dow
falls below 7,500—
global financial crisis
and recession

Troubled Asset
Relief Program
(**TARP**) signed into
law

UK Banking Special
Provisions Act
allows for bank
seizure and
nationalization

Tea Party
movement
emerges

Rem Koolhaas: **CCTV
Headquarters**

European sovereign
debt crisis begins

SOM: **Burj Khalifa**
is world's tallest
building

BRIC country
leaders hold their
first formal summit

European Central
Bank begins buying
up EU sovereign debt

South Africa gains
entry to BRIC
group, now BRICS

**Occupy Wall Street**
forms

Tunisian President
Ben Ali flees, **Arab
Spring** spreads to
Egypt

US-Iraq War

US-Afghan War

Rem Koolhaas:
**Shenzhen Stock
Exchange**

BIAD UFo: **Phoenix
International Media
Center, Beijing**

2010

WORLD POPULATION: 7 BILLION

2015

# Preface

## Peggy Deamer

This book is the result of two seminars I gave at Yale School of Architecture in 2010 and 2011 entitled, "Architecture and Capitalism." Those seminars were the outgrowth of another that I had given in 2008, "Architecture, Post-9/11," which itself was a development of the final week of a Contemporary Theory class that I taught, the week that was most speculative and hardest for me to present coherently. The move from one topic to the other was my trying to attack the thing that was least clear and most curious to me. It seemed that what I knew from Critical Theory didn't totally explain what I understood was happening to architecture after 9/11, which is to say, architecture was simultaneously being asked to be more relevant—at last we were no longer merely debating blob versus box—at the same time that architecture theory went into retreat. It seemed mysterious that just as theory, like practice, had something meaty to grab onto, it shied away. The students in that 9/11 seminar were fabulous and alert to issues that I had not imagined, many of them economic: who were the players in the rebuilding of the WTC site; how was the Superdome in New Orleans being financed; how was environmentalism being sold to us (or not)? I realized from this that one could not disengage architectural discussions—professional or theoretical—from issues of money, and that I wanted to know more.

But the foregrounding of money then sat oddly with my architectural interest in craft and design; a direct $ = artifact formula was inconceivable. What was not inconceivable was my conviction that craft was an attitude of the maker/designer (that itself is a funny schism in architecture); that that attitude was linked to a person's (or group of people's) feeling about the work they were given to do; and that that was linked to their economic condition. One couldn't disengage design from subjectivity or subjectivity from the circumstances of labor. This part of my interest—visiting firms and factories in the US and China where architecture was actually being produced (both designed and made)—was supported by two grants from the Yale Grisold Fund, and I am indebted to them for this. The foregrounding of money also seemed so utterly substantive and interesting even if economics was not part of my background; wouldn't all of us theorists love to chew on this issue, particularly as the recession hit us all so hard? Well, yes, but no one really seemed to be doing it other than celebrating the advantages of thinking about architecture like we think of Nike: respond to the market!

Hence the "Architecture and Capitalism" seminars. And here, too, the students were stimulating. Not only did they research subjects that were enlightening, but they gave me faith that in an era of post-criticality, criticality was still alive. A number of those students deserve special thanks, but in particular, Carmel Greer, whose paper on risk mitigation and coolness needs to be published, and Nathan Rich, whose paper on Gurgaon developed into one of the chapters here, deserve particular recognition.

When Routledge asked if a book could be produced on Architecture and Capitalism, it was a chance to engage authors who were experts in areas that my students and I had waded through inelegantly. And I am indebted to all of these authors who in every case offered more than I had expected. But thanks must go to Wendy Fuller from Routledge for providing this opportunity and making it happen and then to Laura Williamson for so cheerfully moving it along.

Beyond that, there are people who I have worked with over the last years whose thinking, even if not directly on architecture and capitalism, has influenced mine regarding the state of the profession at this (really bad economic) time. Phil Bernstein, with whom I co-sponsored two symposia and co-edited two books on building in the future and BIM, is one of these. He has been an excellent and committed colleague. Paolo Tombesi, with whom I collaborated on grant proposals and articles on BIM, is another. A chapter by him on how BIM is affected by and affecting the finances of the profession needs to be part of the next book. Likewise, I owe thanks to Mary McLeod, who was a sounding-board for the book along the way and whose "Architecture and Politics in the Reagan Era: From Post-Modernism to Deconstruction" (*Assemblage* 8, February 1989) is one of the few examples of an in-depth examination of an economic context and its implications for architectural production. It is an article that needs to be read by anyone who is interested in this topic. Likewise, I need to thank Reinhold Martin for his patience with my back and forth with him on this topic.

Finally I need to thank Dariel Cobb for taking on the task of assisting me in editing this book. It is not just that she has done the (huge amount of) grunt work in making sure that everything from text to image is as it should be; she has also been an invaluable intellectual colleague that has made what would have been a lonely endeavor spirited, fun, and shared.

# Introduction

## Peggy Deamer

Because building a building costs so much money, construction—and within it, architecture—necessarily works for and within the monetary system. One could say that the history of architecture is the history of capital. But, while this is obvious, architectural history, especially as it is handed to us in the US, is oddly devoid of examinations of this relationship. Either it is assumed that this connection is less interesting than one which traces the relationship of one architectural style to another style or to a philosophic position, or the dominance of theories of architectural autonomy overtly exclude such an examination. After all, autonomy insists that architecture speaks and develops its own language in its own history relatively independent of world events. This anthology wants to make clear that there is a relationship, and not just to world events in general, but to the economic condition that enfolds those events.

Having said this, *Architecture and Capitalism: 1845 to the Present* starts from the position that this relationship is rarely direct; that the economy at a given time and place sets the stage for certain cultural productions to be desirable, with architects acting out their design positions accordingly. For all that Heinrich Wolfflin is disparaged today for his formal and formulaic approach to art history, he was wise in pointing out that certain periods of history can only "see" in certain ways, having no consciousness of alternative organizational, visual, or formal schemas. He certainly did not link the circumstances defining these limits to the economy, but he lays out the condition that we wish to pursue here: that it is our cultural desires that shape what architects talk about and see. This anthology suggests that capitalism, in different ways, in different cultures, and in different historical periods shapes those cultural desires and, indeed, makes those desires so desirable that they often seem to fill natural needs.

Another way of saying this might be that this anthology assumes, in the Marxist distinction between base and superstructure, that architecture operates as much in the superstructure as in the base. While the construction industry participates energetically in the economic engine that is the base, architecture (particularly as a design practice) operates in the realm of culture, allowing capital to do its work without its effects being scrutinized. This position then mediates the above indication that this volume challenges the tenants of architectural autonomy. It suggests rather that the issues shaping architectural practice *are* particular to architecture *per se*, but insists that that particularity does not exclude the discipline from the effect of complex extra-architectural conditions, like money. But here, too, it has to be said that historically, the connection between capital and architecture has not been *so* mysterious; architects in the not-so-distant (European) past actually did build their practices around their overtly formulated economic positions. One of the things that inspired this book was the opportunity to expose how politically and economically engaged many of our admired historical architects really were.

If all of architecture is a manifestation of capital, what forms the selections in this anthology? The first consideration, the time frame and sequence, is determined by the advent of industrial society and with it, the self-conscious awareness of the working of capitalism. While this ostensibly begins with Adam Smith's *The Wealth of Nations* in 1776, its connection to the built environment via the conditions of industrialization comes to the fore in the mid-nineteenth century with the work of John Stuart Mill (*Principles of Political Economy*, 1848) and Karl Marx (*Das Kapital*, 1867). Therefore, the anthology begins at this period and moves up to the present in a chronological manner. Capitalism is an unstable phenomenon—what it is and how it operates changes constantly and not just via movements between bull and bear markets, recessions and expansions, *laissez-faire* advocacy and regulation, but in its relationship to culture and power. If, as was mentioned above, the connection between capital and architecture is indirect, it is also nimble and mutant. The chronology is essential to grasping capitalism's changing character and, hence, its changing relationship to architecture.

The second consideration, the determination of what constitutes "architecture," is more dicey. Certainly, architecture excludes the world of construction that excludes architects; that is, it excludes those developments that are guided by a profit margin unable or unwilling to pay for professional architectural services. It also excludes the larger category of urban development that is so closely tied to politics and economics that it, again, would be a history of the built environment everywhere. Indeed, these chapters adhere to projects and productions that are, for the most part, squarely in the pantheon of "architecture history," the aim being to re-examine old stories, filling in information regarding the effects of the economic context. The intention is not to unearth new projects that expose links between power brokers; rather, the chapters here are meant as historiographical adjustments. In this way a conversation ensues; if the time frame and chronology are set by capitalism, the actual choice of stories is shaped by architecture history.

The third directive is to follow case studies rather than fill out general periods of architectural history. While this precludes comprehensiveness, it allows the specifics of the relationship between capital and architecture to be examined more closely. From the standpoint of architecture, the economy shows its effects in a number of ways. Money has implications for those who own the property, who develop the property, who design the building, who actually build the building, who experience the architecture visually, who occupy the building, and who control its dissemination through media. The "subject" of architecture, like that of capital, is not stable, and the specificity of the case studies is instrumental in covering the various and differing ways in which economics affect architecture. In some cases, the architectural issue is labor; in others, it is affordability; in others still, image and propaganda. We could say more bluntly that sometimes the pertinent architectural condition is on the supply side and other times on the demand side. Likewise, the emphasis on case studies allows a specific examination of the political context in which a group of architects are working. If these various case studies aim to expose the particular connections between architecture and the economy, they also expose the particular way that each nation state, either overtly or not, administers the mechanisms of these connections.

Having said this, it proved less interesting (or less possible) to stick with an emphasis on architecture in all cases. Early on, in Chicago at the turn of the century, the skyscrapers under analysis are as much a structural condition as they are one of design. And as the chapters move into the twenty-first century, practices that become interesting are often oblivious to the hand of the architect. Globalization obliterates national differences and it smooths out the distinction between major and minor architects as both are invited to design Asian and Southeast Asian towns from scratch, as the example of Gurgaon shows. The final chapter, "Liberal," is seen as a coda because it leaves the case study model altogether as it discusses not architecture, but infrastructure, and reflects back critically on the terms that we today associate (even in this anthology) with the politics and economics of the built environment.

Despite all of this rationalization, the make-up of this book has to be largely arbitrary and certainly incomplete. For every chapter that is here, there are three others that rightly can be seen as absolutely essential. There are gaps in time and there are gaps in practices and certainly there are gaps in adjudication. The hope of this book is to act as a first foray that will initiate the production of a more thorough history of the relationship between architecture and capitalism. The timeline included in this anthology as well as the short introductions to each chapter are meant to bridge the gaps between chapters and contextualize the diversity of case studies within the history of capitalism. But they are meant as well as invitations to imagine and then write the stories that are left untold here.

Clearly, this book, while about capitalism, is indebted to those who have devoted themselves to its critique, Marx in particular. As analyses of capitalism's multifarious modes of operation, Marxism, neo-Marxism, and the Critical Theory of the Frankfurt School has informed the terms by which this editor and a number of the authors understand the subject-matter. It has as well shaped the thinking of the various cultural analysts who direct architectural debates in a given architectural era, influencing the intellectual arena of cultural production of their time. And finally, more than has traditionally been told, a number of the architects discussed *themselves* approach(ed) their work with a socialist agenda. For contemporary readers, especially in the US, it is still surprising to learn that many of the masters we revere for their formal expertise understood their work as a critique of capitalism. Whether they were largely deceived in their faith in this critique, as Manfredo Tafuri claims, does not disallow the affect it had on their work. The hope is that this anthology will open up debates about the relationship of architecture and capitalism that include non-Marxist orientations. There must be a contemporary Ayn Rand out there that architecture could hear from.

All of this intellectual positioning shapes scholarly allegiances and the choice of authors invited to contribute to this volume; so does appreciation of the expertise of the authors in the relevant periods. Still, in almost every case, the authors brought something much newer and unexpected to both the topics and to their analyses than had been imagined, such that the book as a whole has taken on a life of its own, one that is considerably richer than the one planned and certainly much more fun to be a part of. I am indebted to all of them for both the wealth of information that they have brought to the table and for their enthusiasm and commitment to the topic of this book.

# Chapter 1

# Context: 1800–1860

Morality, progress, and criticism of progress: all of these were bound up in the architectural thinking of the nineteenth century, as witnessed by the moral fervor attending the Gothic Revival as it reacted to the Industrial Revolution. John Ruskin for his belief in the moral labor that seemingly attended the making of the Gothic; William Morris for his support of the vernacular epitomized by medieval ad hocism;[1] Augustus Pugin for the Gothic style's link to Catholicism: these were varied projections put on the Gothic as the architectural community fashioned a way to take a stance against the physical indignities that accompanied the Industrial Revolution.

Placed in the context of a market economy, the Gothic Revival was a shock response to the full-blown emergence of capitalism, itself a latent reaction to the rise of mercantilism in England over the two centuries prior. Mercantilism is a nascent form of capitalism in that labor is contractual, and trade is made for profit. This early capitalist economy was preceded by the collapse of the medieval manorial system in England, which created a class of free tenant-farmers. Rather than relying on fealty and taxation, Lords had to hire labor to work their estates, thus creating incentive to invest in efficient production technologies.[2]

During a concomitant period of enclosure, public lands were transferred to these same large (aristocratic) landowners who used the surplus to graze sheep rather than produce food. As England's wool exports grew in the fifteenth century, the process of single-owner land expansion accelerated, forcing many tenants to give up farming and seek wage-labor.[3] Yet commodities were still produced by non-capitalist production methods. Merchants operated within large monopolies backed by state (i.e. royal) control and state subsidies, such as the British East India Company, in which the state superseded local guilds as economic regulator. This period also saw overseas merchants "discover" new lands, resulting in the rapid growth in overseas trade.

Economic theorists, led by Adam Smith, challenged fundamental mercantilist doctrines. In *The Wealth of Nations* (1776), Smith sought to reveal the nature and cause of a nation's prosperity, therein introducing the terms and tenants of industrial capitalism. One of these was his famous dictum that the laborer is "led by an invisible hand to promote an end which was no part of his intention," his intention being selfish but the outcome benefitting all in the expansion of the economy. Another lasting notion was his production of pins analogy supporting the division of labor: ten workers could produce 48,000 pins per day if each of eighteen specialized tasks was assigned to particular workers, but absent the division of labor, Smith pointed out, a worker would barely be able to produce one pin per day.

In the 1830s, reality caught up with these theoretical observations. England's economy became characterized by a competitive labor market, the investment of capital into machinery, the division of labor, the routinization of tasks, and the replacement of the merchant by the industrialist as the principal player in the economic system. Industrial capitalism had now emerged.

This new form of capitalism emerged with further theoretical assistance. In *Principles of Political Economy* (1848), John Stuart Mill posits that capital has nothing to do with the actual product produced, but rather with the purpose to which the labor of the product is put, which is to say, *productive reinvestment*. He also describes how the value of labor is not set by the product nor even by the sustenance of labor, but by the "convenience" of reimbursing skilled over unskilled labor. Mill was, in other words, expounding on the arbitrary nature of wages.

Karl Marx, a contemporary of Mill (but much less widely read; Marx's *Kapital* was not translated into a volume in English until 1887),[4] also analyzed the arbitrary nature of wages, but saw in it not just a fact of capitalism but rather its degrading essence. Marx's historical perspective—his Hegelian *dialectic* of thesis (agrarian serfs), antithesis (capitalist manufacturing), and synthesis (communism)—and his social agenda—his anti-Hegelian, anti-idealism *materialism* (man's alienated material, labor existence under capitalism)—were part of a larger awakening regarding social "progress" and historical determinism, as seen in the contemporary Victorian work of Charles Dickens and Charles Darwin.

It is in this tumultuous context that Robert Hewison examines the lives and work of contemporaries John Ruskin and Henry Cole. The former may be distilled as the revivalist "romantic," the latter as the modern "pragmatic," but in fact each man had a nuanced view of the economy and of the role of architecture and design within it.

Peggy Deamer

## Notes

1  William Morris alone of these was a reader of Marx. He was a socialist in both practice—his workshop, Morris, Marshall, and Faulkner, being based on the guild model extolled by Marx; and in theory—his utopian novel, *News from Nowhere* (1890), speculating on a society where work was not paid for but voluntary and communally enjoyed.

2  Niall Ferguson, *The Ascent of Money* (New York: Penguin, 2008).

3  Quentin Skinner, *The Foundations of Modern Political Thought, vol I: The Renaissance; vol II: The Age of Reformation* (Cambridge: Cambridge University Press, 1978).

4  Marx's initial volume of *Kapital* appeared in Germany in 1867, but did not appear in English until the journal *To-day*, under Hyndman's editorship, began to serialize it in 1885. *Kapital* lacked an English translation in one volume until the publication of Engels's edition in 1887.

Chapter 1

# Straight lines or curved? The Victorian values of John Ruskin and Henry Cole

Robert Hewison

This essay describes the points of intersection between two figures who have equal right to be described as Great Victorians who shaped the conditions of aesthetic production, yet whose individual personalities, attitudes and ambitions are so diametrically opposed as to represent the longitude and latitude of Victorian cultural values: John Ruskin and Henry Cole. While Ruskin was almost an exact contemporary of Queen Victoria, born the same year and dying just one year ahead of her, Cole was born in 1807 and died in 1882. This calendrical discrepancy is somewhat adjusted, however, by Ruskin's withdrawal into silence after 1889, and the fact that both came into prominence in the early 1840s, at a time of social and economic distress, when industrialization and the expansion of British cities raised important issues of morality and aesthetics for architecture and design. Their intertwined legacies reveal the issues that emerged in the developing conditions of industrial production in the nineteenth century.

Both were larger-than-life personalities, figures who not only shaped their own age, but who left an intellectual and institutional legacy as reformers. Ruskin—"the Professor"—became a Victorian sage who dedicated himself first to the reform of the Victorian visual economy, and then to the reform of the nation's moral and political economy as a whole. Cole—"King Cole"—was a man of administrative action, whose monuments not only include London's early cultural quarter "Albertopolis," the Victoria and Albert Museum and the Royal

Albert Hall of the Arts and Sciences, but the institution of the Public Record Office, the establishment of the Penny Post, reform of patent law, the standard railway gauge, and the National Training School for Cookery.

Both had an interest in that great, now much neglected Victorian legacy, drains—Ruskin with his schemes to dam the waters of the Alps, Cole with his unhappy involvement with Scott's Sewage Company, of which he became Managing Director on his retirement from the South Kensington Museum (later the V&A) in 1873. Both wrote for children: Ruskin's *The King of the Golden River* remains in print to this day; Cole published a series of picture books under the genial *nom-de-plume* of Felix Summerly.

As reformers, both had to be communicators. Ruskin published the first volume of *Modern Painters* in 1843 as the anonymous "graduate of Oxford," but in the 1850s he discovered his power as an enthralling lecturer, and the force of his personality was a significant energizer of his arguments. The much-expanded medium of the Press played an important part in their efforts to influence people. Like Cole, Ruskin was an inveterate writer to the newspapers, though unlike Cole, he was not in the habit of answering his own letters under other, assumed names. Cole, thanks to his family lodging in the house of the novelist and man of letters Thomas Love Peacock, had early experience as a theater, music and art critic, and was in the habit of launching newspapers and journals to promote his ideas. Ruskin published his first articles on architecture as an undergraduate. In 1871 he was to launch his own public newsletter, a Victorian form of blog, *Fors Clavigera*, addressed to the workmen and laborers of Great Britain.

Cole fully understood, much better than Ruskin, the art of public relations. He describes in his uncompleted memoirs, *Fifty Years of Public Work*, how "the proprietors in the London and North Western Railway engaged my services to create a public opinion to support Uniformity of Gauge as best for national interests."[1] It was Cole who ensured that the Press should have free tickets to the Great Exhibition.[2]

Both men, as forceful characters, could be hated. Cole's daughter describes him as "acting more or less as a despot with plenary powers on various occasions" over the dispositions of Albertopolis.[3] During his campaign to promote the building of the Royal Albert Hall in the 1860s, the Prime Minister Lord Derby described Cole as "the most generally unpopular man I know."[4] *The Birmingham Town Crier* satirized his sewage schemes:

> Sir Henry Cole was a funny old soul
> A funny old soul was he:
> His hat and his locks
> His collar and stocks
> Proclaimed him a rarity.[5]

Ruskin's views on art, as well as his views on political economy, could make him unpopular, too. In 1856, *Punch* published the following "Poem by a Perfectly Furious Academician":

> I takes and paints
> Hears no complaints
> And sells before I'm dry;
> Till savage Ruskin
> Sticks his tusks in
> Then nobody will buy.[6]

Both were, in the best sense, amateur artists, though Ruskin was undoubtedly the greater of the two. Cole had drawing lessons from David Cox— an artist collected by Ruskin's father—and attended lectures at the Royal Academy, though he found Turner's lectures on perspective "almost perfection in mumbling and unintelligibility."[7] Ruskin—for whom Turner was hero and friend—was taught by the best drawing masters of his day. This personal experience of art helps to explain their belief in art as a vehicle for reform, though, as will be shown, their opinions on what kind of art diverged. (Cole boastfully records in his memoirs: "I believe I originated, in 1845, the term 'Art Manufactures', meaning Fine Art, or beauty applied to mechanical production."[8] This was something Ruskin was instinctively against, and would have regarded as an oxymoron.)

In both cases, whatever the difference of definition, they believed in the redemptive possibilities offered by access to good art and architecture for members of the working class. They concurred that the fundamental means of understanding and appreciating art was through the practice of drawing. Both established drawing schools: Ruskin his School of Drawing at Oxford in the 1870s—today's Ruskin School of Drawing and Fine Art—Cole the national system of art education formulated in the 1850s, of which the national training school was to become the Royal College of Art. And both believed in the concomitant value of museums as teaching institutions and places of moral recreation. While the Victoria and Albert Museum has its origins in Cole's decision to form a Museum of Ornamental Art following the Great Exhibition, Ruskin's modest Museum of the Guild of St George, now rehoused in the Millennium Galleries in Sheffield, was just a fragment of a grand design.

An important social factor that these young men had in common was that they were both, in Marx's terms, *bourgeois*. Cole was the son of a Dragoon officer wounded in a street riot in Dublin who as a result of his injuries was forced to become a recruiting officer, and then became a coal merchant. Ruskin was altogether wealthier, but his origins were modest. His grandfather had been an Edinburgh grocer who failed in business, and later committed suicide. His father, John James Ruskin, worked hard as a London clerk, and founded the sherry firm of Ruskin, Telford and Domecq, making a fortune that bought his son a gentleman's education at Christ Church, Oxford, and the freedom never to have to work for a living. Cole was poor, but had a scholarship to Christ's Hospital in London where he learned a good enough writing hand to secure, in 1823, the position of a copyist in the Record Commission, the start of his civil service career.

As members of the rising middle classes, the key moment for both of them was the passage of the Reform Act of 1832, which did away with a decayed and corrupt system of parliamentary representation. This was the symbolic moment of the entry into power and at least partial enfranchisement of a new class with new attitudes, and new tastes. It is here that the differences appear.

As the older man, Cole was the one who experienced most directly the political ferment and agitation that preceded the passage of the Reform Bill. Cole was closely connected to the promoters of the Bill, the so-called Philosophic Radicals grouped around James Mill, and his son John Stuart Mill. Cole was introduced to Mill by his landlord, Thomas Love Peacock, who, like Mill and his father, was an official at East India House. They first met on 7 November 1826, not long after Mill's nervous breakdown as a result of the rigorous education imposed by his father. Thus Cole joined Mill's circle at the beginning of the second stage of the Utilitarian project, when Mill's liberalism began to influence the management of government. Although Jeremy Bentham's principles for administrative reform are mentioned almost immediately in Cole's memoirs,[9] Cole was not oppressively Benthamite in the manner evoked by Michel Foucault in his *Surveiller et Punir*. He did read Saint-Simon, but an entry in his diary for 7 January 1831 casts an interesting light on his views. "In the evening reading a review of Tennyson's poems in the W.R. [The *Westminster Review*, organ of utilitarianism.] The reviewer is a utilitarian and like the rest of that species knows little of poetical criticism or poetry itself." The source of this opinion must have been Mill, who had cured his depression by reading Wordsworth, and offended his stricter friends by asserting the virtues of his poetry in their debating society. Cole likewise read Wordsworth and Coleridge, and joined Mill on his 1831 walking tour in the Lake District, when Mill met and dined with Wordsworth. Cole, however, being too young, or too undistinguished, had to stay behind at the hotel.

Cole's, then, was what Raymond Williams has called "the humanized Utilitarianism" of John Stuart Mill.[10] After that first meeting in 1826 he saw Mill frequently until some years after the passage of the Reform Act. He joined Mill's debating society, and attended the early morning discussion group led by the historian George Grote. Through Mill he met the future administrative reformers and radical MPs of the post-1832 era. The group became Cole's informal university. He was caught up in the fervor of the Reform Bill years. He joined the pro-Reform Act National Political Union on its formation in November 1831, and it was in 1832 that he began his own campaign for a reform of the public records. His diary for 7 June 1832 reads: "The King's assent was given to the Reform Bill which shortens his or his successors' notice to quit by some years." These apparently republican sentiments did not prevent Cole from later hitching his star to the Royal Consort, Prince Albert.

Ruskin was only 13 in 1832, but his political formation, with its Scottish Tory background, was quite different to Cole's. As he famously states in the opening sentence of his unfinished memoirs, *Praeterita*: "I am, and my father was before me, a violent Tory of the Old School."[11] The Ruskins were closely connected to a group of Ultra-Tory Evangelicals who rejected both the Reform Act and, even more importantly, Catholic Emancipation. Ruskin revised his views on Catholicism, but he was never a democrat, and many of the ideas of his romantic anti-capitalism stem from Ultra-Tory roots. There was also an early, though indirect, brush with Cole on this score. One of the parliamentary leaders of the Ultra-Tories was the Evangelical Member for Oxford University, Sir Robert Inglis, who was friendly with the Ruskins. Inglis was also a member of the Record Commission and the one who gave Cole the most trouble when Cole, who was sacked from the Commission for his criticisms of the jobbery and corruption there, was pushing for reform through a Parliamentary Select Committee.

Religion is another difference between the Romantic and the Utilitarian: faith—and the difficulties of sustaining it—was absolutely central to Ruskin's ideology, while Cole was a conventional churchgoer. According to Bonython: "He always said . . . he had become an agnostic, while a very young man, under the influence of Thomas Love Peacock."[12] Cole's agnosticism, however, did not prevent him putting some of his spare energies into instituting weekday musical church services at Holy Trinity, Brompton, for the particular benefit of the working classes.

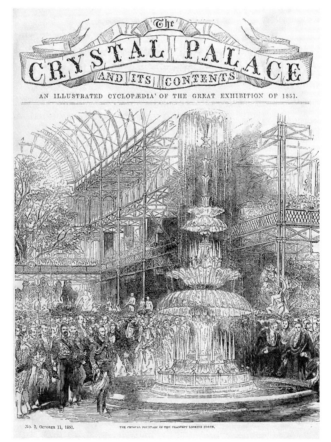

1.1
Frontispiece, *The Crystal Palace and its Contents: An Illustrated Cyclopædia' of the Great Exhibition of 1851*, "The Crystal Fountain in the Transept Looking North." (London: W.M. Clark, 11 October 1851)

Even before the building of Paxton's Crystal Palace, home of Cole's masterwork, the Great Exhibition of 1851, Cole had triumphed over political reaction, and with the aid of Mill and his radical contacts in the House of Commons had helped to secure the establishment of the Public Record Office as an exemplary government institution. He had also straightened out the matter of a standard railway gauge and contributed to the creation of the Penny Post. And as a reformer, he had found his true vocation: the reform of design. And since design had to be done by somebody, it was necessary to reform public art education. This was entirely consistent with the utilitarian worldview. The economic rationale was that the country needed good design, while art education had to be wrested from the *ancien regime* of the Royal Academy and its schools. Cole told a Select Committee in 1849: "I think to act upon the principle of 'every one to his own taste', could be as mischievous as 'every one to his own morals.'"[13]

Much more than an administrator, Cole had become a cultural entrepreneur. In 1846 he joined the moribund Society for the Encouragement of Arts, Manufactures and Commerce, and helped to revive it with a series of exhibitions of—as he had christened them—"art manufactures." He also went into business with Felix Summerly's Art Manufactures. A prize-winning design for a tea service helped to seal an alliance between Cole and the President of the Society of Arts, Queen Victoria's husband Prince Albert. Together, they brought the Great Exhibition—what the architectural historian Jules Lubbock has called "the transformation of Smith's *The Wealth of Nations* into a tableau"[14]—into being. With his typical administrative accuracy, Cole noted that during the course of the Exhibition in Hyde Park, the public had consumed one million eight hundred thousand buns.

Ruskin was skeptical, rather than outright hostile, towards what he described as "a greenhouse larger than any greenhouse built before."[15] He was in the middle of writing *The Stones of Venice*, and he began to write the second volume on the very day the Great Exhibition opened. His virgin wife, Effie, went to the opening on her own. Apart from some passing comments, Ruskin remained silent on the Great Exhibition until 1854, by which time the building had been re-erected at Sydenham—possibly uncomfortably close to Ruskin's home on Denmark Hill. He was actually in Switzerland when reports of the reopening inspired him to publish a pamphlet, *The Opening of the Crystal Palace, considered in some of its relations to the prospects of art*. Typically, this is not really about the Crystal Palace at all, but he comments on the direction in which Cole's great achievement appeared to be leading. "It is impossible, I repeat, to estimate the influence of such an institution on the minds of the working-class" he writes.[16]

> Let it not be thought that I would depreciate . . . the mechanical ingenuity which has been displayed in the erection of the Crystal Palace, or that I under-rate the effect which its vastness may continue to produce on the popular imagination. But the mechanical ingenuity which has been displayed is *not* the essence of either painting or architecture.[17]

In Ruskin's terms, this was building, not architecture, since it lacked expression. (He did, however, countenance the use of iron in the construction of that truly Ruskinian Gothic building, the Oxford Museum, where the wrought iron capitals express his organic aesthetic.)

What concerned Ruskin was that the Crystal Palace's emblematic modernity might cause people to neglect the past. He remarks that Turner had died in 1851, and that his great legacy to the nation was still stuck in a law dispute in Chancery because of the objections of Turner's relatives. Ruskin then makes an explicit reference to Venice as he had seen it in 1851.

> When all that glittering [Crystal Palace] roof was built, in order to exhibit the paltry arts of our fashionable luxury—the carved bedsteads of Vienna, and glued toys of Switzerland, and gay jewellery of France—that very year, I say, the greatest pictures of the Venetian masters were rotting at Venice in the rain for want of roof to cover them, with holes made by cannon shot in their canvas.[18]

He is referring to the Austrian bombardment following the unsuccessful Venetian uprising in 1848, which dropped shells through the roof of the Scuola di San Rocco, home to Tintoretto's great cycle of masterpieces. This lack of concern for the past extended to the contemporary vogue for restoration, and Ruskin concludes with an eloquent protest against the restorations then taking place, and calls for the formation of a society that would preserve buildings for public good rather than private pleasure—a call heeded by William Morris in 1877.

The contrast between the Crystal Palace and the Ducal Palace is legitimate, for they represent two different kinds of society. For Cole it was indeed an instrumental society, a society for getting on, even if the working man and the shilling ticket holder were included in the scheme. Ruskin's was a conservative image of an organic society of rights and duties, where each man knew his place, and was secure in it. Cole's Crystal Palace represented an industrial meritocracy that looked forward to modernity; Ruskin's Ducal Palace a closed oligarchy that looked back to an imagined medieval past.

\* \* \*

So, a utilitarian view on the one hand, an Ultra-Tory on the other. Yet when it came to what both men saw as essential to the well-being of their societies, that is to say, *creativity*, from the moment Ruskin published the central chapter of *The Stones of Venice*, "On the Nature of Gothic" in 1853, it was Ruskin who had the more radical position. This can be demonstrated by a brief account of Cole and Ruskin's direct dealings with each other.

On December 19, 1849, Ruskin wrote a somewhat cool letter to Cole, thanking Cole for sending him a review of *The Seven Lamps of Architecture*, which had appeared in Cole's latest propaganda vehicle, *The Journal of Design and Manufactures*, in October.[19] The review is anonymous, but Ruskin's letter implies that Cole had written it, as seems very likely. It shows that at this stage the two men were not so far apart. It approves of Ruskin's dislike of "shams" and advocacy of truth in the use of materials.

> But with very sincere admiration for portions of this work, and for its excellent spirit generally, we think Mr Ruskin is often led to take narrow and half views, especially of many existing and inevitable circumstances which influence art at the present time. He seems to us to have altogether a very lopsided view of railways and railway architecture, and not to have any consistent theory of mechanical repetition as applied to art.[20]

The review continues: "[Ruskin's] work is a most useful one, but to understand what shape his eloquent doctrines *practically* take see his illustrations—dreamy blotches—and his fantastic book cover."[21] This is very much the Crystal Palace view of the world to which Ruskin became increasingly opposed. His 1854 pamphlet, *The Opening of the Crystal Palace*, might even be a reply.

It is no wonder Ruskin declined to write for *The Journal of Design*. At the heart of Ruskin's central chapter on "The Nature of Gothic" in volume two of *The Stones of Venice* is an examination of the nature of manual labor and the function of the artisan, especially in relation to architecture. Ruskin's analysis is conservative and revolutionary at the same time. He knew nothing of Marx, but both were addressing the same social and economic conditions at the same period, and both concluded that man's alienation was the consequence of having the value of his labor stolen from him. The difference here was that for Marx, the value was economic; for Ruskin, it was aesthetic. Any man has some capacity, however small, to create, and in that capacity lies his humanity. But the division of labor, Ruskin argued—taking Adam Smith head-on by using the example of pin making that Smith used in *The Wealth of Nations*—meant that "it is not, truly, the labor that is divided; but the men."[22] Atomized, men become mere parts of an industrial machine. Thus it should be no surprise that the "great cry that rises from all our manufacturing cities" was that "we manufacture everything there except men."[23] For Ruskin, Cole's *Journal of Design* was one more example of the moral and aesthetic alienation produced by industrialization.

In 1856 it was Ruskin's turn to go on the offensive against Cole. Following the success of the Great Exhibition Cole had been placed in charge of the Government's Department of Practical Art, with the remit to reform the national schools of design originally established in 1836. Initially located in Marlborough House, it was there that Cole opened his first museum, the Museum of Ornamental Art, based on exhibits purchased from the Great Exhibition. Richard Redgrave, RA, became superintendent of the Schools of Design.

On occasion, Ruskin would attend the meetings of the Society of Arts, which Cole continued to use as a platform for his projects and schemes. On March 12, Ruskin went to hear a paper by the headmaster of the Birmingham School of Art, George Wallis. Wallis had in passing deprecated the continuing preference among ladies for floral carpets, instead of the very best geometric designs available. Ruskin rose to chide Wallis for his "ungallant attack upon the ladies."[24]

What one might call the case of the figure in the carpet in fact goes to the heart of different principles of design, in which Ruskin and Cole appear on different sides. Originally Cole, like his colleague Redgrave, had been a naturalist, limiting his Benthamite design rules to ensuring that the decorative features derived from natural imagery did not interfere with the practical purposes of the object—as in his Summerly tea service. But Cole and Redgrave's experience at the Great Exhibition changed all that, and they switched sides, to promote a non-naturalist aesthetic that had its roots in the abstractions of classicism.

As someone steeped in natural theology, which treated nature as God's design, Ruskin was by contrast a naturalist. His argument for the virtues of Gothic architecture was that the style had flourished as compensation for the loss of association with nature when men clustered in towns. Gothic ornament was rooted in nature, though that did not exclude a degree of abstraction. In *The Stones of Venice*, he published a plate, "Abstract Lines," to show that the most beautiful lines were already present in nature, from the curve of a glacier to the edge of a leaf. The classical sources of Cole's conventionalism were the heathen forms that had corrupted the Renaissance and enslaved the artisan.

In spite of this skirmish, Ruskin and Cole appeared to be friendly. Cole's diary records an "at home" at Lord Ashburton's on May 10, 1856. "Ruskin said he thought we were 'Popes' of doctrine at the Department and glad to hear

1.2
"Abstract Lines,"
Plate VII, John
Ruskin, *The Stones
of Venice*—Vol 1:
Foundations, 1851

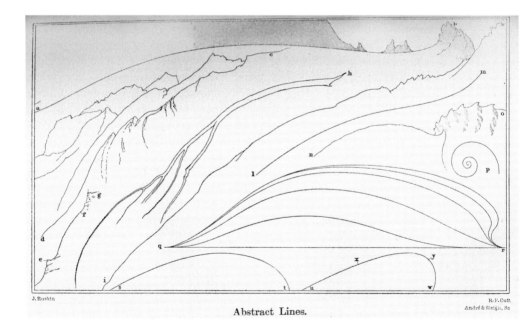

J. Ruskin

R. P. Cuff.
André & Sleigh, Sc

Abstract Lines.

we were beginning with Elementary Drawing." Ruskin had reason to be polite, for it so happens that he and Cole must have seen a good deal of each other at this time. By one of those accidents of fate, when the Turner bequest was released from Chancery, the National Gallery exhibited a selection of pictures at Marlborough House—and Ruskin supplied the catalogue notes. Ralph Wornum, future Keeper of the National Gallery and with Ruskin responsible for the destruction of some of Turner's so-called erotic drawings, was originally employed by Cole. On February 10, 1857, Cole's diary records a day at the office: "Ruskin came and examined all the drawings carefully. Would be glad to assist, especially in promoting Natural History." In letters to two different corres- pondents at this time Ruskin describes "the Marlborough House people" as "fraternizing" with him.[25] In July 1858 he went as far as telling his father that he hoped "to get my system taught at Marlborough House."[26]

But that was not to be. By "my system," Ruskin meant the somewhat freer approach he used at his own drawing classes, which he had begun at the London Working Men's College in 1854. It was Ruskin's Tory principle that his efforts "were directed not at making a carpenter an artist, but to making him happier as a carpenter."[27] At the Working Men's College, he saw the work of students who had attended classes at Cole's Schools of Design, and on January 13, 1858, he took the battle to the enemy with a lecture in the newly opened, but still provisionally housed Museum at South Kensington. The occasion was the opening of the Architectural Museum at South Kensington, a separate institution that Ruskin had sponsored since its creation in 1850, to whose collection of archi- tectural casts, some of them donated by Ruskin, Cole was giving temporary house room.

Ruskin's lecture, "On The Deteriotative Power of Conventional Art over Nations," turned on the distinction between naturalistic and convention- alizing, abstract design, and was particularly critical of Indian design, which had been a revelation to Cole at the Great Exhibition, and many examples of which he had acquired for his museum. Cole was there, and noted Ruskin's theme in his diary, and that it was a "Full meeting." But he clearly didn't like what he heard. According to The Times, that year's annual report of the Department of Science and Practical Art stated that: "in allowing certain persons, including Mr Ruskin, the author, to give illustrative lectures, the department is not responsible for their opinions."[28]

There was another cause of friction between Ruskin and Cole. When the Marlborough House collections moved to South Kensington, the Turner watercolors that Ruskin had taken such pains to conserve and catalog went too, and were hung in galleries illuminated by gas. On April 29 Cole noted in his diary: "To private view of Royal Academy. A high average of interesting pictures. Ruskin asked if we were 'Baking' the pictures, and if Turner's drawings had become white."

When Ruskin and Richard Redgrave, Cole's Art Superintendent, shared a platform at the inauguration of the Cambridge School of Design on October 29, 1858, fraternization was over. By this time Cole and Redgrave had turned the teaching of design into a magnificent self-perpetuating, self-financing system that reached from the National School at South Kensington through branch schools in every manufacturing town, right down to classes in elementary schools. The system trained up students who graduated as art teachers who could then go back and teach more students. Considerable income was drawn from the fees paid by middle-class students. At Cambridge, Redgrave announced:

> Under the old, exclusive system [that is to say, one exclusively devoted to artisans, and excluding classes for children or fee-paying young ladies and gentlemen] nineteen schools were established, and about three thousand artisans availed themselves thereof; the cost to the state per man averaged three pounds two shillings and fourpence; in some cases—at Leeds for instance—the cost was seven pounds. Under the new system, up to 1856, the number of Art Schools amounted to sixty, and there were forty-two thousand, four hundred and twenty six scholars, the average cost per head being only thirteen shillings, one penny three-farthings.[29]

For those concerned with university teaching today, these calculations have a strangely contemporary ring.

In a memoir, Redgrave writes that while the actual teaching system was his creation, "Cole's clever invention of rules, his administrative abilities, his self-assertion have been wonderful co-agents; as without his firmness of purpose I should never have succeeded in carrying the system through."[30] Redgrave and Cole believed that it was as important to be able to draw as to read and write. Ruskin believed so too, but in order to manage this vast system, it was necessary to impose a uniformity on the teaching that must have crushed nearly all tendrils of individual creativity, which for him was the moral purpose of the exercise.

The National Course for Instruction was a fixed, twenty-two-stage series of exercises that led from the elementary school class up to South Kensington. The vast majority of students would be involved in laboriously copying from two-dimensional reproductions, using examples of decoration printed and distributed by the Department. An examination had to be passed before going on to the next stage, and most pupils were on stages one to ten, with up to half at stage two. The Primary Course omitted all drawing from life, landscape or natural objects. It was a rigorous training for the hand and eye, but death to the imagination.

During the 1860s, as Cole's system spread its tentacles across the land, Ruskin turned his attention from the visual economy as such to the political economy that sustained it. His lectures on art, such as the two entitled "The Political Economy of Art" given during the Manchester Art Treasures Exhibition of 1857, had signaled the change of direction that led to the publication of his articles Unto This Last in 1860. Here Cole's friend John Stuart Mill was the emblematic target of Ruskin's attacks on laissez-faire economics and the exclusion of the moral calculus from notions of value. What mattered to Ruskin was value in use, not value in exchange, a principle that can be translated into a view of architecture and design.

Ruskin's economic views were largely ridiculed and rejected at the time of their first publication. But in 1869 he at last was given what he regarded as an official platform from which to promulgate his ideas, when he was elected as the first Slade Professor of Fine Art at Oxford. At his inaugural lecture in 1870 he announced that he intended to *teach* art, as well as talk about it—and from this came Ruskin's answer to Cole, the Ruskin School of Drawing.

From this also came many of Ruskin's woes. The reason was that a branch school of the government system, the Oxford School of Science and Art, was already established in the University Galleries, and was backed by the very same university politicians who had secured his own election. The school taught Artisans—mainly boys and apprentices—as well as Ladies, Governesses, and Gentlemen. The Art Master, Alexander MacDonald, was a product of the South Kensington system. In 1871 Ruskin announced in *Fors Clavigera*: "After carefully considering the operation of the Kensington system of Art-teaching throughout the country, and watching for two year's its effects on various classes of students at Oxford, I became finally convinced that it fell short of its objects in more than one vital particular,"[31] and he went on to explain that he had obtained permission to start his own school on his own lines.

Unfortunately, as is the way with universities, Ruskin's idea was fatally compromised. His backers insisted that the first Ruskin Drawing Master, funded out of Ruskin's own money, should be none other than Alexander MacDonald. Secondly, while the teaching of undergraduates in "The Professor's Class" and of the middle classes in the "Town Class" were reformed on Ruskinian lines, with the study of nature and the enjoyment of art as its primary motives, Ruskin was forced to allow the continuation of the government's "artisans" class, taught on the South Kensington system, by gaslight in the basement.

There are many reasons for the failure of Ruskin to achieve his ambitions with his Drawing School—though the School thrives to this day. He had over-expended his energies on so many projects to reform Victorian society, including the Guild of St George, a utopian scheme he had launched in 1871 that was intended to own land and manage it without use of machinery, while providing its workers and organizers with opportunities for education and creativity. At least some of his failure can be accounted for by the power of the national institution he had set himself up against. In July 1877 Ruskin told his readers in *Fors Clavigera*: "The Professorship of Sir Henry Cole at Kensington has corrupted the system of art-teaching all over England into a state of abortion and falsehood from which it will take twenty years to recover."[32] Earlier that year he had had his first complete mental breakdown, and in 1878 resigned his Professorship, although he was to return from 1883 to 1885.

Cole had in fact retired from South Kensington in 1873—by which time the South Kensington empire had expanded to 120 schools—but that clearly had not assuaged Ruskin's animosity. Cole made no reply at the time—possibly because he was not a subscriber to *Fors Clavigera*. But the following year, on November 28, 1878, Cole traveled to Portsmouth for the prize giving at the government school of Art. He writes in his diary: "Ruskin's abuse of me made a good text. Speech much applauded, and the Committee well pleased. Ruskin's attack on me was a source of fun." We would not know which of Ruskin's attacks it was, had not Cole helpfully glued into his diary an extract from a court report from the previous day's *Times*.

The case in question was one of the great trials of the Victorian period, one that marks a cultural watershed, when Victorian moral authority is challenged, and defeated, by a new, amoral aestheticism. It is *Whistler versus Ruskin*, which had opened on November 25, 1878. Ruskin had written in *Fors Clavigera* that for Whistler to charge 200 guineas for paintings such as *The Falling Rocket* was like "throwing a pot of paint in the public's face."[33] In order to prove the "personal and malicious" tone of *Fors*, Whistler's counsel Sergeant Barry cited other passages:

> In the same publication he twice described Professor Gordon Smith as a 'goose'—(Laughter in court)—and spoke of the Presidency of Sir Henry Cole at Kensington as having 'corrupted the system of art-teaching all over England into a state of abortion and falsehood from which it will take twenty years to recover.' (Laughter). That was pleasant for Sir Henry Cole. (Laughter).[34]

It may have been, as Cole remarked in his diary, "a source of fun," but for Ruskin it was not. He had been unable to attend the trial because of his breakdown, and the verdict against him was another cause for resignation from Oxford. Ruskin's personal star began to wane from this point.

\* \* \*

In the short run, it would appear that Cole had the greater success in his lifetime, and has left the larger legacy, notably the Albert Hall, which Cole had constructed, not in the Ruskinian Byzantine-Gothic proposed by Gilbert Scott, but the Renaissance style that Ruskin abhorred. Cole knew how to get things done, while Ruskin's dealing with institutions, even the ones he created himself, ended in lamentable failure.

And yet.

The National Course of Instruction was abandoned in the 1890s. In 1896, the National Art Training School changed its name to the Royal College of Art, and in the words of Christopher Frayling's history of the College "The Art Workers' Guild Takes Over"[35]—notably with the appointment of the Ruskin and Morris-influenced William Lethaby as the College's first Professor of Design in 1901. Ruskin's "twenty years to recover" had come to pass, and it was Ruskin's "arts and crafts" rather than Cole's "art-manufactures" that became the aesthetic legacy that shaped the early twentieth century.

So too—and paradoxically—with politics. When in the 1880s and 1890s the newly enfranchised and better-educated artisan class broke their traditional concordat with the Liberal Party and sought their own voice, the language they found was Ruskin's. *Unto This Last*, which sold fewer than a thousand copies in the 1860s, sold in hundreds of thousands, and became a shaping text for the founders of the Labour Party. When you consider that many of the authors of the post 1945 settlement—notably William Beveridge and Clement Atlee—had been devotees of Ruskin in their youth, Ruskin can be described as a grandfather of the Welfare State. Ruskin's Tory anti-capitalism ultimately inspired a democratic socialism that sought to soften the harshness of industrial exploitation and provide every citizen with the cultural and educational resources that would overcome the alienation of modern life.

Cole once said: "Straight lines are a national want."[36] Ruskin sought national revival through the curving, organic forms of the Gothic. These two traditions, the utilitarian and the romantic anti-capitalist, the rationalist and the imaginative, are as present in the twenty-first century as they were in the nineteenth.

In death, there is one, final, link between Ruskin and Cole. In April 1882, Henry Cole, then aged seventy-three, was as busy as ever, but he had over-exerted himself. In spite of feeling unwell, he insisted on turning up for a sitting for his portrait. After the sitting he had a seizure, and died the following day. The artist working on this unfinished portrait was James McNeil Whistler. Thus Whistler, victor over Ruskin in the law courts, harbinger of twentieth-century modernism, can be said to have been the nemesis of not one, but two truly Great Victorians.

## Notes

1 Sir Henry Cole, *Fifty Years of Public Work of Sir Henry Cole, K.C.B., Accounted for in His Deeds, Speeches and Writings*, ed. Alan Summerly Cole (London: George Bell and Sons, 1884), 1:82.

2 Cole, *Fifty Years*, 1:194.

3 Ibid., 1:226.

4 Elizabeth Bonython, *King Cole: A Picture Portrait of Sir Henry Cole, KCB, 1808–82* (London: V&A Museum, 1982), 2.

5 R. Clark, *A History of the Royal Albert Hall* (London: Hamish Hamilton, 1958), 103.

6 John Ruskin, *The Works of John Ruskin*, Library Edition, ed. E.T. Cook and Alexander Wedderburn (London: George Allen, 1903–12), XIV:xxvii.

7 Sir Henry Cole, "The Diary of Henry Cole" (unpublished manuscript and typescript, transcribed and indexed by Elizabeth Bonython, National Art Library, Victorian and Albert Museum, 1992), January 14, 1828. The dates of entries further cited are given in the text.

8 Cole, *Fifty Years*, 1:103.

9 Ibid., 1:6.

10 Raymond Williams, *Culture and Society 1780–1950* (London: Chatto & Windus, 1958; Harmondsworth: Penguin Books, 1961), 83.

11  Ruskin, *Works*, XXXV:13.

12  Bonython, *King Cole*, 61.

13  Cole, *Fifty Years*, 1:286.

14  Jules Lubbock, *The Tyranny of Taste: The Politics of Architecture and Design in Britain* (London: Yale University Press, 1995), 270.

15  Ruskin, *Works*, XII: 456.

16  Ibid., XII: 418.

17  Ibid., XII: 419.

18  Ibid., XII: 420–1.

19  Ibid., XXXVI:105.

20  John Ruskin, "The Seven Lamps of Architecture," *The Journal of Design and Manufactures* 2, 8 (October 1849): 72.

21  Ruskin, "Seven Lamps," 72.

22  Ruskin, *Works*, X:196.

23  Ruskin, *Works*, X:196.

24  Ruskin, *Works*, XVI: 427.

25  Virginia Surtees, *Sublime and Instructive: Letters of John Ruskin to Louisa, Marchioness of Waterford, Anna Blunden and Ellen Heaton* (London: Michael Joseph, 1972), 36.

26  Ruskin, *Works*, XVI: xxix.

27  Ibid., XIII: 553.

28  *The Times*, June 14, 1858.

29  A. Burton, "Redgrave as Art Educator, Museum Official and Design Theorist," in *Richard Redgrave 1804–1888*, ed. S.P. Casteras and R. Parkinson (London: Yale University Press, 1988), 48.

30  Burton, "Redgrave," 56.

31  Ruskin, *Works*, XXVII:159.

32  Ibid., XXIX:154.

33  Ibid., XXIX:160.

34  *The Times*, November 27, 1877.

35  Christopher Frayling, *The Royal College of Art: One Hundred and Fifty Years of Art and Design* (London: Barrie & Jenkins, 1987), 66.

36  Stuart MacDonald, *The History and Philosophy of Art Education* (London: University of London Press, 1970), 228.

# Chapter 2

# Context: 1860–1890

While upper-class European intellectuals generally looked on commerce with disdain, most Americans—living in a society with a more fluid class structure—enthusiastically embraced the idea of moneymaking. The late nineteenth century became the "Gilded Age" of American tycoons who amassed vast financial empires: John D. Rockefeller in oil, Jay Gould in railroads, J. Pierpont Morgan in banking, and Andrew Carnegie in steel. Considerable amounts of money and power were based in Chicago, transformed from frontier outpost to metropolis during this tumultuous period, a place Joanna Merwood-Salisbury takes us to in this chapter.

The Gilded Age was enabled by the evolution of the US economy after the end of the Civil War in 1865. With the development of the Bessemer Process, perfecting the mass production of steel, the second wave of the Industrial Revolution began. The half-century between the Civil War and the beginning of World War I witnessed the emergence of the US as the world's dominant economy, surpassing Britain in gross domestic product by 1868. By 1914—the dawn of World War I—the US economy was larger than that of industrial superpowers Britain, France, and Germany combined.

This incredible growth was fueled by US protectionism. At the end of the Civil War, Republicans in control of Washington developed a program of economic modernization that permanently altered the economy. The Morrill Tariff (1861) served not only to raise revenue but also to encourage the establishment of factories protected from British competition, assuaging the South's evolution away from its slave-labor economy. In addition to tariffs, congress, via the Legal Tender Act (1862), allowed the government to issue bonds in small denominations, sold directly to the people, in part to pay for the cost of the war. The following year it created a system of banks via the National Bank Act (1863) which not only provided sound currency but required all new banks to purchase government bonds, thereby monetizing the wealth represented by farms, urban buildings, factories, and businesses for the Treasury.

Parallel to these economic policies was the development of the nation's natural resources: abundant coal in the Appalachian Mountains from Pennsylvania south to Kentucky, oil in western Pennsylvania, iron ore mines in the Lake Superior region. Steel mills thrived in places where coal and iron ore could be brought together, the birth of what in its decline is known as "the rust belt." The discovery of gold in California provided incentive to fulfill the popular notion of "manifest destiny," and as America moved west, infrastructure followed. Free land provided to farmers by the Homestead Act (1862) paved the way, in addition to land grants to railroad construction companies to open up the western plains and link the east coast to California. Besides drastically cutting the cost of moving freight, stimulating new industries such as steel and telegraphy, and encouraging the profession of civil engineering, the railroads were the first businesses to encounter managerial complexities, labor union complications, and problems of geographical competition. How they dealt with these problems as the first large-scale business enterprise became the model for most large corporations to come.

The organization of financing represented by and fueling Gilded Age tycoons was unprecedented, and marked the beginning of not just new industries but new forms of finance. On the organizational side, Frederick W. Taylor's "scientific management" re-calibrated the efficiency of worker production. His books describe the most efficient body movements for a given task as well as the high level of oversight needed to ensure control of workers' performance. On the labor side, the first significant labor union, the Knights of Labor, was created in 1869. The Knights collapsed in the 1880s and were displaced by strong international unions that banded together as the American Federation of Labor. These unions were often formed by immigrants who brought revolutionary ideals with them from Europe, as Merwood-Salisbury details. Factories created after the Civil War had attracted tens of thousands of European immigrants seeking high-wage jobs. In 1900, one-third of the labor supply were either foreign born or the children of foreign-born parents, making immigration a political issue for the first time, and entangling social politics with Anglo-American xenophobia. In part as a way to demonstrate their American bona fides, the AFL unions formally rejected socialism and negotiated with owners for higher wages and better working conditions—within the capitalism system.

These were the men and women who built the US in the twentieth century, piecing together and inhabiting the Chicago skyscrapers that instantly became the icons of global capitalism.

Peggy Deamer

Chapter 2

# The first Chicago school and the ideology of the skyscraper

Joanna Merwood-Salisbury

The most celebrated products of the first Chicago school of architecture, a series of skyscrapers constructed between the early 1880s and the early 1890s, are not only monuments signifying the emergence of the modern style; they are also monuments to the institutions that powered the incredible economic growth of the United States in the nineteenth century: financial exchanges, banks, railways, insurance companies, and department stores. However, in modernist architectural histories the association between the form of these buildings and their economic function was not much discussed. By the 1940s they came to signify the spontaneous appearance of a modern aesthetic removed from the influence of European history and taste, unconsciously derived from new construction technologies.[1] This new building type, wrote the historian Sigfried Giedion, quoting Chicago architect John W. Root, should by its "mass and proportion convey in some large elemental sense an idea of the great, stable, conserving force of modern civilization."[2] While contemporary historians of the early American skyscraper have refocused attention on their origins in commerce and real estate development— "form follows function" has become "form follows finance"—a renewed understanding of the relationship between architecture and capital does not yet account for the broader social impact of capitalism on the culture of building in this place and time.[3]

From its first appearance in the 1880s the skyscraper was the subject of an ideological battle, the symbol of capitalism's triumph; it was also the target of anti-capitalist protest. The struggle to define its meaning was carried out in the press, including mass-market newspapers and magazines, and specialist journals aimed at architects and real estate interests (the *Inland Architect* and *Building*

*Budget*), as well as the newly radicalized labor movement, a movement dominated by the building trades unions (the German-language *Arbeiter-Zeitung* and the English-language *Alarm*). While anarchists vilified the skyscraper as an instrument of class oppression, architects, borrowing from European architectural theorists, published essays heralding it as the organic product of its environment, the entirely natural product of the evolution of European styles, particularly the Gothic, to the unique environment of the American Midwest.

By the 1930s the rhetoric of stylistic evolution espoused by Chicago architects was transformed into one of entirely positive technological and aesthetic revolution. The creation of the steel-framed skyscraper became viewed as a catalyst for the appearance of a new modern style in the United States, and any sense of ambivalence about, or resistance to, the symbolism or functions of the new building type was lost. This became the defining narrative of the first Chicago school of architecture, a narrative so successful that by the mid-twentieth century it had assumed the mantle of modern "mythology" in the sense described by the literary critic Roland Barthes: an historical construction whose ideological origins are suppressed. A rereading of the skyscraper through issues of class and labor helps recover the essential instability of the skyscraper as both form and idea, reminding us that these icons of modern architecture were the creation of a tumultuous historical period characterized by uncertainty and agitation brought about by "constant revolutionizing of production [and] uninterrupted disturbance of all social conditions."[4]

* * *

When Marx and Engels published the *Communist Manifesto* in 1848, their contemporary model for the capitalist city was Manchester, the city where Engels worked for his father's company and that Marx visited in exile from Germany.[5] Though the industrial revolution that had begun in the Lancashire cotton industry in the eighteenth century had reached its most advanced form there, they believed the Mancunian model would soon spread all over the world, not only repeated, but also intensified. Indeed the future they predicted was already emerging in the present. In 1848, just as they were completing their tract, a new capitalist city was emerging on the North American frontier.

As Manchester was to London, Chicago was to New York: the second city, the place where things were made. While Manchester assumed the role of production and processing center for an empire, Chicago was designed to fulfill that role while it was still a notional mark on the map of world trade. As the environmental historian William Cronon has shown, the city was founded on the presumption of future greatness as a metropolis linking the northeastern seaboard to the American west.[6] In 1822, the Federal Government authorized the Illinois and Michigan Canal Commission to build a waterway linking Lake Michigan and the Mississippi River. This was to be the western-most component of a vast transportation system connecting New York City to emerging agricultural markets in the west via the Great Lakes and the Erie Canal. The land on which this canal was built was taken from Native American tribes under a series of treaties brokered and broken in the first decade of the nineteenth century. In 1830, the Canal Commission platted a town at the mouth of the Chicago River on the site of Fort Dearborn, a military camp built to secure the site during the recent land wars. Based on a simple grid plan with lots about 350 feet square, this town was a speculative venture, effectively an agreement between the Canal Commission (now the Canal Company) and prospective real estate developers: the company would provide business to the area in the form of river traffic, and the new landowners would provide the capital to build the canal. The venture was successful and the banks of the Chicago River were soon dotted with businesses serving the trade in goods. In the 1850s, canal traffic was supplemented by the railways and by the 1870s the city was threaded by train tracks bringing grain, lumber, and live animals to Chicago from the great plains, where they were processed for delivery back east.

**2.1**
Joshua Hathaway Jr., Chicago With the School Section, Wabansia and Kinzie's Addition, 1834. The original grid plan of Chicago drawn up by the Illinois and Michigan Canal Commission lies over the main branch of the Chicago River in the middle of the image. Additions to the grid are shown to the north and south. Courtesy Newberry Library

By 1890 Chicago more than exemplified the characteristics of what Marx and Engels called the "bourgeois political economy": a large city controlling the economy of a vast productive landscape around it, created to serve the global market; the agglomeration of a large labor pool, made up in this case of recent immigrants, first from England and Ireland and more recently from Germany and Eastern Europe; the concentration of property in the hands of a few, many living far from the city in Boston, New York, and Philadelphia; and the constant revolutionizing of means of production driven by the need to reduce the cost of labor, in particular the introduction of mechanization into agriculture and construction. With these conditions in place, Marx and Engels argued that capitalism had already "accomplished wonders far surpassing Egyptian pyramids, Roman aqueducts and Gothic cathedrals," and would go on to create "more massive and more colossal productive forces than have all preceding generations together."[7] But while the two men referenced the great architectural monuments of history, they showed little interest in the aesthetic of their own time.

Paris has long served as the European example of the urban transformation of capitalism, and Chicago was its American equivalent, a city that attracted not only businessmen but also huge numbers of tourists eager to witness the spectacle of industrialization.[8] Early visitors were directed by guidebook authors to view the Union Stockyards on the southern edge of the city and the

2.2
In the heart of the Great Union Stockyards, Chicago, USA, c.1909

**2.3**
The Chicago skyline with the "El" visible in the left foreground. Kaufman, Weimer and Fabry Co., Bird's Eye View of Chicago, 1912

forest of tall buildings lining La Salle, Dearborn, and State Streets in the center. Together these sights represented the most visible and awe-inspiring symbols of the astonishing productive forces that the new world order had brought into being. Built in 1865, the Stockyards were created by the consolidation of individual meatpacking companies, all for the sake of efficiency. With its gridded streets and alleys of pens, it was built on a square mile of drained marshland, a huge slaughterhouse and meatpacking factory designed to be serviced by railway cars. Similarly, the skyscrapers containing the businesses that organized the movement of goods around them were serviced by a sophisticated transportation infrastructure: a web of elevated streetcar lines that brought office workers and consumers in from the suburbs and home again, and a series of railway lines linking the city to the east.

Searching for an explanation for this unlikely vertical landscape rising from the horizontal plain on the shores of Lake Michigan, guidebook authors found one in the image of the mythical Phoenix. The forest of towers, they claimed, had risen from the ashes of the great fire of 1871. This fire burned for three days, destroying an area four miles long and more than half a mile wide, including most of the Loop but sparing the industries on the periphery of the city.[9] In its wake, new city ordinances required all construction in the burnt over district to be fireproof, effectively restricting wooden residential dwellings to the periphery. But while these building regulations did help create a segregated commercial core, the fire did not produce the iconic tall buildings later celebrated in architectural history.[10] Immediately after the disaster the city was repopulated with much the same kind of buildings that had existed before: four-, five- and six-storey masonry buildings, many designed in the fashionable Gothic Revival style. The post-fire generation of so-called "commercial Gothic" structures included several buildings by Peter B. Wight and his firm, Carter, Drake and Wight, including the Lenox Building (1872), and others by William Le Baron Jenney, such as the polychrome Portland Block (1872). Taller buildings incorporating new building technologies and with new aesthetic qualities did not appear until about a decade later.

The first tall office buildings constructed in Chicago owed their appearance not to the *tabula rasa* produced by the fire, but to a rise in property prices that began to accelerate as the country emerged from the recession of 1873. The cycle of boom and bust that had driven Chicago's exponential growth since the 1830s was about to enter an epic but short-lived boom period. Beginning in the early 1880s, whole swathes of post-fire buildings were demolished and replaced with higher ones in an act of economic destruction and reconstruction that was almost equal in its force to the great fire. Burnham and Root's ten-storey Montauk Block, built in 1882 on Monroe Street between Dearborn and Clark, was an early example and is generally considered the first high-rise building in Chicago. At the same time that rising property prices encouraged building developers to think taller, the geography of capitalism was at work reorienting the center of the city away from the river and southward in search of cheaper land and access to newly built railway terminals.[11] La Salle Street was the first skyscraper corridor, prompted by the completion of W. W. Boyington's Chicago Board of Trade at La Salle and Jackson in 1885. Dearborn Street south of Jackson saw a boom in skyscraper development around 1890, prompted by the construction of another Burnham and Root building, the Monadnock, in 1889.

These buildings were testament to the power of combined capital. While some early Chicago skyscrapers were commissioned by large companies, many were speculative ventures created not to house particular organizations but to make a profit via rental return. The limited liability corporation, a kind of joint stock company, was the mechanism that made this possible. As Robert Bruegmann has explained, "the use of corporate organization and the issuance of stocks and bonds made possible much larger capital pools than those available to any individual or private partnership."[12] These investments were considered safe because they were protected by limited liability law and individual investors were not personally responsible if the project failed.

The men who commissioned these buildings were less interested in artistic effect than they were in profit. Developers such as the Boston-based brothers Peter and Shepherd Brooks, who began investing in Chicago real estate in the 1860s, rarely visited the city and were absentee landlords.[13] Regular clients of Burnham and Root, they commissioned the Monadnock, directing their architects through an agent and by correspondence. Wanting his buildings to be as plain as possible, Peter Brooks asked his architects to restrict themselves to "the effect of solidity and strength, or a design that will produce that effect, rather than ornament for a notable appearance."[14]

The form of the skyscraper was largely dictated by the profit motive. As Carol Willis has shown, architects were restricted not only by building regulations and by structural considerations but also by the charge to produce offices of standard dimensions, well supplied with daylight.[15] These restrictions amounted to real estate formulae that varied little from building to building and Chicago architects were well acquainted with them. According to these formulae, the height of the skyscraper was not dictated by the limits of engineering but by economics. By 1889 the equation balancing rentable office space and the cost of construction dictated that sixteen stories was the most profitable, or "economic height," and this became the new norm. (Beyond this height, the additional requirements for foundations, elevators, and mechanical services meant a diminished return on the capital invested.)[16] Most buildings of this height incorporated some metal framing, but this was not always the case. The 16-storey Monadnock, for example, had thick masonry load-bearing walls. This was an anomaly, however. As soon as they discovered the means by which to build a 16-storey office building out of masonry, Chicago architects rejected this solution. In 1893 the Brooks commissioned Holabird and Roche to design a southerly addition to the Monadnock, legally two new buildings called the Katahdin and Wachusett. The Katahdin, planned first, has skeleton framing inside and masonry exterior walls like the original. The Wachusett is entirely steel framed.

During the real estate boom of the 1880s, the desire to accrue high rents from speculative office buildings led to rapid and extreme changes to the building industry, most significantly the invention of a new system called the "Chicago construction." This system is often conflated with the skeleton frame,

2.5
Monadnock
Building, Chicago,
IL, 1889–1891.
Burnham and Root,
north building
architects. Holabird
& Roche, south
building addition
[1893]. Historic
Architecture and
Landscape Image
Collection, Ryerson
and Burnham
Archives, The Art
Institute of Chicago.
Digital File # 60321
© The Art Institute
of Chicago

but in fact it denoted a whole series of changes to the practice of construction, including the development of a new kind of foundation system, the use of mass-produced, prefabricated components including terracotta tile and plate glass, along with developments in fireproofing, plumbing, and elevator technologies.

The Chicago construction had several economic benefits: it allowed for taller buildings because the metal frame could carry a higher load than masonry, and it was much faster to erect. It also enabled thinner walls, creating more rentable area per floor. Cheaper than stone and lighter than brick, terracotta tile could be produced and fabricated relatively quickly. At the same time architects took advantage of new supplies of inexpensive plate glass from local manufacturers to design larger window openings at a time when electric light was not yet strong enough to service offices and stores. The result of this new

2.6
Tacoma Building, Chicago, IL, 1888–1889. Holabird & Roche, architects, J.W. Taylor, photographer. Historic Architecture and Landscape Image Collection, Ryerson and Burnham Archives, The Art Institute of Chicago. Digital File # 2392 © The Art Institute of Chicago

2.7
Reliance Building,
Chicago, IL,
1889–1895. D. H.
Burnham and Co.,
architects

system was startling in its appearance. For example, Holabird & Roche's Tacoma building constructed on the corner of La Salle and Madison Streets in 1889, and D. H. Burnham and Co.'s Reliance Building on the corner of State and Washington Streets, completed in 1895, both presented a gently undulating terracotta tile and glass curtain wall to their two street facades, an effect so unexpected that they were highly criticized in the popular press.[17]

The advent of the Chicago construction not only produced a new aesthetic, it also initiated a remarkable and tumultuous reorganization of traditional building practices, including the work of contractors, architects, and building tradesmen. The Tacoma and the Reliance were both erected by the

George A. Fuller Company. Trained as an architect at the Massachusetts Institute of Technology, Fuller started his construction company in Chicago in 1882, just as the revolution in building practice was beginning. His firm was a new kind of contractor, a coordinator of all the aspects of building rather than a specialist in one particular trade, responsible for purchasing and assembling materials, hiring subcontractors, as well as financing building projects in some cases.[18]

The work of the architect was similarly reorganized, exemplified by the changes that took place in Daniel Burnham's office after the death of his partner John W. Root in 1891. Burnham rationalized his office, basing it on the corporate model of his big business clients. He created three separate departments, each with its own responsibility and controlled by one of his three partners: Ernest Graham, his long-time assistant, was the office manager; Edward Shankland, an engineer, was in charge of construction management; and Charles Atwood, the young architect responsible for the Reliance, was the designer.[19] The name of the office changed from "Burnham and Root" to "D. H. Burnham and Company," and eventually included satellite offices working in a number of cities. This model set a precedent for a new kind of architectural office with national and even international commissions, one in which the work produced should be seen as the creation of the whole company and not that of one or two individuals.

As the organization of contracting companies and architecture offices changed, so did their relationships with the building trades.[20] The Chicago construction allowed the contractor and the architect to reposition themselves as managers of the building process, at the expense of the building tradesmen's traditional autonomy. As the production of building materials and the construction of buildings became industrialized, building workers saw the value of their labor reduced. Not only could machines replicate some of their tasks, they worked more quickly and for no pay. As old trades disappeared, new ones took their place. In the 1880s a distinct category of ironworkers appeared, men who worked solely on building construction, rather than bridges and railways, and they quickly came into conflict with masons and carpenters over matters of jurisdiction.[21] As the tall steel towers rose above the city, they became highly contentious symbols of a new economic and industrial system.

By the late 1880s, the success of the skyscraper seemed assured in the popular imagination; its limits appeared almost infinite as science fiction writers and utopians confidently predicted future fifty- and one hundred-storey buildings made of steel and glass. But at the same time the new building type came under attack as the pace of industrial change created serious civil unrest. The combination of an unstable economy with periods of low wages and high unemployment, the mechanization of the building industry, and the threat of decline for the traditional building trades created a volatile situation, one in which labor unions became increasingly radical, and tall office buildings became highly visible targets.

From the time of its first appearance, the skyscraper was, in fact, the center of an architectural ideological battle. In art and architectural journals, critics from Europe and the east coast condemned Chicago and Chicago architecture as ugly and uncultured.[22] Indeed, they barely recognized the tall office building as architecture at all. Instead they saw it as a product of engineering and construction, built in the service of capital, and therefore not art. An 1892 article in the English *Builder* claimed, "The Chicago architect does not build high because he likes it, but because the problem presented to him forces him to do so."[23] In 1894 the French architect Jacques Hermant criticized the plain Monadnock as "no longer the work of an artist responding to particular needs with intelligence and drawing from them all of the possible consequences. It is the work of a laborer who, without the slightest study, superimposes fifteen strictly identical stories to make a block then stops when he finds the block high enough."[24] In this way the tallest and most imposing of Chicago's commercial buildings was dismissed as the work of a builder, not a designer.

At the same time that the skyscraper was being dismissed by foreign critics, local labor groups were picketing building sites in downtown Chicago, pointing to the new building type as evidence of capitalist greed and exploitation. Between 1883 and 1900, building disputes in Chicago grew exponentially as the process of building became industrialized and the economy continued to be extremely volatile. The strikes began in the spring and summer of 1883 when the powerful bricklayers union struck, demanding a fixed daily wage of $4 and a ten-hour working day. Because the bricklayers were so indispensable to the building process, this strike was ultimately successful and it spurred others, including one by the carpenters' union in 1886. The success of these strikes also prompted further changes in the building industry. There is evidence, for example, that the success of the bricklayers' strike encouraged architects to utilize the Chicago construction more fully. As Henry Ericsson, a builder and early member of the bricklayers' union, later claimed, the use of the iron and steel frame "soon released building from dependence upon the prior erection of massive walls of brick and stone, and thus set in motion a revolution in the technology of modern building and altered fundamentally the brick and stone mason's relation to the building industry."[25]

This transfer of power in the building industry had far-reaching consequences. Responding to the threat industrialization posed to traditional crafts, the labor movement became increasingly radicalized, aligning itself first with the national Eight Hour Movement, and then with radical groups such as the International Working People's Association (IWPA). Understanding the advantages of the popular press, the IWPA organized mass meetings and published their own broadsheets. The most radical members of the IWPA were recent German immigrants affiliated with revolutionary movements in Europe, such as August Spies, editor of the German-language labor newspaper *Arbeiter-Zeitung*. They also included some American-born members like Albert Parsons and his wife Lucy, editors of the English-language *Alarm*. Spies and Parsons were not factory workers but skilled tradesmen with some education: before turning to journalism, Spies was an upholsterer and Albert Parsons was a printer, while Lucy Parsons was a seamstress.[26] Just as Marx did, these revolutionaries believed in the power of the strike to incite revolution. Their alliance with unionized labor in the service of that goal became known as the "Chicago idea": the strike would be the first line of attack on the capitalist system, leading ultimately to its destruction. Modeled on the Declaration of Independence, the IWPA's manifesto declared the group's dedication to the "destruction of the existing class rule, by all means i.e. the energetic, relentless, revolutionary and international action."[27]

This destruction would begin with the skyscraper, the most obvious symbol of capitalistic speculation and private property ownership. Lucy Parsons utilized its image in her criticism of the city's treatment of the poor. Drawing a direct relationship between the tall office buildings in the Loop and the conditions of the destitute living in their shadows, she described these buildings as symbols of capital's oppression of the workers. In 1885, she wrote:

> We build magnificent piles of architecture whose dizzy heights dazzle us, as we attempt to follow with our eye along the towering walls of solid brick, granite and iron, where tier after tier is broken only by wondrous panes of plate glass. And as we gradually bring the eye down story after story, until it reaches the ground, we discover within the very shadow of these magnificent abodes the homeless man, the homeless child, the young girl offering her virtue for a few paltry dollars to hire a little room way up in the garret of one of them . . . Yet it was their labor that erected these evidences of civilization.[28]

Through the pages of the *Alarm*, the Parsons tried to co-opt the "mechanic," or skilled building worker, arguing that effort expended in building "jails, court-houses . . . law and insurance offices" was an ultimately useless form of production benefiting only property owners.[29] It also printed recipes for the manufacture of dynamite and encouraged its use in bombing banks and other public buildings.[30] With these publications, Chicago anarchists joined like-minded European groups in turning towards dynamite as a way to violently reject a state they saw as intolerable. This became known as "propaganda of the deed" and resulted in a large number of political attacks and assassinations in Europe and the United States between 1880 and the beginning of World War I.[31]

During this period, anarchist bomb threats were frequent and while they were more often rhetorical than real, in Chicago at least, the police and the military took them very seriously. In an 1884 report, Philip Sheridan, commanding general of the United States Army and leader of the Chicago militia, warned that anarchists could easily manufacture explosives, and that "mercantile houses" represented prime targets.[32] This danger appeared to be realized in January 1885 when an anonymous messenger left what appeared to be a crude explosive device at the main office of Burnham and Root's recently completed Chicago, Burlington and Quincy Railway offices on the corner of Franklin and Adams Streets, one block from the Board of Trade on La Salle Street. The railway companies were the most powerful businesses in the city, and the choice of a railway company building was highly symbolic. Though anarchist leaders dis-owned the purported bomb—they accused local Pinkerton agents of planting it in order to precipitate a showdown between the two sides; the package was thrown into the Chicago River before it could be examined—its existence was widely reported as evidence that the anarchists were about to abandon words for action.[33]

The same ambiguity surrounds the Haymarket bombing which took place a year later, though in this case the consequences were much more severe.[34] On the evening of May 5, 1886, a relatively small group gathered to listen to speeches by Albert Parsons and other anarchist leaders at the Haymarket, a market square in a working-class area west of the Loop beyond the Chicago River. As the meeting began to disperse, an unknown assailant threw a bomb, killing several police officers and wounding others. The effects were immediate and catastrophic for the labor movement. The police rounded up and arrested hundreds of suspects. On June 5, 1886, 31 men were indicted for the crime and eventually eight were charged with conspiracy to commit murder. After a lengthy and highly publicized trial, four men, including Parsons and Spies, were hanged as accessories to murder. Though talk of social revolution was effectively put to an end by the Haymarket bombing, the events of that year—mass demonstrations by the working classes, violent strikes followed by a dynamite attack and effective martial law—solidified middle-class opinion that labor leaders, those responsible for strikes in the building trades as well as in other industries, were nothing but foreign fanatics intent on destroying the American way of life.

In their publications, Chicago architects joined ranks with the mainstream press in opposing the unions, seeing them as incubators for anarchist activity, organizations in which incompetent foreign agitators exploited honest and worthy "American" workers (as in the *Harper's Weekly* cartoon, Figure 2.8). An August 1886 editorial published in the real estate journal, the *Building Budget*, argued that the profession of architecture and the system of anarchy were purely antithetical. The author had nothing but praise for the prosecution of the men indicted for inciting the Haymarket bombing:

> Architecture and massive masonry are symbols of law and order, and the iconoclast longs to pull them down . . . When society becomes unsettled, and property is rendered insecure, men are not disposed to launch out in beautiful and substantial structures . . . The anarchist is the plain and practical foe of the architect and builder. Art, indeed, and anarchy cannot exist together. They are as antagonistic as light and darkness, cosmos and chaos, order and confusion.[35]

In this turbulent environment, Chicago architects argued that, rather than the structurally fragile and temporary physical manifestation of an unstable financial system, the skyscraper was the natural product of the frontier landscape. Throughout the 1880s the *Inland Architect*, the professional journal of the Western Association of Architects, published editorials condemning strikes by the building trades unions and vilifying labor activists, side by side with articles justifying the

2.8
"Too Heavy A Load for the Trades-Unions. The Competent Workman Must Support the Incompetent,"
*Harper's Weekly*, March 17, 1883

TOO HEAVY A LOAD FOR THE TRADES-UNIONS.
THE COMPETENT WORKMAN MUST SUPPORT THE INCOMPETENT.

skyscraper as the organic product of its environment, the result of a biological process in which European architectural forms evolved into a robust new American style. These articles were, in effect, an attempt to "naturalize" the forms assumed by capitalism.[36] The common practice of naming the skyscraper after a Native American tribe or mountain range (the Tacoma, Monadnock, Katahdin, and Wachusett to name but a few) is testament to building developers' efforts to promote their constructions as native and organic objects. In their published writings, architects took on the same project, describing the skyscraper as the most progressive example of the evolution of architectural form.

In making their argument for the skyscraper's naturalness, Chicago architects drew on the writing of the English art critic, John Ruskin. At the heart of Ruskin's philosophy was an argument about the relationship between art and labor, and the veracity of this position was one of the few things that both architects and anarchists agreed upon: the great man was frequently quoted in both the *Inland Architect* and the *Alarm*. For Ruskin, the Gothic cathedral was an authentic form of architecture because it represented a society in which the workman was given aesthetic freedom, and collaboration between all participants in the building process was the norm. He held up the collaborative efforts of medieval craftsmen in building the great cathedrals as an allegory of the participation of the working man in the governance of society.[37] Moreover, he believed that the Gothic style was a living mode of expression, changeable and adaptable to new contexts and uses, new places and peoples. Experiments in the commercial Gothic in the years after the 1871 fire by architects like Wight and Jenney reflected Ruskin's influence, both stylistically and intellectually.[38]

The moral associations of the Gothic style were particularly important as Chicago grew into a powerful city. Even more so than New York, Chicago was considered the American Gotham, the capital of capitalism, a city dedicated entirely to making money, by fair means or otherwise. Given this reputation, the adaptation of the Gothic style for office buildings, housing, banks, financial exchanges, and insurance companies provided new and often financially precarious institutions with the moral authority previously held by sacred architecture. Implying intellectual and spiritual correctness, if not strict stylistic authenticity, the "commercial Gothic" ensured prestige for the architect and, with luck, high returns for his patron and longevity for the building itself.[39] Jenney's Portland Block, in particular, became a well-loved monument, one of the few of the post-fire buildings to survive longer than ten years.

Ironically, given Ruskin's celebration of the working man, the symbolism of the Gothic Revival style was also useful for architects in pitting themselves against building trades unions and anarchist groups. In architectural journals as well as in the popular press labor conflicts were cast in explicitly ethnic terms: business owners with roots in the American North East were represented as "native" Americans, and labor leaders, often recent immigrants from Germany and Eastern Europe, were represented as foreigners, ethnically "other." In the mythology of national identity, a new American race was evolving at the frontier: a strong, practical, and independent tribe that had descended over many centuries from roots in Northern Europe. More recent immigrants who had not undertaken that process were assumed to be racially inferior.[40] Borrowing liberally from Viollet-le-Duc, Jenney argued that the architectural style evolving in the American West was a reflection of its builders, the modern-day Aryans. The Aryans, he said, are "again migrating westward and spreading themselves over the United States from the Gulf of Mexico to Canada and the Pacific to produce a new center of civilization."[41] For Chicago architects, the local adaptation of the Gothic was the solution to the intellectual struggle to find an indigenous style for the United States, one that had evolved, like the new American, from medieval Europe.

But despite the connection between the commercial Gothic and the supposed patrimony of building developers, it became increasingly difficult to reconcile this style with the Chicago construction. Initially, the Gothic cathedral, an historical precedent relying on buttresses rather than masonry walls for its primary structure, was the obvious reference point for steel-framed structures.

The New York critic Schuyler hinted at its adaptability to the new building method when he wrote, "We must own that the Chicago construction in its latest development, (sic) has not yet found its artistic expression; that no designer has yet learned to deal successfully with a structural change so radical that it has abolished the wall, which is the chief datum of every one of the historical styles of architecture, excepting only the developed Gothic."[42] Burnham and Root, in particular, were praised for their free adaptation of the Gothic style in ever-higher steel-framed buildings, including the Woman's Temple and the Masonic Temple, both completed in 1892. However, the physical form and interior requirements of these large buildings, along with the practical conditions of their construction, soon made overt Gothic styling go out of favor. The skyscraper was a rationalized building type, designed by newly bureaucratic architecture practices and erected by newly bureaucratic contracting companies using newly industrialized construction processes. In 1889 the Kansas City-based architect Henry Van Brunt rejected the Gothic as a model for the Chicago construction. "Such a problem does not call for the same sort of architectural inspirations as the building of a vaulted cathedral in the Middle Ages," he wrote. "The one required a century of deliberate and patient toil to complete it; the other must be finished, equipped, and occupied in a year of strenuous and carefully ordered labor."[43]

Influenced by the writing of Viollet-le-Duc, Chicago architects increasingly made a distinction between Gothicism as a style with recognizable external form (as in the Venetian Gothic), and Gothicism as a philosophy based on the principle of "constructive" expression in which materials were used "truthfully"; that is, their structural capability was made visible. The fact that the new structural system was an industrial one and its use transferred power out of the hands of traditional building craftsmen and into the hands of architects was viewed as a positive development. Viollet-le-Duc provided the last word on this. Significantly, he did not object to cast-iron, as Ruskin did, but saw in it the potential for a new modern style based on Gothic principles. Chicago architects soon adopted Viollet-le-Duc's rationalist understanding of structure and materials and in the process the Gothic Revival was transformed from a morally correct style into a rational constructive principle, a transformation that enabled local architects to unleash the Gothic from its anti-modern associations and to embrace industrialization.

Louis Sullivan is the architect most celebrated for his ability to adapt the naturalism of the Gothic style to new functions and new materials, but when viewed in the context of the labor conflicts dividing his city (conflicts in which he was professionally involved on a daily basis), his work can be seen as an attempt to create a new aesthetic that expressed the triumph of business and technology over the forces that threatened to destabilize the city.[44] While his version of the Gothic was true to the characteristics of its materials (iron, terracotta tile, and plate glass), its structure (an internal steel skeleton), and to its method of production (semi-industrialized processes), the all-important Ruskinian ideals of handicraft and collaborative effort had been replaced by an architect-driven, aestheticized representation of rationalized modern building processes. In 1896,

Sullivan famously claimed the skyscraper as a monument to American demo-cracy,[45] and for him, the ideal American was not the building trades worker but a member of the managerial class.

Echoing this idea, Frank Lloyd Wright in 1901 argued that the stone-mason's chisel was the tool of the slave. Only by embracing industrialized building methods could Americans free themselves and begin a new tradition. "The machine does not write the doom of liberty," he claimed, "but is waiting at man's hand as a peerless tool, for him to use to put foundations beneath a genuine democracy."[46] The transfer of the Ruskinian ideal of the medieval mason to the architect versed in the Chicago construction, from pre-industrial to industrial culture, was complete. For the architects of the first Chicago school, the curtain wall facade was an advertisement for an optimistic view of the future of American society under capitalism.

* * *

As we know, the appropriation of the skyscraper for anti-capitalist purposes occurred not in the United States, but in the drawings and rhetoric of the European avant-garde, where Expressionist, Constructivist, and Functionalist architects experimented with versions of the glass-clad, steel-framed tower in the service of socialism.[47] In the United States, the brutal aftermath of the Haymarket bombing put an end to this particular revolutionary moment in the nation's history. While labor unions still struck, it was in service of better pay and conditions, and not an attempt to overturn the social system. At the turn of the twentieth century the biggest threat to the skyscraper was not the anarchist's bomb but the wrecking ball as the country entered a steep depression in 1893. Faced with an oversupply of office space, the tall office building was no longer a sound business investment, and many early skyscrapers were demolished to make way for shorter and more profitable buildings. Inspired by the World's Columbian Exposition held in Chicago in the same year, Burnham began a second career as an urban planner in which he imagined the future of global capitalism in terms of horizontal rather than vertical expansion. The era of the skyscraper seemed to be over. But of course this was not the case: this particular form of accumulated capital merely lay in abeyance until the next boom period during the 1920s.

The dialectical nature of history is the organizing theme of Marx's analysis of capitalism, but he could not predict the ultimate challenge to capi-talism's global expansion presented by our limited natural resources nor the complex organizational, urban, and architectural forms in the twentieth century. His writing ultimately is best seen as an argument about the interconnectedness of the technical and social revolutions of the nineteenth century. In these terms, the Chicago of the 1880s and early 1890s presents a vivid illustration of his understanding of the workings of capitalism. Rereading the history of the first Chicago school through his lens of labor and class is useful in reminding us that the monolithic form of the skyscraper arose, paradoxically, out of conditions of transience, uncertainty, and conflict; that the technological revolution of the Chicago construction was inextricably tied to intense economic and social upheaval. One of the most visible manifestations of the massive and colossal productive forces created by capitalism, the skyscraper participated in a continuous dialectic of dismantlement and reconstruction, and this perpetual re-invention applied just as much to its cultural signification as it did to its material form.

## Notes

1 The history of the term "Chicago school of architecture" is discussed in: H. Allen Brooks, "Chicago School: Metamorphosis of a Term," *Journal of the Society of Architectural Historians* (May 1966): 115–118; Robert Bruegmann, "The Marquette Building and the Myth of the Chicago School," Thresholds 5, 6 (Fall 1991): 7–18, reprinted as "The Myth of the Chicago School," in *Chicago Architecture: Histories, Revisions, Alternatives*, ed. Charles Waldheim and Katerina Ruedi Ray (Chicago: University of Chicago Press, 2005), 15–29; and Daniel Bluestone, "Preservation and Renewal in Post-World War II Chicago," *Journal of Architectural Education* 47, 4 (May 1994): 210–223.

2 Sigfried Giedion, *Space, Time and Architecture: The Growth of a New Tradition* (Cambridge: Harvard University Press, 1941), 304.

3 As the first architectural historians to apply a Marxist lens to the discipline, Manfredo Tafuri and his students were especially interested in the early American skyscraper, understanding it as an instrument of ideology in the terms set out by philosopher Louis Althusser. See Giorgio Ciucci, Francesco Dal Co, Mario Manieri-Elia, and Manfredo Tafuri, *The American City: From the Civil War to the New Deal*, trans. Barbara Luigia La Penta (Cambridge: MIT Press, 1979). See also Andrew Leach, *Manfredo Tafuri: Choosing History* (Ghent: A&S/books, 2007), 34–43. More recently, Carol Willis has examined the early American skyscrapers in New York and Chicago in terms of their relationship to economic development and real estate practices in *Form Follows Finance, Skyscrapers and Skylines in New York and Chicago* (New York: Princeton Architectural Press, 1995).

4 Karl Marx and Friedrich Engels, *The Communist Manifesto* (1848; London: Penguin Books, 1967), 83.

5 A. J. P. Taylor, introduction to *The Communist Manifesto*, 18–19.

6 William Cronon, *Nature's Metropolis: Chicago and the Great West* (New York: W.W. Norton and Co., 1991). On the origins of the city, see also Harold M. Mayer and Richard C. Wade, *Chicago: Growth of a Metropolis* (Chicago: University of Chicago Press, 1969), 10–18; John Reps, "Urban Planning on the Great Lakes Frontier," in *Town Planning in Frontier America* (Princeton: Princeton University Press, 1969), 344–381; Janet L. Abu-Lughod, *New York, Chicago, Los Angeles: America's Global Cities* (Minneapolis: University of Minnesota Press, 1999), 33–34, 48–54.

7 Marx, *Communist Manifesto*, 85.

8 David Harvey discusses the transformation of Paris in these terms in *Paris, Capital of Modernity* (London: Routledge, 2003).

9 Mayer and Wade, *Chicago: Growth of a Metropolis*, 106–122.

10   Karen Sawislak has described the post-fire building regulations that hastened the physical segregation of Chicago into downtown business district and outlying suburbs in *Smoldering City: Chicagoans and the Great Fire, 1871–74* (Chicago: University of Chicago Press, 1995).

11   Homer Hoyt, *One Hundred Years of Land Values in Chicago* (Chicago: University of Chicago Press, 1933).

12   Robert Bruegmann discusses the role of this new financial entity in developing skyscrapers in *Holabird & Roche/Holabird & Root: An Illustrated Catalogue of Works, 1880–1940* (New York: Garland, 1991), 1:71.

13   In 1859 the New York-based magazine of arts and architecture, *The Crayon*, claimed that half of Chicago's buildings were owned by New Yorkers. "Notes on the West," *Crayon* 6 (1859): 223. On the Brooks and other patrons of Chicago real estate, see Miles L. Berger, *They Built Chicago: Entrepreneurs Who Shaped a Great City's Architecture* (Chicago: Bonus Books, 1992), 29–48.

14   Donald Hoffman, *The Architecture of John Wellborn Root* (Chicago: University of Chicago Press, 1973), 156.

15   Willis, *Form Follows Finance*, 19–34, 49–77.

16   Ibid., 46.

17   On the Tacoma, see Bruegmann, *Holabird and Roche*, 1:11–21. On the Reliance, see Joanna Merwood, "The Mechanization of Cladding: The Reliance Building and Narratives of Modern Architecture," *Grey Room* 4 (Summer 2001): 52–69.

18   The George A. Fuller Company built the majority of tall office buildings erected in Chicago in the 1880s and 1890s before expanding to New York in the early twentieth century. See *Fireproof Building Construction. Prominent Buildings Erected by the George A. Fuller Company* (New York: T. D. Rich and G.A. Fuller, 1904); Raymond C. Daly, *75 Years of Construction Pioneering: George A. Fuller Company, 1882–1957:* (New York: Newcomen Society in North America, 1957); David Van Zanten, "The Nineteenth Century: The Projecting of Chicago as a Commercial City and the Rationalization of Design and Construction" in *Chicago and New York: Architectural Interactions* (Chicago: Art Institute of Chicago, 1984), 42–45.

19   On the reorganization of Burnham's firm after Root's death, see Peter B. Wight, "Daniel Hudson Burnham and His Associates," *Architectural Record* 38, 1 (July 1915): 3–7; Charles Moore, *Daniel Hudson Burnham: Architect and Planner of Cities* (1992; repr., New York: Da Capo Press, 1968), 82–86; and Thomas Hines, *Burnham of Chicago: Architect and Planner* (Chicago: University of Chicago Press, 1974), 268–269.

20   Richard Schneirov provides a detailed history of the changes to labor practice in late nineteenth-century Chicago in *Labor and Urban Politics: Class Conflict and the Origins of Modern Liberalism in Chicago, 1864–97* (Urbana: University of Illinois Press, 1998).

21   Earl McMahon, *The Chicago Building Trades Council: Yesterday and Today* (Chicago: Chicago Building Trades Council, 1947).

22   Arnold Lewis describes European critical reaction to Chicago architecture in *An Early Encounter With Tomorrow: Europeans. Chicago's Loop, and the World's Columbian Exposition* (Urbana: University of Illinois Press, 1997).

23   "New Business Buildings of Chicago," *The Builder* (Great Britain) 63 (July 9, 1892): 23–25.

24 Jacques Hermant, "L'architecture aux Etats-Unis et à l'exposition universelle de Chicago," *L'Architecture* 7 (October 20, 1894): 341–346.

25 Henry Ericsson, *Sixty Years A Builder: The Autobiography of Henry Ericsson* (Chicago: A. Kroch and Sons, 1942), 71.

26 On the lives of Lucy and Albert Parsons, see Lucy Parsons ed., *The Life of Albert R. Parsons* (Chicago: L.E. Parsons, 1889); Albert R. Parsons, "Autobiography of Albert Parsons," in *The Autobiographies of the Haymarket Martyrs*, ed. Philip S. Foner (New York: Humanities Press, 1969); Carolyn Ashbaugh, *Lucy Parsons: American Revolutionary* (Chicago: Charles H. Kerr, 1976).

27 "International Workingmen's Proclamation," *Alarm*, July 23, 1886. On the principles of the IWPA, see Schneirov, *Labor and Urban Politics*, 173.

28 Lucy Parsons, "Our Civilization. Is it Worth Saving?" *Alarm*, August 8, 1885.

29 *Alarm*, November 1, 1884.

30 "Dynamite: The Protection of the Poor Against the Armies of the Rich," *Alarm*, December 6, 1884; "Dynamite," *Alarm*, February 21, 1885; "How to Make Dynamite," *Alarm*, March 21, 1885; "Explosives: A Practical Lesson in Popular Chemistry. The Manufacture of Dynamite Made Easy," *Alarm*, April 4, 1885; "Dynamite: Instructions Regarding its Use and Operations," *Alarm*, June 27, 1885; "Voice from the People: Nitro-glycerine," *Arbeiter-Zeitung*, January 4, 1885.

31 See Andrew R. Carlson, *Anarchism in Germany*, 2 vols (Metuchen, NY: Scarecrow Press, 1972); Jean Maitron, *Le mouvement anarchiste en France*, 2 vols (Paris: François Maspero, 1972–1975); Hermia Oliver, *The International Anarchist Movement in Late Victorian London* (London: Croome Helm, 1983); Richard B. Jensen, "Daggers, Rifles and Dynamite: Anarchist Terrorism In Nineteenth Century Europe," *Terrorism and Political Violence* 16, 1 (2004): 116–153; and John Merriman, *The Dynamite Club: How a Bombing in Fin-de-Siècle Paris Ignited the Age of Modern Terror* (New York: Houghton Mifflin, 2009).

32 The *Alarm* quoted from Sheridan's report of November 10, 1884 in which he warned of the dangers of dynamite. *Alarm*, December 6, 1884.

33 "Another Infernal Machine. A Curious Package Which Frightened Several Chicago People," *New York Times*, January 2, 1886; "The Chicago Socialists. How They Have Prepared for a Threatened 'Revolution.' Bombs and Infernal Machines for Future Use— Plans for Fighting in the Streets and from the Housetops," *New York Times*, January 15, 1886.

34 On the Haymarket bombing, see Henry David, *The History of the Haymarket Affair: A Study in American Social-Revolutionary and Labor Movements* (New York: Russell and Russell, 1936); Paul Avrich, *The Haymarket Tragedy* (Princeton: Princeton University Press, 1984); Carl Smith, *Urban Disorder and the Shape of Belief* (Chicago: University of Chicago Press, 1995), 101–146; and James Green, *Death in the Haymarket: A Story of Chicago, the First Labor Movement, and the Bombing that Divided America* (New York: Pantheon, 2006).

35 *Building Budget* 2, 8 (August 1886): 90.

36 Marx, as we know, derided attempts to "transform into eternal laws of nature and of reason, the social forms springing from your present mode of production and from property." Marx and Engels, *The Communist Manifesto*, 100.

37 On the influence of Ruskin's writing in the United States, see Michael W. Brooks, "Ruskin's Influence in America," in *John Ruskin and Victorian Architecture* (New

Brunswick: Rutgers University Press, 1987), 277–297; and Lauren Weingarden, "Gothic Naturalism and the Ruskinian Critical Tradition in America," in *Louis H. Sullivan and a Nineteenth-Century Poetics of Naturalized Architecture* (London: Ashgate Press, 2009), 71–96.

38  Wight's long-standing advocacy of the Gothic as the most appropriate way of building began with his early career in New York City, and his connections to the art journals the *New Path* and the *Crayon* in the 1860s. Peter B. Wight, "The Development of New Phases of the Fine Arts in America," *Inland Architect* 4, 4 (November 1884): 51–53; *Inland Architect* 4, 5 (December 1884): 63–65. On Wight's career and intellectual influences see Sarah Bradford Landau, *P. B. Wight: Architect, Contractor, and Critic, 1838–1925* (Chicago: Art Institute of Chicago, 1981).

39  Though this was the goal, not all critics were convinced as to the beauty or authenticity of the Chicago version of the neo-Gothic. The New York critic Montgomery Schuyler derided local attempts at what he called the "American eclectic Gothic." Montgomery Schuyler, "Glimpses of Western Architecture: Chicago" (1891), in *American Architecture and Other Writings*, ed. William Jordy and Ralph Coe (Cambridge: Harvard University Press and the Belknap Press, 1961), 2:253. Upon visiting the city in 1882 Oscar Wilde famously described the Water Tower as "a castellated monstrosity with pepperboxes stuck all over it." Arthur Seigel, *Chicago's Famous Buildings* (Chicago: University of Chicago Press, 1965), 48.

40  On the popularity of the Aryan myth in nineteenth-century America, see Reginald Horsman, *Race and Manifest Destiny: The Origins of American Racial Anglo-Saxonism* (Cambridge: Harvard University Press, 1981), and Richard Slotkin, *The Fatal Environment: The Myth of the Frontier in the Age of Industrialization 1800–1890* (New York: Atheneum, 1985).

41  William Le Baron Jenney, "Architecture. Lectures Delivered at the University of Chicago," pt. 2, *Inland Architect* 1, 3 (April 1883): 33–34.

42  Montgomery Schuyler, "Architecture in Chicago: Adler and Sullivan" (1896), in *American Architecture and Other Writings*, 2:387; emphasis added.

43  Henry Van Brunt, "Architecture in the West" (1889), in *Architecture and Society. Selected Essays of Henry Van Brunt* (Cambridge: Belknap Press, 1969), 187.

44  David Van Zanten and Lauren Weingarden have explored the ways in which Louis Sullivan carried on the Gothic tradition in his ornament. David Van Zanten, *Sullivan's City: The Meaning of Ornament for Louis Sullivan* (New York: W. W. Norton, 2000); Lauren Weingarden, "Ruskin's Reception in the Chicago School," in *Louis H. Sullivan and a Nineteenth-Century Poetics of Naturalized Architecture*, 183–212. Robert Twombly and Joseph Siry have discussed the effects of strikes on the construction of the Auditorium Building and on Chicago in general. Robert Twombly, "Cuds and Snipes: Labor at Chicago's Auditorium Building, 1887–89," *Journal of American Studies* 31 (1997); Joseph Siry, *The Chicago Auditorium: Adler and Sullivan's Architecture and the City* (Chicago: University of Chicago Press, 2002).

45  Louis Sullivan, "The Tall Office Building Artistically Considered," *Inland Architect* 27 (February 1896): 32.

46  Frank Lloyd Wright, "The Art and Craft of the Machine" (1901), in *America Builds: Source Documents in American Architecture and Planning*, ed. Leland M. Roth (New York: Harper and Row, 1983), 376.

47 Jean-Louis Cohen explores the fascination that American industrial architecture held for the architects of the European avant-garde in *Scenes of the World to Come: European Architecture and the American Challenge 1893–1960* (Paris and Montreal: Flammarion and Canadian Center for Architecture, 1995).

# Chapter 3

# Context: 1870–1914

Germany in the late nineteenth and early twentieth century traces another chal-
lenge to Britain's industrial hegemony. During the Second Reich (1871–1918),
Germany emerged as the third most powerful industrial economy behind the
United States and England. This required geo-political unity, achieved under
Wilhelm I and his Prussian prime minister, Otto von Bismark, and later by
Wilhelm's grandson, Wilhelm II. The unification of Germany after the Franco-
Prussian War brought with it a coordinated effort to brand the new state—as
much for itself as for others. It is in this context that Lauren Kogod examines
the intersection of economic politics, design, and consumerism through the
Deutscher Werkbund (German Work Federation).

The Werkbund is symptomatic of the many worker organizations that
came with the upsurge in population, energy, and territory following German
unification. In thirty years, exports and chemicals tripled, manufacturing quadru-
pled, coal production and machinery exports quintupled, and steel production
multiplied 12 times. Germany became the largest steel producer in Europe and
developed an expansive network of railroads that made internal exchange very
efficient. The annexation of Alsace-Lorraine in 1871 allowed it to incorporate a
significant part of France's industrial base. Germany rapidly learned Britain's
industrial lessons and, investing more heavily in research and development,
captured one-third of the Nobel prizes of this period. It surpassed Britain in key
areas such as dyes, chemicals, and electrical engineering. The German cartel
system, allowing trusts to be highly concentrated, made exceptionally efficient
use of capital. And unlike the European neighbors with which it competed,
Germany was not yet burdened with the cost of building up and defending an
extensive empire.

Politically, Bismark devoted his attention to combating opposition
within and limiting unrest from the working class of the Marxist Social
Democratic Party (SPD). Despite his natural conservative tendencies, the Prussian
prime minister forged a modern social welfare state: the German worker canteens
and changing rooms, the health benefits, and the national pensions. Despite this—

and partly because work was still a 12-hour day and an 80-hour week—the SDP gained in strength, becoming Germany's first political party.

Culture, too, was a political tool. Bismark's Kulturkampf (1871–1880) was aimed against the Catholics of Prussia who were seen by liberal intellectuals as a reactionary, anti-modern force. Given the context of overt concern for culture, sociology as a discipline was born, taking on the task of investigating the meaning of modern society. Max Weber (1864–1920) and Georg Simmel (1858–1918) continued the social critique initiated by Marx without his singular emphasis on the proletariat. Weber maintained that the rationalization of economic action can only be realized when it is supported by a positive ethical sanction that satisfies, sanctions, and maximizes the self-interests of the actor—for him, the Protestant Ethic. Simmel, in *The Metropolis and Mental Life* (1903), describes in detail the numbing quality that the city, the center of commodification, has on the individual experiencing it; and in his *Philosophy of Money*, he analyzes how money flattens qualitative differences between things as well as between people.

The Deutscher Werkbund was motivated by these social critics, anxious to prove the pessimism wrong. Like the German government which supported it, the Werkbund, as Kogod describes, was a project of active citizen indoctrination. German officials were key players. Friedrich Naumann, who helped devise the Werkbund's nationalist organizational structure, held a Reichstag seat. He linked the Werkbund to Germany's Navy League in advancing German hegemony, but unlike the League, he said it would fund itself. Hermann Muthesius lived in England as the Cultural Attaché for the German ambassador and reported regularly on advances in English architecture, crafts, and industrial design, cultivating relationships with the leaders of the Arts and Crafts movement. In 1904, now working for the Prussian Ministry of Commerce in Berlin, he resumed his architectural career and built houses in the "English Style" for the wealthy bourgeoise of the capital. Thus the dialog between, and the boundaries around, British and German culture became more fluid leading up to World War I.

Peggy Deamer

Chapter 3

# The display window as educator: the German Werkbund and cultural economy

Lauren Kogod

> We are in a battle that goes on behind the display windows, but is none the
> less passionate for it.
>
> Else Oppler-Legband[1]

It is axiomatic in architectural history that the work of Peter Behrens for the
German *Allgemeine Elektricitäts-Gesellschaft*, and his Turbine Factory building in
particular, is synecdochic for the German Werkbund. In 1907 Behrens was
appointed *AEG* artistic adviser, responsible for the planning and architecture of
its factories, administration buildings, exhibit pavilions and employee housing
estates. He was interior designer of industrial showrooms, retail shops and
traveling exhibits, and industrial designer of products and household appliances.
As graphic artist, Behrens designed the *AEG* logo, advertising and typeface. Even
at the time, Behrens's fellow Werkbund members identified his comprehensive
and coherent corporate branding as their ideal of the empowered artist in the
factory, conducting a visual symphony of industrial capital. The unadorned
simplicity and geometric clarity of Behrens's formal vocabulary provided monumentality for architecture, and, in product design, represented the spirit of
machined production, communicating the modern, industrial process in-its-
totality.

The privileging by historians of production over consumption and dis-
cernible protagonists over mute crowds evinced by this reading has camouflaged

significant aspects. The Werkbund was an association of designers and manufacturers intending to transform the German finished goods industries from a
piecemeal assortment of individual businesses into a unified and unifying
enterprise of cultural-economic agency.[2] We might interpret a pluralism of
commodity form to indicate egalitarianism in the market, or the calculated ability
of the market to reach every diverse sector; in the discourse of the Werkbund the
synchronicity of form and content insisted on a more troubling conclusion,
namely, a socially fragmenting effect of the capitalist economy. The *cultural* crisis
brought on by modern capitalism was only in part a problem of industrial
production; the bulk of critical anxiety was focused, rather, on mass consumption.
Insofar as their collective project was to create an operative—and remediating—
praxis of mass culture, as Frederic J. Schwartz argues, then Behrens's factory
should no longer serve as Werkbund icon.[3] Enlightened factory owners might
grasp the benefit of hiring artists to improve the design of their products, but
it was uncertain that consumers would buy them. In place of the productive
and monumental factory, it is the retail-store window, as reformed through its
interventions, which should be recognized as most emblematic of the German
Werkbund.

## Culture and civilization

The idea of a "display window reform" shouldn't be entirely surprising. The later
decades of the Wilhelmine Empire exploded with a spectrum of radical and
radically conservative "rebirth," protection, preservation and liberation movements that test a simple opposition between "progressive" and "conservative."
Every phenomenon of life was a candidate for transformation. Protecting nature
and animals, the landscape and local history was accompanied by vegetarianism,
homeopathy, nudism, artists' communes, new spiritualisms, women's equality,
youth groups, hiking groups, sexual freedom, eugenics and "social hygiene"
movements, housing reform, clothing reform, toy reform, nonprofit cooperatives and land-use reform, not to mention avant-gardist upheavals in the
performing and fine arts. Implicit in each was education—*Erziehung*—the guidance for a new orientation to life. Even political parties—Christian Socialists
and Communists alike—functioned as life reform movements, offering evening
instruction and social clubs.

Reviewing the Berlin Trade Exhibit of 1896, the sociologist Georg
Simmel identified "what could be termed the shop-window quality of things,"
by which he meant the attempt to arouse visual interest in objects by means of a
"tempting exterior," an artificial differentiation of form and surface among
similar products. "Competition no longer operates in matters of usefulness and
intrinsic properties," he wrote, "indeed, it strikes one as curious that the separate
objects in an exhibition show the same relationship and modifications that
are made by the individual within society."[4] In a tranquil, pre-capitalist
"before," objects were created to fulfill needs and, being necessary, required no
aesthetic surplus. The literature of social thought in Germany at this time was an
extended meditation on the antitheses between this idealized "before" and the

incomprehensible present, whether mournful, like Ferdinand Tönnies's 1887 *Community and Society*, or neutral, like Simmel. Pre-capitalist and "Oriental" populations enjoyed a rooted and collective community; modern conditions offered only a restless, competitive society. In small communities, useful tools were made by commission between mutually known individuals; in metropolitan societies, commodities, most of which were gratuitous, were produced speculatively and exchanged anonymously by means of abstract equivalence. Market capitalism created not the meaningful *Kultur* of shared values and references, but merely a *Zivilization*, technically advanced and spiritually hollow. The corrosive symptoms were observed in the cheap and ugly soullessness of its products, in "what the eulogists of the good old days," Simmel wrote, "complain of . . . [as] the ubiquitous and growing formlessness of modern life," and the increasing rapidity of its destructive pace.[5] To be clear, the Werkbund as a movement had no interest in alternative economic or political systems. They joined not to threaten the production/consumption machine of this "new age"; but to intervene among its inner relations.

The *locus classicus* of *Großkapital* was the urban department store, where consumers encountered objects divested of any evidence of their manufacture. The alienation was so complete, Simmel noted, that even "the worker is compelled to buy his own product."[6] Berlin's first department store, Gerson's, opened as the barricade embers of 1848 were barely extinguished, and fifty years passed before the program emerged as a coherent and respectable architectural type. Alfred Messel's 1907 addition to the *Warenhaus* Wertheim on Leipzigerstraße was to the department store what Behrens's Turbine Hall was to the factory: a masterpiece whose elegant resolution conferred dignity, elevating the previously mundane program to a work of *Kultur*.

In his 1908 study of this new urban presence Leo Colze wrote:

> The transformation of Berlin into a major city, into an international metropolis, is closely tied to the arrival of these shopping palaces. The impartial observer, without political agenda, must admit it was the department stores that got the ball rolling here in the commercial areas. When one shopping palace after another lines the thoroughfares of the imperial capital today, when light-permeated display windows not only incite us to buy the most amazing merchandise of every industry from the civilized nations, but also speaks to our purely aesthetic sense, when today even the little man is in a position, for a low price, to possess luxury items for which he has no useful need—then it is the sole doing of the modern department store organism.[7]

Colze was an astute observer whose apparent appreciation for the urban development produced by these stores slipped into an ambiguous tone when focused on their windows. Does Colze imply, "Today the 'little man' may aspire to more than the meanest subsistence; such small luxuries will improve his happiness?" Or does he mean, "The cornucopia on display incites even those who have so

3.1
August Messel,
Wertheim
Department Store,
Leipzigerplatz
(Berlin: 1907), *Kunst
in Industrie und
Handel; Jahrbuch
des Deutsches
Werkbundes*, 1913,
(Eugen Diederichs,
Jena, 1913), 63

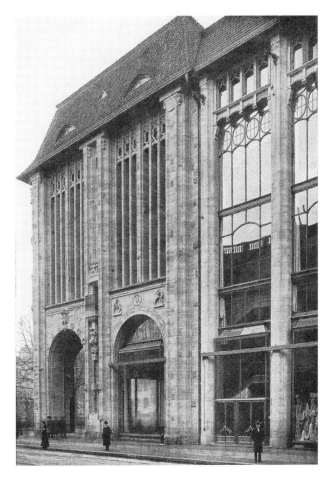

little, to waste on useless trinkets what ought to be saved for necessities?" The department store was an unassailable fact of modernity, a powerful economic conduit; but like many others, Colze considered the illuminated parade of merchandise lining the boulevards to be an endless assault on self-restraint.

Not only luxury was flaunted in store windows. Uncannily lifelike, female wax mannequins were under-clothed and provocatively posed, unlike the Greek statuary in museums, modeling immodesty and stimulating erotic desire.[8] Their diorama-like scenography was indistinguishable from the narrative tableaux of the "Panopticon" (as the wax museums were called), consolidating the opinion that window-dressing pandered to the lowest instincts of the widest audience. The average consumer knew no better, preferring shallow entertainments to edifying activities and purchasing cheap imitations of "fancy" wares instead of the tasteful and well made. Joseph August Lux wrote, "The masses can only be made bearable if bad products are withheld and only good ones served up. They can't be consulted because they have no judgment."[9]

3.2
Unknown artist,
advertising stamp,
Otto Freyberg,
*Mess- und
Geschäftshaus.*
Author's collection.

That the contemplation of the fine arts was a worthy practice of personal improvement and cultivation was a matter of faith in nineteenth-century Germany: art imparted moral instruction and civic virtue, a value to which the rise of the public museum attests. In 1897, Jean-Louis Sponsel argued that the modern metropolis itself could be considered a public museum in which the entire urban throng was a potential audience.[10] Advertising posters and shop windows were its paintings and vitrines, where emerging artistic principles were conveyed to the mass public. Even Colze, despite his implicit critique, recognized the display window as an aesthetic phenomenon. If craftsmen had once created tools and wares to satisfy specific needs, under the reign of *Großkapital* it was consumers that were produced—fashioned through their longing gazes—to insure the continuous circulation of money.[11] Its flow would pause while merchandise in the glazed between-space awaited "the mystery of the wedding between customer and product."[12] If the desiring subject was successfully interpolated and window-looker transformed into buyer, the whirring gears of the healthy economic machine would cycle forward. But in a new capacity, the role of the display window as a provocateur could be disciplined and put to pedagogic use, determining the kind of consumer it produced.

3.3
Top: Julius Klinger
for J. Lowenstein,
Hagen. Bottom:
Karl Bernhart for
TET-Packungen
(Leibnitz-Keks),
*Kunst in Industrie
und Handel;
Jahrbuch des
Deutsches
Werkbundes* 1913
(Eugen Diederichs,
Jena, 1913), 123

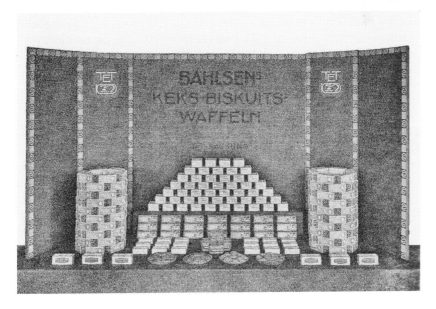

Window-dressing emerged as a specialized profession in these years: in 1904 Elisabeth von Stephani-Hahn was hired as Wertheim's first full-time supervisor of window display. In 1910 her colleague there, the Arts and Crafts department director Else Oppler-Legband, became director of a new Professional School of Decorative Arts founded with the support of the Werkbund, the German Association of Commercial Education and the Berlin Association of Specialty

Retailers. Oppler-Legband emphasized the window-dressing department, telling the 1911 Werkbund congress, "almost every student leaves us with an obvious enthusiasm for the important mission he can and must provide as a promoter and educator of taste."[13] At the proto-productive end of the production-consumption chain, Hermann Muthesius reorganized more than thirty German applied- and fine-arts schools including staffing and curricular changes. One of these was requiring some preparation for industrial production be included in applied arts instruction.[14] In the distributive middle, according to Heinrich Wolff, "the taste education of the German merchant" was among "the national-economic tasks of the Werkbund."[15]

Indeed, the Werkbund organized a traveling lecture series in 1909 called "The Taste Education of the German Merchant," held in partnership with a Commercial Employees Association and hosted by local chambers of commerce. John Maciuika reports, "By 1910 more than 5,000 salespeople had attended lectures, seminars and courses on the education of consumer taste."[16] Every gear in the distribution machine—business owner, merchant, window-dresser, and salesperson—was a potential teacher. Muthesius, Oppler-Legband, and Karl Ernst Osthaus traveled through Germany teaching these potential "teachers" how to "teach." In arranging products in his windows, wrote Friedrich Naumann, "the merchant works as an artist, not only as a distributor. At his glass panes, women and men learn what is beautiful . . . This creates a new profession: painting with beautiful objects, an architecture of diverse products."[17] Retailer and customer were both elevated in this exchange. When he acted as an educator, the merchant became more than a middleman; he and his picturesque (or architectural) display window were redeemed by their service to what Naumann called the Quality-Movement.

In September 1909, the first of three Greater Berlin Display Window Competitions was held with the guidance of the Werkbund, the support of the Berlin Association of Specialty Retailers and the Central Office for Berlin Tourism.[18] Although it lasted only three days, over 200 stores took part. In preparation, the Berlin Chamber of Commerce petitioned the Upper Brandenburg state council to suspend the prohibition against the display of merchandise on Sundays. After some resistance, the law requiring wares be covered or windows shuttered on the holy day was lifted, even during the 10:00 a.m. to 12:00 p.m. church hours.[19] "The latest victory of artists in Berlin is the conquest of the display window for cultural purposes," Stephani-Hahn declared.[20] The precise value of this victory was tempered by a consequence of the visual availability of merchandise on Sunday. Suddenly the stained-glass windows of church were put in direct competition with "cathedrals of consumption," and the lessons of scripture vied with a window-shopping promenade.

## Culture and state

At the 1911 Werkbund Congress, Muthesius outlined an historical trajectory (not, as is generally assumed, describing a putative scope of work) when he said, "'from the sofa cushion to the city plan' could characterize the path traveled by the applied arts-architectural movement of the last 15 years."[21] He was most likely referring to the previous year's meeting, which had been held in association with the Berlin General Urban Design Exhibit, where the 1910 Master Plan for the Development of Greater Berlin competition entries were presented.[22] Historical context clarifies Muthesius's intended meaning and yet his syntax suggests an additional implication. Apparently linear, "from the sofa cushion to the city plan" could be also understood as centrifugal, like a *Matryoshka* doll. Such constructions permeate Muthesius's ideas about change, for example, in *Style-Architecture and Building-Art*, where he argued: "only he who takes on the artistic interest in his [own] four walls, who has a natural impulse to artistically design his personal space, will take this feeling from his own rooms onto the street and into the wider environment."[23] And, "transformation can proceed only from the small to the large, above all from the interior to the outside before one[self]."[24] The artistic cultivation of each individual was necessary for the creation of neighbors, then communities, German citizens, and Europeans, in expanding concentric rings. Just as the sofa cushion informs the room, the room integrates within the house, the house with the neighborhood, the neighborhood connects to the town, and the town functions within the regional plan, the sphere of German aesthetic influence might reverberate ever outward, like the platitude of the pebble's rings. The construction encapsulates the German ideal of *Bildung*, the effect of personal cultivation in transforming self-seeking and callow youths into responsible, socially directed citizens.

In its discourse, the Werkbund regarded the mass German society as just this subject whose wholesale taste-cultivation (*Geschmacksbildung*) would guarantee a proper developmental trajectory, off an imaginary path of philistinism and some vague ruin toward a mature freedom. To develop a coherent, modern, German language of form—which went by the revered name *Style*—would demonstrate unity, vitality and, as the symbolic content of the shared good taste, the spiritual legitimacy of German ascendance. Becoming a leader in matters of taste and exporting products, to Britain and France no less, was as tantalizing to many citizens as it was to the Kaiser. Through the nineteenth century, German wares were of such low quality as to threaten trade imbalances. Maiken Umbach recounts that the British Merchandise Act of 1887 required all German products shipped to Britain and British colonies to be labeled "Made in Germany" as a warning to customers. Only ten years later, "Made in Germany" was "identified with goods of a high technical and aesthetic standard. English manufacturers even began to forge the label, printing it on their English-made products."[25] In 1896, Muthesius had been sent to London to research English artistic, technological and educational trends with the mission to recreate those achievements at home. In 1910, the *École d'Art* graduate from La Chaux-de-Fonds, Charles-Édouard Jeanneret, was sent to study German applied arts reform.[26] Within French decorative arts circles, the patent improvement of German design was experienced with consternation as an attack on the manifest hegemony of French style, as Jeanneret wrote, a "German invasion."[27]

In their founding year, 1907, the Werkbund was delighted by the support of its government for their unifying cause of *Geschmacksbildung*. But by 1914, some members chafed under the increasing pressure exerted by Muthesius as emissary of the commerce and interior ministries.[28] The debate between Muthesius and Henry van de Velde at the 1914 July congress in Cologne is presented in histories of architecture as a clash between *Realpolitik* "moderns" advocating for incipient type-forms (Muthesius) against a residual *Jugendstil* sentiment (joined by the errant proto-expressionist) mourning the death-knoll of artistic individuality (van de Velde). In fact, of the ten guidelines Muthesius expected to ratify, only two mentioned "typification" (*Typisierung*). Seven argued that the further development and expansion of the German export industry was the "question of life" for the nation.[29] As the coherent syntax of the nascent German brand identity, Muthesius's type-form was the formal means to a nationalist, economic-political end. At the heart of the dispute, then, was less the freedom of form from constraining norm, but the necessity to serve an end rather than be one. *Was the shared goal of the Werkbund the elevation of German culture? Or was it the elevation of the German state?*

## Culture and mass culture

Van de Velde delivered the counter-theses but he spoke for a group that included Karl Ernst Osthaus, an unusually persistent patron of the arts who had lectured on display windows and store design with the Werkbund merchant-education tour. Having opened his private Folkwang Museum in 1901 in Hagen, in 1909 Osthaus founded the German Museum for Art in Trade and Industry, also in Hagen. In the Folkwang Museum was Osthaus's collection of neo-Impressionists, van Gogh, Cézanne and *die Brücke* expressionists, paintings of the kind state museums were consistently denied municipal and royal permission to exhibit. These were displayed with and among his collection of ethnographic ritual and utilitarian objects according to Osthaus's personal aesthetic sense of "resolution of form bound by inner laws."[30] The German Museum for Art in Trade and Industry, operating as the *de facto* Werkbund museum of *Qualität*, collected contemporary advertising posters, packaging, letterheads and trademarks, published monographs of advertising artists, housed a materials library, a slide library and organized traveling exhibits. The Folkwang Museum was dedicated to avant-garde art and radical—because so purely formalist—curating. What the Museum for Art in Trade and Industry was—a museum which showed "work" that could be seen on any streetcar or advertising column and that could circulate duplicate exhibits because its artworks were already mass reproductions—is less clear. Neither avant-garde nor kitsch, this museum created an in-between, culturalist space for *Geschmacksbildung* and *Qualität* distinct, also, from the pious aspirations of what later was called "middlebrow."

The *Qualität* that the Museum for Art in Trade and Industry promoted was a visual simplicity or essentialism bordering on abstraction which Osthaus, Muthesius, Lux, Naumann and others called *Sachlichkeit*. With the artistic leadership of the commercial artists (and Werkbund members) Lucian Bernhard and Julius Klinger, the modern advertisement had developed as a *Sachplakat*, an object-poster, which reduced its graphic elements to product image and brand name in richly saturated color.

**3.4**
Lucian Bernhard,
advertisement for
Manoli cigarettes.
The black
background has no
indication of depth,
such as a division
between horizontal
(tabletop) and
vertical (wall)
surfaces; the
cigarette pack is
rendered in an
extremely
rudimentary
perspectival
recession and is in
front of the brand
name only because
the A (and a bit of
the M) is covered
by the open top of
the case; Bernhard
communicates
"planarity"
by creating
incommensurability
between flat and
deep. Kunst in
Industrie und
Handel; Jahrbuch
des Deutsches
Werkbundes 1913,
Eugen Diederichs,
Jena, 1913

"The most important principle of poster-art," wrote Lux, "is that it should appear as a surface," just as the display window "must avoid becoming a little stage."[31] The *Sache* or "thing" of the poster was less the merchandise pictured than its own "poster-ness"; the interplay of flat (text and color) and deep (simple perspective or isometric product image) communicated its planarity.

In the same year Lux had suggested the curtailment of consumer choice for the masses, he also published *Taste in Daily Life: a Lifebook for the Nurturing of Beauty* (1908) which offered practical advice for the aesthetic improvement of everyday objects and practices, almost all of which centered on the middle-class home. Lux employed the didactic model of example and counter-example to show, for instance, the setting of a beautiful or fussy table, good and bad flower arrangements, tasteful and unspeakable furniture, handsome and unbearable wall clocks, and artistic and un-artistic family photographs.

Read with Werkbund literature in mind, the book illuminates the extent to which the movement was driven by middle-class (*bürgerlich*)—specifically educated, upper-middle-class (*Bildungsbürgerlich*)—values. Their dream of social cohesion was to be built on this foundation: self-restraint and discipline, sincerity in work and unpretentious, refined taste. By discursive consent, the taste-aesthetic of this class was *Sachlichkeit*: objective, object-ness, practicality, straightforwardness, simplicity, a kind of ideological *transparency*, without the aesthetic surplus Simmel had identified in 1896 on the surface of competing commercial goods. *Sachlichkeit* was the disciplining of surfaces.

The persistent synchronism of *Sachlichkeit* and *Qualität* throughout the Werkbund reveals an undercurrent of nearly mystical faith in the transformative

3.5
Top: "an unspeakable Jugendstil comedy", bottom: "a sachlich cabinet." J. A. Lux, *Geschmack im Alltag: ein Lebensbuch zur Pflege des Schönen,* (Dresden,Gerhard Kühtmann 1808), 240–241

Eine unsägliche Jugendstilkomik. Möbelzeichnerphantasie,
die auch „in Sezession" arbeitet. Falsche Moderne.
Echte Moderne gibt sich sachlich und angemessen.

Hier ist ein sachlicher Schrank im Gegensatz zu der vorigen Möbel-
zeichner-Entgleisung. Sorgen wir also, daß das Salonmöbel zu
unserm Salonrock paßt, daß es so sachgemäß geformt ist, wie dieser.

power of objects on what Simmel called the individual "psychic life-process."[32] Despite their differences, Lux, Osthaus, Muthesius, Naumann, van de Velde and others of their fractious alliance shared the belief that, redeemed by a high aesthetic and material *Qualität*, mass-produced utensils of daily life could function as indoctrination, transmuting *formal* principles of objects, such as simplicity, proportion and functionality, into the *personal* values of individuals, such as sobriety, serenity and diligence. With Simmel, they understood individual cultivation to be "consummated in a unique adjustment and teleological inter-weaving of subject and object," whereby the "more elevated and perfect [the] objects" incorporated, the more beneficial the "measure of development of persons thus attained."[33] The consummation was visual over haptic. Further, the qualitative or potential value of each object was determined not by inner empathy or affinity but by its distance: "The more separated a product is from the subjective spirituality of its creator, the more it is integrated into an objective order—the more distinct is its *cultural* significance and the more suited it is to become a general means for the cultivation of many individual souls."[34] In a sense, Simmel provided a benediction for *Sachlichkeit*.

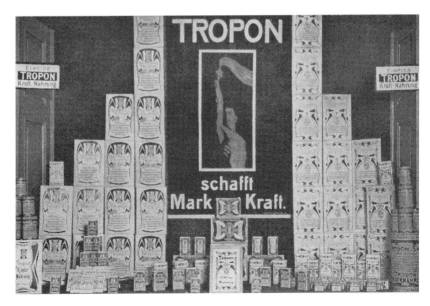

**3.6**
Top: Julius Klinger for J. Loewenstein, Hagen. Bottom: Henry van de Velde for Tropon, *Kunst in Industrie und Handel; Jahrbuch des Deutsches Werkbundes* 1913 (Eugen Diederichs, Jena, 1913)

The display window was both a *where* for *Geschmacksbildung* and a *what*; re-formation demanded it "catch up" to aesthetic concepts emerging in reform theater and contemporary advertising. In "The Display Window," published in the 1913 Werkbund Yearbook "Art in Trade and Industry," Osthaus suggested looking to the products themselves to inform their composition: "The objects that surround us fall into two categories: those that attract us by their color and such, and those through form and [out]line. All products of an essentially painterly nature can tolerate crowding; those of a sculptural nature need to be displayed separately."[35] In his examples, the objects of a plastic, or sculptural, nature were not in every case human (but if so, the new anti-illusionism demanded their decapitation), yet their compositional structures are familiar from the humanist formal canon, above all the still life.

But the windows displaying merchandise of a "painterly nature" are entirely unexpected. While for the most part symmetrical, they yet have in common a repetitive, abstract rhythm which indexes the later aesthetic of construction.[36] Non-referential, geometric shapes are built up by stacking goods like building blocks. Van de Velde's display for Tropon nutritional supplement no less than Lucian Bernhard's windows for Stiller shoes "is determined by repetitive and serially structured formation that is the very nature of mass-reproduced commodities."[37] Briefcases, bath oils, biscuits, cigarettes and shoes tap out the rhythm of the Tiller Girls, in whose precisely synchronized dances Siegfried Kracauer later identified the mass ornament, the ideational figure of the mass subject. As in their dances, no less than in these displays or with the norma-tive type-form, sameness trumps difference, and any individuality is subsumed to the abstract whole. In the perpetual "teleological interweaving of subject and object," the display of "sculptural" goods re-enacted abstractly an aesthetic known, the "painterly" display prepared for a future.

Among its countless initiatives, the reformed display window describes most articulately the invisible forces the Werkbund was founded to confront. Just as its own glazed space joins indoors and out, store and street, the group created a discursive space begrudgingly shared by artistic culture and commercial civilization, by "non-political" culture and ambitious state, by humanist and posthumanist subject-formation. Its members intended to recapture some inher-ited memory of social harmony with the tools, forms and "psychic life process" of the imminent future-present. By bringing those repetitive, constructed rhythms into cultural representation and reproduction, the Werkbund unintentionally enabled a subject yet to come.

\* \* \*

The following is a translated excerpt from Karl Ernst Osthaus, "The Display Window" ("*Das Schaufenster*"), *Jahrbuch des Deutschen Werkbundes 1913: Kunst in Industrie und Handel* (Jena: Eugen Diederichs, 1913).[38]

\* \* \*

The Orient knows nothing of the shop window. There, the storerooms of the craftsman and peddlers are lined up in covered bazaars. The front walls are open during the day and boarded up at night. Shelves surround the small space from which the trader, smoking and gossiping on his yellow straw mat, keeps an eye out for customers. The entire shop is, as it were, the shop window.

But it is also a workshop. For in the Orient, one "trades" only in goods that come from foreign lands: spices from India, precious stones, European junk. The weaver, the shoemaker, the metalsmith and the cook ply their trades in plain sight, and the miller himself pours the corn into the trough around which his harnessed donkey makes round after round. The appeal of the bazaar is based on the interest we take in the creating and forming. By watching we understand and learn, and this is the final reason why the Orient—as it was in antiquity—has not lost its style in its crafts.

The shop window of the North shows us the product and not the production. It lacks the thrill of Becoming that the Oriental bazaar makes so attractive. One thinks only of the use of the product, not about the work that created it. The Becoming is completed in a closed workshop, and only those authorized have the opportunity to observe it. Thus, for most people, the most important source of interest in the work has dried up, a feeling for style deprived of its most indispensable foundation.

What is the consequence of this for the window display? It must attempt to elevate itself by artistic means. It must show off, tempt, and stimulate desire. All the more so now that easier production has increased competition, making advertising a decisive factor for success. Today's window display has become advertising, so much so that many stores have given up displaying the goods for sale. They want simply to attract, to amaze, and to push the city throng into a sense of excitement through the never-ending wonders of decorative art.

A few years ago on Leipzigerstraße in Berlin there was a window that contained a whole pile of birthday presents: a rocking horse, a sailor suit, a toy train and cigars (!); only the cake on the table quietly indicated that it was a pastry shop offering this tempting spectacle. At the same time, Jacoby's Shoe Store displayed a dressing room with furniture, items of clothing and pictures on the walls; of everything the display offered, only the little slippers on the arctic pelt in front of the dressing table were taken from that store's inventory. In Berlin, there are associations for the mutual lending of set pieces, which account for this kind of display.

You can trace examples like those described above to the hypertrophic atmosphere of the display window competitions; clothing stores have not yet outgrown the habit of panoptical presentations. One sees women at their toilette to show lingerie, a picnic under palm trees for tropical clothing, fox hunting for riding or hunting apparel, arctic hunts with painted icebergs to display furs. The principle of these displays lacks the objectivity [Sachlichkeit] we demand today as the infallible criterion of quality for artistic achievement. No one can deny that these windows cause a sensation, attract countless gawkers and not infrequently create a climax to a street. Nevertheless, their days are numbered simply, you could say, because they're "done." Every visual sensation has its allotted time; as soon as the hunger for each is sated, it fizzles out ineffectively.

Is it still worth considering its virtues and vices in detail? Today we might have to remind ourselves these things had their benefits. The amount of taste and elegance produced in the dressing and color composition in a display window at Gerson's easily outweighs the "art" of dozens of these objective [*Sachlich*] displays already boring us today by those who can't grasp that art relies on sensitivity, not on the application of a theory. The Gerson's are few, however, and even they haven't managed to resolve this contradiction entirely. [. . .] Those Bismarck-monuments made of chocolate or bars of soap, that temple made from candles, and the ham decorated with lard Raphaël-angels, all these prompt embarrassing memories of that time when the store window—like the stage—was supposed to signify the whole world.

The new store window aspires to be objective [*sachlich*]. Every product wants to be itself instead of telling stories. The display wants to be a display, something that is arranged but isn't apparently held together by any "literary" binding. The dress is a product, not the sheath for an expectantly eavesdropping wax beauty. This will require a reversal of terms. It's the rejection of romanticism applied to the shop window. It's merely the corollary of that huge turning point [*Wende*] that did away with historicist style in architecture and painted set decoration in theater, and which formed its economic-political organ in the German *Werkbund*.

\* \* \*

Another issue is no less important. In our capital city streets, window displays are lined up like paintings in an artist's studio. The frames are missing. Wherever possible, their interior walls are even mirrored. We see thousands of criss-crossing reflections of light and color. A veritable feast for eyes sensitive to impressions, but an insult to objectivity [*Sachlichkeit*]. The merchant who wants to sell his goods cannot be indifferent to whether the human stream parading past is simply intoxicated by the atmosphere of sparkle and light. He has to lure this crowd, hook it and reel it in; the commodity must become endowed with meaning, declare itself, drive off the intoxicating glare and become alone with each individual. So alone that the magic spell spins its web and the bewitched can't break free from the thought: I must possess you.

But the mystery of the wedding between customer and product requires focus. All means should come into play to isolate the product. And above all the window requires a frame.

[August] Endell, the greatest magician among the display artists in Berlin, has understood this best. Wherever he has the opportunity to design the facades of his shops, he puts wide pilasters between the windows and decorates the window infill with such a precious setting that we're overcome with a feeling of wonder even before we step up to the pane.

3.7
August Endell,
Salamander
Shoe Store (Berlin:
Tauentzienstraße).
*Kunst in Industrie
und Handel;
Jahrbuch des
Deutsches
Werkbundes* 1913,
(Eugen Diederichs,
Jena, 1913)

It was also Endell who gave lighting its best solution. Others anticipated him in eliminating external arc lamps, which blind instead of illuminate. Concealed lighting, which hides the light source from the onlooker and allows products to stand out all the more clearly, had already come to window display as a legacy of the stage. But light first achieved a mysterious magic in Endell's hands. The fixtures above, from which light shines down onto the wares, are closed to the street in glittering planes of jewel-colored glass. Transformed into magical signs, the (Salamander) logos glow in the warm rays. The whole thing breathes that mood experienced by a child in front of the curtain that will open the world of dreams to him for the first time. What is presented in this magic shrine is always something precious, even if it's only a pair of black leather boots . . .

And herein lies the secret of good display: fantasy, the merchant's most faithful helper, wants to be summoned. However, this art is difficult, and inspirations soon turn into rigid rules if the eternally playful goddess withholds her blessing from the artist's hand. The modern department store, invented by Messel and refined by Olbrich, has brought the shop window to its latest architectural version. It is like a glass vitrine between stone pillars, which strain against the roof in a powerfully striving ascent. These glass cases offer the most unrestricted opportunities for objects of several sizes. Elisabeth von Hahn, the Wertheim display-artist, has laid the historic foundation for arrangement in them.

\* \* \*

Objective unity that puts everything on display under the rule of a guiding idea is achieved only in rare cases. And even this is expendable compared to the more important visual unity. Display windows are still lives, not historical paintings.

In recent years, the question, "should one exhibit more or less?" has animated the decorators' thoughts. They came to the realization that a random and disorderly accumulation of objects is hardly conducive for the purpose of sales. Only in the suburbs does one still see today those towering piles of pants, bureaus and china tableware that constituted the schema of every dependable store back in the 1890s. But the theory of the modern display window has overshot its goal many times. It's not true that a display window has a better effect the less it contains. The nature of the goods themselves ought to decide between more and less.

The objects that surround us fall into two categories: those that attract us by their color and such, and those through form and line. Tomatoes and oranges, as well as fabrics, sponges, many flowers and colonial goods rarely claim our feeling for the plastic. Their allure lies in their color. Conversely, furniture, lingerie and clothing interest us primarily with the dignity or elegance of their (out)lines. This has to be taken into account when designing displays. You can stack up a hundred oranges, or let entire waterfalls of lovely fabrics cascade down, but even a few large figures in a window will be unbearable. All products of an essentially painterly nature can tolerate crowding; those of a sculptural nature need to be displayed separately. And each painterly value requires we group like with like; a full planting bed of red tulips has a stronger effect than tulips, narcissi, mignonettes and forget-me-nots together. A statue works well next to an arm-chair, a chest, curtains and a flowerpot, but not with another one of itself or even a similar work with which it has no inner relationship. Naturally there are some who push the edges. One example is shoe display, which has literally become an elevated school of window display culture in Berlin.

\* \* \*

Of course nothing stands in the way of composing a window as freely as a still life by Heda or Cezanne. But then it should also hold together as tightly as those artists' works. To create the fullest resolution of form bound by inner [laws] belongs to a great artistic talent. Gipkens has made frequent efforts with refined taste at Friedmann & Weber. And we recall with delight the cascades of color Mrs.

Oppler-Legband created out of sofa cushions and wool blankets for Brühl on the occasion of one competition. But the danger of lapsing into banal chaos is never greater than with the attempt to do just this kind of thing. In general, the decorator should leave this to the artist.

It wasn't the task of this essay to give (precise) advice and instructions for window-dressing. Its one and only purpose is to show the larger context of our cultural movement within which the display window operates. It has no independent existence. The regeneration of taste that we observe in all fields today has been integrated into its growth. It has become a venue for artistic experimentation, which is all the more important as it takes place in front of everybody on the street. More attention is paid to the display window than to the facade. Thus the effect it produces is all the greater. The store owner has therefore become an educator of the people, or at least a mediator, on whom the fate of taste among the wider public depends. He didn't seek out this role for himself; it's fallen to him. But if he thinks well of his profession, he'll take it up with joy. It leads him out from the confinement of his guild again into the intellectual life of his people, where, in addition to gold, the man is also weighed.

## Notes

I am eternally grateful to David and team Smiley.

1  Else Oppler-Legband, "Die Höhere Fachschule für Dekorationskunst," in *Jahrbuch des Deutschen Werkbundes 1912: Die Durchgeistigung der deutschen Arbeit* (Jena: Eugen Diederichs, 1912), 110; hereafter JDW 1912. Translations are my own unless otherwise noted.

2  The formulation "finished goods industries" is owed to John V. Maciuika, *Before the Bauhaus: Architecture, Politics, and the German State, 1890–1920* (Cambridge: Cambridge University Press, 2005), 14.

3  Frederic J. Schwartz, *The Werkbund: Design Theory and Mass Culture Before the First World War* (New Haven: Yale University Press, 1996).

4  Georg Simmel, "Berliner Gewerbeausstellung," in *Simmel on Culture*, ed. David Frisby and Mike Featherstone, trans. Sam Whimster (1896; London: Sage Publications, 1997), 257.

5  ——, "The Conflict of Modern Culture," in *Simmel on Culture*, ed. David Frisby and Mike Featherstone, trans. D.E. Jenkinson (1918; London: Sage Publications, 1997), 77.

6  ——, "Philosophie des Geldes," in *The Philosophy of Money*, ed. David Frisby, trans. Tom Bottomore and David Frisby (1900; London: Routledge, 1978), 454.

7  Leo Colze, *Berliner Warenhäuser* (1908; Berlin: Fannei & Walz Verlag, 1989), 11.

8  Sherwin Simmons, "Ernst Kirchner's Streetwalkers: Art, Luxury, and Immorality in Berlin, 1913–16," *The Art Bulletin* 82, 1 (March 2000): 117–148.

9  Joseph August Lux, *Das Neue Kunstgewerbe in Deutschland* (Leipzig: Klinkhardt & Biermann, 1908), 250.

10  Sponsel advocated for the equivalence of the placard with fine art; see Jeremy Aynsley, *Graphic Design in Germany, 1890–1945* (Berkeley: University of California Press, 2000).

11  Schwartz is excellent here; see 26–60 and 82–91.

12 Karl Ernst Osthaus, "Das Schaufenster," in *Jahrbuch des Deutschen Werkbundes* 1913: *Kunst in Industrie und Handel* (Jena: Eugen Diederichs, 1913), 62; hereafter *JDW* 1913.

13 Oppler-Legband, "Die Höhere Fachschule für Dekorationskunst," *JDW* 1912, 105–110.

14 Maciuika, *Before the Bauhaus*, 104.

15 Heinrich Wolff, "Die Volkswirtschaftlichen Aufgaben des D.W.B," *JDW* 1912, 89.

16 Maciuika, *Before the Bauhaus*, 169. Schwartz, *The Werkbund*, 102–103.

17 Friedrich Naumann, "Werkbund und Handel," *JDW* 1913, 13–14.

18 Gudrun M. König, *Konsumkultur: Inszenierte Warenwelt um 1900* (Vienna: Böhlau, 2009): 126–127.

19 Ibid.

20 Elisabeth von Stephani-Hahn, "Die Kunst der Schaufensterdekoration," in *Was die Frau von Berlin wissen muß*, ed. Eliza Ichenhaeuser (Berlin: Herbert G. Loesdau, 1913), 273.

21 Hermann Muthesius, "Wo stehen wir?" *JDW* 1912, 16.

22 Wolfgang Sonne, "Ideen für eine Großstadt: der Wettbewerb Großer-Berlins, 1910," in *Stadt der Architektur/Architektur der Stadt: Berlin, 1900–2000* (Berlin: Nicolai, 2000), 67–78.

23 Hermann Muthesius, *Stilarchitektur und Baukunst; Wandlungen der Architektur im XIX. Jahrhundert und ihr Heutiger Standpunkt* (Mülheim a.d. Ruhr: K. Schlimmelpfeng, 1902), 59.

24 Ibid.

25 Maiken Umbach, "The Deutscher Werkbund and Modern Vernaculars," in *Vernacular Modernism; Heimat, Globalization and the Built Environment*, eds. Umbach and Bernd Hüppauf (Stanford: Stanford University Press, 2005), 120.

26 Le Corbusier, *A Study of the Decorative Art Movement in Germany*, trans. Alex T. Anderson (Weil am Rhein: Vitra Design Museum, 2008), 139.

27 Ibid., 204.

28 See Maciuika, *Before the Bauhaus*, 248–282.

29 Hermann Muthesius, "Leitsätze und Vortrag," in *Die Werkbund: Arbeit der Zukunft* (Jena: Eugen Diederichs, 1914), 32–33. Guideline five mentioned neither.

30 Osthaus, "Das Schaufenster," *JDW* 1913, 68.

31 Joseph August Lux, "Das Plakat" and "Das Schaufenster," in *Geschmack im Alltag: ein Lebensbuch zur Pflege des Schönen* (Dresden: G. Kuhtmann, 1908), 346, 349.

32 Georg Simmel, "Subjective Culture," in *On Individuality and Social Forms*, ed. and trans. Donald N. Levine (1908; Chicago: University of Chicago Press, 1971), 227–234.

33 Ibid.

34 Ibid.

35 Osthaus, "Das Schaufenster," *JDW* 1913, 67.

36 Naumann's "painting with beautiful objects, an architecture of diverse products" is a better description of these categories; cf. note 27.

37 Describing Hannes Meyer's 1925 Co-op Vitrine, see K. Michael Hays, *Modernism and the Posthumanist Subject* (Cambridge: The MIT Press, 1992), 32.

38 Osthaus, "Das Schaufenster," *JDW* 1913, 59–69. Translated and abridged by author. First draft by William L. West, Yale School of Architecture Teaching Assistant, 2005.

Chapter 4

# Context: 1918–1935

The transition from the Werkbund to the Bauhaus traces the ongoing importance of Germany culturally, economically, and politically, and tells the story behind the introduction and popularization of Modernism. The Weimar republic, formed after the abdication of Wilhelm II at the end of the November Revolution of 1918 (itself a shade of the Russian Revolution), marked a period of dynamic instability. This instability was less the result of Germany's defeat in World War I than its own internal struggles. Numerous challenges—the loss of pre-war industrial exports, the cessation of food supplies and raw material from Alsace-Lorraine, deepening debt, war reparations, and eventually, hyperinflation as the government just printed more money—led both the proletariat and the industrialists to fear the chaos of the free market and to support strong governmental control of the economy. However, the nature of this control was disputed. The Social Democratic Party (SDP) was divided between those who wanted a parliamentary system and those who wanted a socialist, council-based one and the Communists played an increasingly significant role in shaping the new Germany. While the left was appeased by a number of SDP-led social decrees—the eight-hour workday, national health insurance, and universal suffrage—the period between 1920 and 1923 was one of widespread chaos and bloody confrontation. When Germany defaulted on its debt in 1923 and experienced massive inflation, financial reforms were introduced to stabilize the German economy, and the Americans reluctantly—given their post-war isolationism—intervened. Beginning in 1924 under the Dawes Plan, German bonds were sold to American investors, enabling the German economy to recover and inter-Allied debts to be paid.

From 1923–1929, there emerged a period of relative stability. The chancellor created a new monetary system and Germany was admitted to the League of Nations. This precipitated a surge of cultural experimentation: new street theater, radical political graphics, the liberation of women, the introduction of jazz, the "Americanization" of cultural liberalism, and the rise of the Bauhaus. The Bauhaus, one of the best examples of the creative experimentation in the 1920s, spawned by a zeal for worker empowerment on the part of the liberal intelligentsia. A natural outgrowth of the Werkbund and inspired by Russian experiments with constructivism and productivism, its aspirations, while inter-national, were German in the particulars. It was aided by the promise of "minimal dwelling" written into the Weimar constitution and Weimar's need, given its lack of raw materials, to utilize its skilled labor force to promote exportable innovation and high-quality goods to fuel the German economy. This is still true today: Germany designs quality.

While Gropius, who started the Bauhaus in Weimar in 1919, was on the pro-art side of the art-versus-production Werkbund dispute and while he stated that the goals of the Bauhaus were completely "a-political," his work was clearly aimed at cultural, if not social liberation. While originally supported by the state, anxiety over Bauhaus politics caused the curtailment of funds, leading Gropius to close the school in 1925 and move it to Dessau, a more liberal area. It was then that Hannes Meyer was asked to direct the architecture program and, in 1928, take over the directorship of the whole school as Hilberseimer became director of the building department. Meyer became a controversial figure for the overtness of his Marxist politics as well as its direct inscription into the Bauhaus curriculum, but he also saw the Bauhaus make a profit for the first time and brought in its only two commissions: five apartment buildings in Dessau and the Federal School of the German Trade Unions in Bernau (ADGB). Nevertheless, Gropius fired him in 1930 and asked Mies to take over the school. Mies rid the Bauhaus of its overt politics but in 1933, the year that Hitler came to power, the Nazi party, seeing modernist work as "anti-German," closed the school.

Peggy Deamer

Chapter 4

# Capital dwelling: industrial capitalism, financial crisis, and the Bauhaus's Haus am Horn

Robin Schuldenfrei

"Can't you help me to find capitalists?" wrote Walter Gropius in the early years of the Weimar Bauhaus in an appeal to Lily Hildebrandt, wife of art historian Hans Hildebrandt. "There's no money to relieve the terrible conditions of the students . . . I try to raise funds but I am not gifted at it."[1] Over the course of the next few years, Gropius would hone his fundraising skills with a wide variety of "capitalists" who contributed sums of money, materials, and products to the Bauhaus's efforts. In the same period, Bauhaus member Oskar Schlemmer worried aloud about the effects of capital on art in the pamphlet designed for the Bauhaus's 1923 exhibition—a document which was quickly withdrawn by the school—writing:

> Mathematics, structure and mechanization are the elements, and power and money are the dictators of these modern phenomena of steel, concrete, glass, and electricity. Velocity of rigid matter, dematerialization of matter, organization of inorganic matter, all these produce the miracle of abstraction. Based on the laws of nature, these are the achievements of mind in the conquest of nature, based on the power of capital, the work of man against man. The speed and supertension of commercialism make expediency and utility the measure of all effectiveness, and calculation seizes the transcendent world: art becomes a logarithm.[2]

4.1
Kitchen, Haus am
Horn (architect:
Georg Muche),
Weimar, 1923.
Bauhaus-Universität
Weimar, Archiv der
Moderne, Signature:
BA XII-30

The Bauhaus in 1923 was pulled in many directions: a dire need for financial support as government backing—and its funding—was being withdrawn, a resulting new turn to capitalism to assist it in meeting the economic crises of the day, an ambiguous position with regard to the priority of craftsmanship, technology, and industry, and a radical redefinition of the role of art and the artist in an age of mechanical reproduction. At this economically desperate moment in Germany—the height of the post-World War I inflation which caused the bulk of the population extraordinary economic distress—the school was eager to "collaborate" with capitalist industry, setting the direction that would continue for the length of Gropius's tenure as the Bauhaus's director. At the same time, these circumstances dramatically altered the society for which the Bauhaus was designing.

The Haus am Horn, a seemingly modest single-family show house constructed to communicate ideas and designs fostered by the Bauhaus at its first large-scale public exhibition in 1923, was the first concrete example of architecture to emerge from the school, which famously did not have a formalized program or department of architecture until Hannes Meyer was appointed to succeed Gropius in 1927.[3] This initial architectural exemplar seemingly demonstrates all of the concepts that modernism proclaimed—functionality, technology, hygiene, the use of modern materials and construction methods—and was erected using the latest materials—plywood, plate glass, rubber flooring. From the more romantic, socialist, and Expressionistic post-World War I origins of the Bauhaus, the Haus am Horn represents a turning point in Bauhaus ideas. Its contents were intended to represent the school's practical and visual move away from utopianism and craftsmanship towards a stated desire to produce for and cooperate with *capitalist* industry, concretized with Gropius's concurrent slogan, proclaimed at the exhibition's opening: "art and technology—a new unity." But it was

**4.2**
Georg Muche, Haus am Horn, Weimar, 1923 (photograph: Atelier Hüttich Oemler Weimar). Bauhaus-Universität Weimar, Archiv der Moderne, Signature: BA XII-3

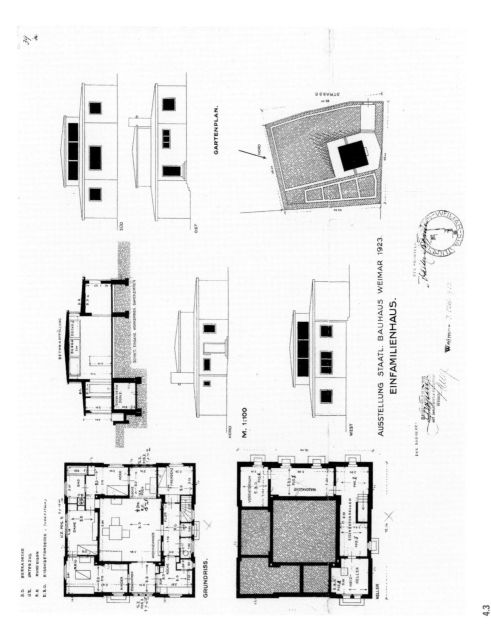

**4.3**
Walter Gropius and the Bauhaus-Siedlung GmbH, Plans submitted for the Haus am Horn construction permit, Weimar, 1923. Klassik Stiftung Weimar, L 2108 A, on loan from the Bauaktenarchiv Weimar © VG Bild-Kunst, Bonn 2013

**4.4**
Living Room
(furniture: Marcel
Breuer), Haus am
Horn, Weimar, 1923.
Bauhaus-Universität
Weimar, Archiv der
Moderne, Signature:
BA XII-10

laboriously designed at great cost for a specific use and place, and never put into mass production.

At the Haus am Horn, not only was the reproducibility of its architecture limited by its costly fabrication and materials but it failed also in the more general sense that, despite the school's ideological and social project, it remained an inaccessible luxury object appropriate only for the period's wealthy, a house speaking mainly to an elite of industrial patrons and their circle, whose taste and favor it sought to cultivate, rather than to a base of potential dwellers for whom it was nominally intended.[4] Positing it as an elite object, a product of the structure of 1920s industrial capitalism more than of any revolutionary social program, the Haus am Horn illuminates the disconnect between modernism's ideals and the realities of the reigning economic structures. Completed at a moment of runaway inflation, it is less a visionary conception of a house of the future than a compromise with the realities of capitalism, albeit under the peculiar and dramatic circumstances of the German currency's collapse. Under these circumstances, the Haus am Horn was less of a vehicle for a *collaboration* with industry, as Gropius had espoused, but rather an uncritical showcasing of its output. It represents an improbable application of industrial capital to design and a very early and noteworthy example of the role capitalism could have in determining architecture, a relationship which would come to its fullest fruition following World War II.

## Building blocks for industry

The Haus am Horn was marketed as a scalable, flexible, mass-producible dwelling within a planned settlement. Although artist Georg Muche is credited as the architect, members of the Bauhaus and Gropius's private architectural office shared the design. (Muche won the competition held at the Bauhaus; Gropius's architectural office took over the execution of the design, with Adolf Meyer in charge of the project.) Muche's plan and elevations are a modification of a system Gropius had been working on since 1911. The Gropius version was less modest, a flexible model likewise consisting of small rooms ringing a central, double-height living room but with two more stories of additional rooms for working and sleeping.[5]

With the assistance of a young architect whom he had recently brought into his office, Fred Forbát, Gropius had returned to the idea, exhibiting it at the Bauhaus in June 1922 and again in the Exhibition of International Architecture held within the Haus am Horn during the 1923 exhibition.[6] The system comprised different basic blocks intended to form variable, two- to three-storey

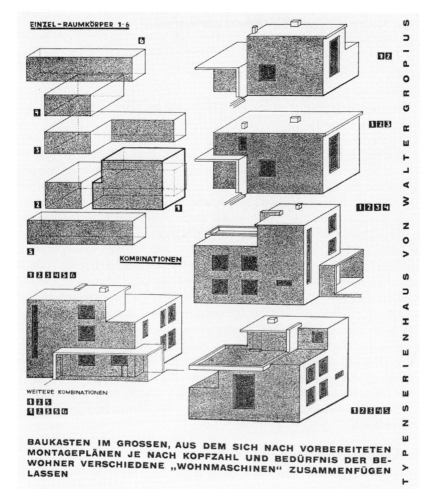

EINZEL-RAUMKÖRPER 1-6

KOMBINATIONEN

WEITERE KOMBINATIONEN

BAUKASTEN IM GROSSEN, AUS DEM SICH NACH VORBEREITETEN MONTAGEPLÄNEN JE NACH KOPFZAHL UND BEDÜRFNIS DER BE-WOHNER VERSCHIEDENE „WOHNMASCHINEN" ZUSAMMENFÜGEN LASSEN

TYPENSERIENHAUS VON WALTER GROPIUS

4.5a
Walter Gropius,
Serial-type house
(large-scale building
blocks), 1922

single- and multi-family houses; mass-produced elementary forms were combined and the results were labeled simply *Typenserienhaus* (serial-type house). Standardization was to be attained via a single module used in conjunction with a set of molds for concrete casting.[7] In reference to the underlying concept of these expandable units, Gropius used the term *Wabenbau* (honeycomb construction), a term which helpfully aligns the conceptually useful modular principle in beehive construction with the term *Bau* (structure, building). The elements themselves he termed *Baukasten im Grossen* (large-scale building blocks), referencing elementary and easily mass-produced children's building blocks. A flexible combination of forms and sizes for variably numbered dwellers and their needs, yet still appropriate for industrialized, serial production, these units or *wohnmaschinen* (literally: living machines), as Gropius referred to them, were designed to be assembled together according to a prepared installation plan.[8]

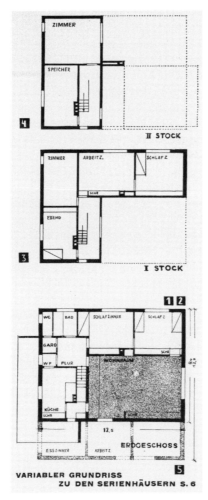

**4.5b**
Walter Gropius, Variable floorplan of the serial-type house, 1922. As published in *Ein Versuchshaus des Bauhauses in Weimar*, 1925. Adolf Meyer, Ed., *Ein Versuchshaus des Bauhauses in Weimar* (München: Albert Langen Verlag, 1925), pp. 8, 9. © VG Bild-Kunst, Bonn 2013

Gropius's goal was "dry-assembly construction . . . that would make it possible to order a house from the factory inventory as one orders a pair of shoes," with "savings to be expected from constructing houses in this way at 50 percent or more compared to traditional methods."[9] Realizing such a design would have required a true collaboration with industry of the sort often associated with the Bauhaus. The underlying intention with this building block system was to produce a socio-economic gain through the development of housing made economically feasible via industrial production methods—and that could be backed, moreover, Gropius hoped, by capitalist enterprise.

## Incorporated planning: the Bauhaus Siedlung GmbH

In order to realize these aims, the Bauhaus undertook an organizational innovation, the Bauhaus Siedlung GmbH, a limited liability holding company registered by the Bauhaus for the purposes of creating a planned housing development in Weimar. This was the first in a series of such companies that the Bauhaus would found in an ultimately unsuccessful attempt to formalize ties between the school, industry, and the wider market.[10] The Bauhaus Siedlung GmbH was established in April 1921 (and granted legal status in May 1922) to create affordable housing for Bauhaus members and to cultivate food for the Bauhaus cafeteria.[11]

The Bauhaus housing estate idea was not a new one; as early as October 1920, Gropius asked the masters and students of the Bauhaus to come up with ideas for a planned community.[12] From 1920 to 1922, organizational meetings were held and an executive committee formed, interested parties—members of the school and of Gropius's office—gave sums of money towards the project, and the intended site was divided into plots. In June 1921, Gropius wrote the Thuringian Finance Ministry asking for a lease to the land.[13] One year later, he requested a plot of land for ninety-nine years, rent-free, as well as a five million mark loan for the construction of dwellings (which were to be sold with inexpensive mortgages, rather than rented), and the development of the Bauhaus garden.[14] Gropius carefully made the case to the Thuringian officials that the Siedlung plan represented an architecturally and economically new, flexible building plan—in contradistinction to the "usual one-sided template" for planned housing communities—addressing a variety of needs.[15]

The intended site was a sizable plot of land in a residential section of the city surrounded by large single-family villas, overlooking the Ilm Park, situated between the streets Am Horn and Besselstraße. The plan by Gropius, Forbát, and other members of Gropius's office comprised a mix of housing types: nineteen free-standing single-family houses (intended for masters), fifty-two single-family row houses, dormitories for forty students, as well as additional workshops and school buildings. Perhaps tellingly, the single-family homes on the slope, intended for the masters, were deemed, in Forbát's recollection, the "most urgent and my first commission to plan these."[16] Like the Haus am Horn, many of the designs featured a central living room surrounded by bedrooms, kitchen, and other service rooms. As early as mid-July of 1922, four house designs merited building permit applications.[17] Although Gropius exerted much effort in

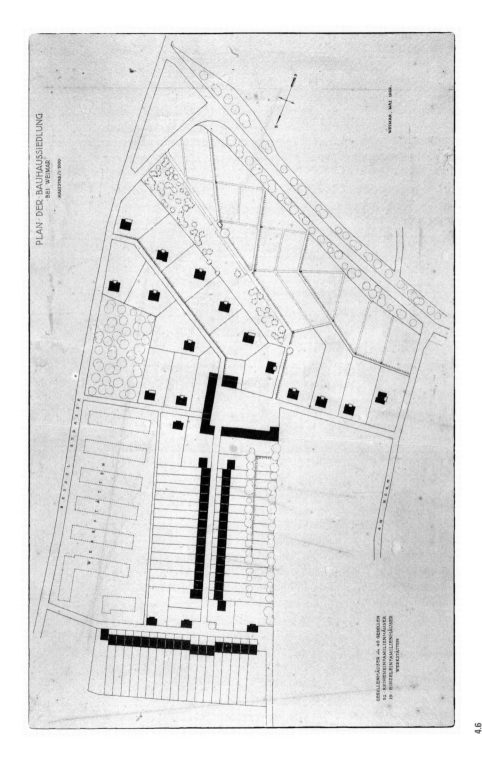

4.6
Walter Gropius, Plan of the Bauhaus Siedlung, Weimar, 1922. Harvard Art Museums/Busch-Reisinger Museum, Gift of Walter Gropius, BRGA.12.1. Imaging Department
© President and Fellows of Harvard College. © VG Bild-Kunst, Bonn 2013

attaining rights to the land and financing for the development, the political situation ultimately deteriorated, and the financial crisis during the period of hyperinflation caused the development to become unfeasible.

The Bauhaus Siedlung GmbH, albeit unsuccessful, was an important step in formalizing Bauhaus initiatives within market economic structures, first in a pragmatic attempt to eliminate the middle-man, and secondly by controlling the intended development site from not only an architectural but also a financial standpoint. Likewise, it points to Gropius's particular take on how housing operated in the market. There was an interest in industrial means of production across a wide political spectrum from the left to the right, from capitalism to communism. Architects such as Hannes Meyer were equally interested in economical building and industrialized techniques, but towards socialist ends, without an engagement with capitalism. The decision to build single-family houses over high-density apartment blocks, and to sell rather than rent, demonstrates Gropius's interest in capitalism on the consumptive side, rather than the most efficient, cost-sensitive, productive side.

## Taking financial stock: the Haus am Horn at the 1923 Bauhaus Exhibition

The 1923 Bauhaus Exhibition and its accompanying celebratory "Bauhaus Week," which brought an initial wave of visitors to Weimar, was deeply tied to the financial status of the school and its future economic outlook. The exhibition represented an attempt to account for state funding and to promote public relations for the school in hopes of continued state—and new external—support. In 1922, the Thuringian government agreed to give an additional loan for the expansion of the workshops under the condition that the school put on a comprehensive exhibition.[18] The Bauhaus was a state institution funded primarily through the regional parliament where political parties were divided with regard to its continued funding. Generally in support of the Bauhaus were the workers', socialist, and communist parties, and against it were the bourgeois and right-wing parties.[19]

Emerging out of World War I, the German economy was in shambles, a condition made manifest in the everyday visibility of the destitute, the severely disabled, the widowed, and the unemployed. The economic upheaval caused by the war generally, and specifically by the loss of the Alsace and Lorraine regions, war reparations, and faltering industry, left citizens' savings and the country bereft.[20] The devaluation of currency had already begun by the Bauhaus's opening in 1919; in proposing his initial budget Gropius noted, "the momentary financial situation does not promise favorable working conditions . . . The value of money today amounts to only about 1/3 to 1/4" of its prior worth.[21] Gropius urged state officials to "put the school into a viable condition" by including the "estimated sum in the state budget." Though the school was allotted an annual budget, Gropius regularly made additional appeals for sums of money and other support, in writing and in person at the parliament. The German economy worsened as inflation rose, reaching its peak precisely during the exhibition's dates. Thus the worth of the annual budget would drastically fall as hyperinflation ensued. Schlemmer described the dire situation: "This exhibition, which will decide the fate of the Bauhaus, is so much at the mercy of attacks from right and left, shortage of money, and the spirit of the times, that it becomes a question of survival, of victory or total destruction."[22]

The school sprang into action, organizing an exhibition committee which met regularly and which carefully organized publicity in order to maximize its impact. Already in November 1922, for example, the school designed an ink stamp with the text "Bauhaus Exhibition Summer 1923," which Gropius declared would be placed on all outgoing mail.[23] The exhibition was also advertised on the sides of trains and in major train stations.[24] The economic opportunity posed by the exhibition was never far from discussions that went into its planning; March 1922 meeting minutes, for example, record the desire, through exhibitions generally, to find "individuals who would economically support the Bauhaus."[25]

In meetings held throughout the fall of 1922, it was also decided to offer objects for sale at the exhibition, the aim being to draw attention to their designs in order to sell more objects in the future, to try to arrange contracts for products, and to drum up more government support as well as space for a permanent Bauhaus exhibition in the city museum.[26] A flyer available at the exhibition underscored—in bold type—the degree to which all wares on display were for sale: with regard to the workshop wares, copy stated "all of the objects are for purchase or available for later orders"; about the Haus am Horn it was noted, "house and interior available for purchase"; and with reference to the Bauhaus exhibition installed at the Weimar Landesmuseum, "all works are for sale."[27] Exhibition sales did in fact raise 4,500 goldmarks (less than had been hoped, and of that amount only a little more than half were actually collected), which was earmarked for use in setting up a corporation to keep the workshops in supply of working capital (*Betriebskapital*).[28]

In September 1922, it was decided that "at least one house" from the *Bauhaus Siedlung* should be constructed, furnished, and made accessible to the exhibition's visitors. Rather than a single show house encompassing the ideals and products of the school, as it is normally presented, the emphasis was on an exemplary dwelling within the context of the planned community.[29] The flyer available at the house alerted visitors that the overall site plan for the Bauhaus development was completed, noted that the government lacked necessary financial resources, and called for interested parties to support the project.[30]

In comparison to the Bauhaus's first commission—the expansive 1922 Sommerfeld House with its handmade decorative elements and high quality of craftsmanship—the modestly scaled Haus am Horn was straightforward in its design and seemingly devoid of superficial ornamentation. Instead, the use of new materials and building techniques gave it its distinguishing characteristics, namely a machine-like precision that belied the costly provision with industrial products and mechanical systems. Color was an important aspect of this emerging modern aesthetic; its use in the interiors further emphasized the house's rarified modern materials, from the black glass baseboards ringing the bedroom's cream

4.7
Kitchen (design:
Benita Otte and
Ernst Gebhardt),
Haus am Horn,
Weimar, 1923. Adolf
Meyer, Ed., *Ein
Versuchshaus des
Bauhauses in
Weimar* (München:
Albert Langen
Verlag, 1925), 52

white walls, to the red, white, and blue rubber flooring of the dining room, to the black frames around the African plywood doors.[31] The interior comprised a central living space lit from above by atrium windows and one ground-level set of windows in the work niche, while small bedrooms and a kitchen and dining room ringed the other three sides (see Figure 4.3). These spaces featured a mixture of industrially produced elements such as exposed metal radiators, steel windows and door frames, appliances, and modern-appearing but handmade, mainly wooden, furniture from the Bauhaus's workshops, exemplified by pieces such as Marcel Breuer's armchairs and bedroom vanity. The furnishings, in particular, were expensive; for example, the constructivist women's dressing table by Marcel Breuer was valued at 350 goldmarks, the divan in the living room with cushions and covers at 290 goldmarks, the glass cupboard at 550 goldmarks, and the desk in the niche at 520 goldmarks.[32] The total sales price for all Bauhaus-produced furnishings was 6,692 goldmarks.

The kitchen, designed by Benita Otte and Ernst Gebhardt, featured a light-filled space with windows which tipped open, white opaque glass protective backsplash surfaces, a modern radiator, a ventilation fan, ample work surfaces, storage units, and two sinks, one with hot running water thanks to the installation of a gas-powered hot water heater (see Figure 4.1, 4.7). The electric stove was celebrated for alleviating the former necessity of wood or coal transportation and of lighting it, and for being both adjustable and extinguishable.[33] As famous and forward-thinking as this kitchen appears—it predates the 1926 Frankfurt Kitchen, which was successfully mass produced—in reality it represents the acquiring and insertion of industrial materials and technical objects in a modern layout. Beyond the simple cupboards, shelves, and counters, the only other items of design from the school were Theodor Bogler's stoneware storage jars, supplied

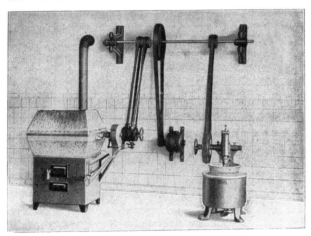

# HAUSWÄSCHEREI 63
# EINRICHTUNG

**J. A. JOHN, AKTIENGESELLSCHAFT**
**ERFURT - ILVERSGEHOFEN**
**HAUSWÄSCHEREI-EINRICHTUNG MIT GAS-**
**HEIZUNG UND ELEKTRISCHEM ANTRIEB**

Mechanisierung der groben Arbeit
75 % Ersparnis an Heiz- und Waschmitteln, an Zeit und Personal schont die Wäsche

**4.8**
Gas and electric laundry facility (supplied by the firm of J.A. John AG), Haus am Horn, Weimar, 1923. Adolf Meyer, Ed., *Ein Versuchshaus des Bauhauses in Weimar* (München: Albert Langen Verlag, 1925), 63

by the Steingutfabriken Velten-Vordamm, which were never reproduced in that period. In an environment where the newest hot water heater and stove could be celebrated next to the new, pared-down storage jars, a modern aesthetic emerged. But whereas the technical products from existing firms were readily available, the Bauhaus objects were not and did not, in any case, align with factory owners' notions of potential consumer desire. It was largely these *outside* products that gave the house a seductive, modern patina.

4.9a
Bathroom, Haus am Horn, Weimar, 1923. Adolf Meyer, Ed., *Ein Versuchshaus des Bauhauses in Weimar* (München: Albert Langen Verlag, 1925), 48

48 TRITON WERKE HAMBURG

WAND- UND DECKENBEKLEIDUNG: WEISSES OPAKGLAS. DEUTSCHE SPIEGELGLAS-A.-G., FREDEN AN DER LEINE

JUNKERS & CO. DESSAU

GASBADEOFEN IM BADEZIMMER

**4.9b**
Bathroom, Haus am Hom, Weimar, 1923. Bauhaus-Universität Weimar, Archiv der Moderne, Signature: BA XII-10

In its provision with technologically advanced amenities, the house was indeed innovative. Specific instances are numerous: the house prominently featured an "in-house laundry facility" connected to gas for heating the hot water and electric motors (see Figure 4.8).[34] Costing 1,260 goldmarks, its technical specifications included a "full-steam" washing machine and a "spinning dryer."[35] Archival records list an extraordinary number of mechanical apparati and appliances—electrical belt pulleys, hot water heaters, vacuum, toaster, iron, hair dryer, electric coffee machine, curling iron, and electric cigar lighter, all supplied by AEG and totaling 1,700 goldmarks.[36] For 580 goldmarks, three telephones were installed, including an extra bell so that the ring could be heard in the kitchen.[37] The critic Paul Westheim wrote enthusiastically in October 1923 about the house's showcasing of objects produced by industry, citing specifically the bath facilities, electrical iron, vacuum cleaner, and electric cigar lighter as "splendid," advising that they should be adopted more widely.[38]

But in this, it was out of step with the economic realities of the time.[39] Corporate sponsorship—an important strategy for obtaining the desired materials and technical objects, many of which were newly introduced to the market—entailed more product placement than true collaboration with industry.[40] In exchange for partially underwriting the cost and installation of goods such as flooring, radiators, windows, mirrors, door handles, and light fixtures, all of the firms' names and wares were listed in the exhibition's accompanying publicity materials and prominently posted on a placard in the living room (see Figure 4.4).[41] The bathroom, for example, featured walls and ceiling covered with white opaque glass from Deutsche Spiegelglas A.G., bathroom fixtures from the Triton-Werke A.G. Hamburg, a gas hot water heater from Junkers & Co. in Dessau, and rubber flooring supplied by the Harburger Gummiwaren-Fabrik (see Figure 4.9).

The corporate firms and wares came from all over Germany: radiators came from the Berlin-Burger Eisenwerk A.G.; the cast bronze, nickel-coated door handle designed by Walter Gropius and Adolf Meyer (in 1922) was manufactured by S.A. Loevy, Berlin; the plywood (Koptoxyl panel) doors came from B. Harras GmbH, Böhlen; and lighting fixtures were supplied by AEG with Osram.[42] These materials and goods were also thoroughly described in the Bauhaus book on the house, *Ein Versuchshaus des Bauhauses in Weimar* ("An Experimental House by the Bauhaus in Weimar"), which featured all of the participating firms, who paid for their inclusion.[43] The book reads accordingly like advertising copy, rather than underscoring any actual collaboration between modern architecture, industry and technology, as Gropius's famous proclamation of "art and technology—a new unity" at the exhibition's opening suggested; it does, however, highlight his acumen for enlisting capitalism's prerogatives for the school's financial benefit.

## Inflation, industrialists, and the Bauhaus

The Haus am Horn was thus a very concrete example of working within the reigning capitalist economic system of the early Weimar Republic in a period of desperate financial crisis and complete insecurity in the banking and monetary system. Gropius's biggest foe in raising funds for the house was the period of hyperinflation that mirrored the time span of the Haus am Horn's conception and construction. Inflation had been a fact of daily life from the beginning of the Weimar Republic, but hyperinflation began in June of 1921 and in earnest in 1922, until the mark's value had finally fallen to the point of 4.2 billion marks to the dollar in November 1923.[44] (The printing of money could hardly keep pace; contributing to the effort, Bauhaus artist Herbert Bayer designed banknotes in denominations of one, two, five, ten, twenty, fifty, one hundred and five hundred million mark notes, issued by the state bank of Thuringia in August 1923.)[45] The Rentenmark—backed by bonds linked to the goldmark and hard assets such as Germany's real estate—was finally introduced on November 16, 1923, replacing the old Reichsbank mark, and stabilizing the currency.

4.10
Children using money as building blocks during the 1923 German inflation crisis, 1923. Photography courtesy Fotolibra

Against this backdrop, Gropius sought to raise money for the house. From November 1922 through February of 1923, he wrote a series of letters translated into English by Lyonel Feininger to Henry Ford, John Rockefeller, William Hearst, and Paul Warburg—labeled in the school's own records as the "dollar kings"—which described the school, its aims, organization and activities and asked for money to build the Haus am Horn, noting that $3,000 was needed, which varied (at that moment) between 30 to 60 million marks or 12,000–13,000 goldmarks.[46] American industrialists, for Germans in general and Gropius in particular, represented the success of capitalism, and their dollars had obvious appeal in the context of inflation. Nothing came of these appeals, however, but a similar letter campaign addressed to German industrialists successfully raised 100 million marks by the time the house opened. Carl Benscheidt Jr., who had hired Gropius to design the Fagus Factory, gave 1.5 million marks.[47] Adolf Sommerfeld initially loaned him 20 million marks, interest free, to be paid back when the house sold.[48] Herman Lange, an industrialist in the silk industry who would later commission Ludwig Mies van der Rohe to design his home in Krefeld, gave the Bauhaus 6 million marks.[49] These donations underscored the extent to which many industrialists, unlike the rest of the population, were doing extremely well during this period—even as the real value of the funds raised continued to diminish.

Archival documents note that Gropius re-estimated the Haus am Horn's construction price at 100 million marks in March of 1923, but by August, the recently opened house had cost 450 million marks, with Sommerfeld having ultimately contributed 208 million marks.[50] The Bauhaus had to contend with a 150-fold debasement of the currency from March to September of 1923, a difference which left them with a 1.5 billion mark deficit for the house. As a result, the business manager of the Bauhaus, Emil Lange, wrote an unsuccessful letter to Sommerfeld in September asking him for an additional 1 billion marks.[51] The Bauhaus's own workshops also faced a 10 to 15 million mark shortfall for their contributions to the house.[52]

Wherever possible, Gropius arranged materials purchases so that their price was fixed to the delivery date's price, taking further pains to arrange prices below the market rate,[53] and generally firms were willing to wait to be paid until the house was finished.[54] The hyperinflation led to complicated payment schedules. For example, for the ordering of the wooden doors, the following arrangement was detailed: on the date of delivery, the firm was to note the day's wood price and what percentage rebate was going to be in effect due to the publicity the firm would receive through its product placement; the firm was to be paid when the house sold at the exhibition's close (at the latest on 1 November), at which point a higher or lower percentage of the bill was to be paid out, depending on whether the price of wood had risen or fallen.[55] The terms of sale for the workshop pieces and artworks in the exhibition also reflected the daily devaluation of currency—the Bauhaus stipulated that prices be calculated for the day of receipt of payment, not the date of sale.[56]

The contributing firms lent materials and money for Haus am Horn's construction, with the intention of its being recuperated through eventual resale.

For example, the glass manufacturer lent five million marks and agreed to put off billing for the glass until the house sold, agreeing to bill at cost.[57] Archival sources reveal many letters from participating firms beseeching the Bauhaus to pay overdue bills.[58] After much correspondence, following the exhibition's closure and as the mark's value continued to plummet, Sommerfeld's firm finally authorized 18 billion marks so that the school could pay the other suppliers.[59]

In 1921, Schlemmer had noted Gropius's business acumen: "Gropius is an excellent diplomat, businessman, and practical genius."[60] But Schlemmer's diary from November of 1922 reveals the disquiet the new direction caused for him, and the difficulties he foresaw for the school:

> Handmade *objets d'art* in the age of the machine and technology would be a luxury for the rich, lacking a broad popular basis and roots in the people. Industry now provides what the crafts once provided, or it will when fully developed: standardized, solid functional objects made of genuine materials . . . Technological progress has resulted in bold innovations . . . I do not believe that craftsmanship as practiced at the Bauhaus can transcend the aesthetic and fulfill more serious social functions. "Getting in touch with industry" will not do the trick; we would have to commit ourselves and merge completely with industry.[61]

He concludes, "But we cannot make that our goal; it would mean turning our backs on the Bauhaus."

## Luxury at the Haus am Horn: the period reception

A product of its time, both in its utopian aspirations about dwelling anew and in its concessions to economic realities, how can we understand the Haus am Horn's situation in relation to the intersection of architecture and capitalism over the longer term? The materials (rubber flooring, plywood) and technology (electric washer and dryer) utilized have now attained an everyday quality, part of what is often expected of even a minimal dwelling. But the extraordinary amenities of the house during a period of uncertainty and economic chaos must be seen in the context of the relationship between industrial capitalism and the housing needs of the time.

The period response to the house was mixed, and criticism often focused on the house's ambiguous position vis-à-vis the economic realities of its day. It was unclear if the house was meant to be a realistic solution for typical middle-class dwelling as part of a larger housing plan, or if it was a show house for an idealized future. The school was careful to chart a middle course. For example, Muche, in his essay about it, specifically points out a desire to ensure that the machine production of furniture and interior fittings would not result in the "barbarism of formlessness."[62] Gropius, too, would talk of the "uncultivated formlessness of a *parvenu*,"[63] suggesting a need to maintain an elite standard of design in the face of its anticipated diffusion. He also sought to maintain a nuanced, critical position on the relationship between living, design, art, and business: "Our informing conception of the basic unity of all design in relation to life was in diametrical opposition to that of 'art for art's sake,' and the even more dangerous philosophy it sprang from: business as an end in itself."[64] In this disavowal of "business," and in his talk of collaboration with the more neutral entity of "industrial production," one might see an attempt to mask his intensive engagement with the powers of German industrial capitalism.

But to observers and critics, regardless of rhetoric, it was clear that the house was not within reach of the average family of the period. As one reporter pointed out, "only a dollar-man" (i.e., only someone possessing hard currency) would be eligible to live in this housing development, quipping that it would be very welcome if the Bauhaus succeeded, in its next exhibition, in meeting local conditions and terms of livability.[65] Architectural critic Adolf Behne similarly found the house to be both irreproducible and unable to meet people's needs: "The Bauhaus affirms the typification and normalization of the dwelling . . . They flirt with machine exactness, but simply *everything* here turns out oblique, false, hollow, artificial, for each individual object, like the whole, lacks necessity, an internal law, a human will of its own!"[66] In another review, Behne articulated the unconvincing, contradictory nature of the house, commenting that it "stands among all these difficulties as somewhat uninteresting and unknowing. It is half luxurious, half primitive; half postulation of an ideal, half product of its time; half handicraft, half industry; half standard-type, half idyll. But it is in no sense pure and persuasive, but again an aesthetic, papery affair."[67] Ernst May commented that despite some fine individual solutions towards the rational management of the household, the rich use of "precious materials . . . that stamp the building as luxury housing" contradicted the efficiencies; he called for atten-tion to problems relevant to "not just 5% but rather 95% of all Germans."[68] In reviewing the show, one newspaper reporter pointed out, in discussing the laundry facilities and their electric dryer, that the designers were clearly most concerned with utilizing all of the products of modern technology, and especially through the heavy use of electric power, to make a home that would be as easy as possible to run: "the aim was thus not to create a low-cost house, but rather a house with the most comfort possible."[69]

And although he continued to subsidize the house's construction, Sommerfeld wrote to Gropius on May 8, 1923 of his own doubts about its aims— "I would like to urgently ask you to rein in your fantasies"[70]—and in September, he again raised his concerns: "What now remains is a strange (*seltsames*) house which one can argue about if one likes, but which, when observed as a sales object, poses great difficulties and which costs many times more than what a solidly built, normal house would cost in comparison."[71]

\* \* \*

Indeed, more than a vision of bourgeois middle- or upper-class single-family living, the Haus am Horn demonstrates the results of the school's ardent desire to work within the strictures of capitalism, however flawed they were in this period. Haus am Horn attempts to convince industry to cooperate with the Bauhaus by making available its products and its financial support, in return for which the Bauhaus showcased industry's products in the context of its own exhibition. Occurring at a moment of rapid impoverishment of German society, the result is ambiguous and anachronistic. The house was a product of its time, itself manifesting the contrast—and contradictions—between the Bauhaus's social ambitions for design and its ideas of reformed "everyday" dwelling on the one hand, and the house's status as a luxury object in its time and a distant, unrealistic, utopian hope, on the other. Unattuned to the needs of the day, the experimental Bauhaus house exhibited expensive industrial products and materials which were not readily available to many, and certainly not objects of everyday life. To be sure, they were products of industrial innovation and mass-production processes, but their development answered to the imperatives of a capitalist industrial economy, not to any collaboration with the artists and designers of the Bauhaus nor to any pressing social needs.

Read unforgivingly, the Haus am Horn was a project doomed to failure, its desire to mix the luxury of avant-garde approaches to design with Taylorist efficiencies inherently naïve. Read generously, one might argue that the school under Gropius sought to cultivate the social potential that might be found within the economic system of its time and with the support of its industrial protagonists. Even though this search did not come to fruition, and despite the fact that the specific material and design solutions the Gropius-led Bauhaus proposed were out of touch with the needs and means of those for whom it claimed to want to design, some observers of the 1923 Bauhaus Exhibition and the Haus am Horn were able to find promise in this apparent contradiction, perhaps seeing in it the potential to harness capitalism towards socially oriented design. Critic Fritz Wichert wrote, "Now there is space for ideas, for inspiration, for being moved. It's almost as if one could see the thoughts and feelings appear like something sculpted on this bare writing table. The force from within, the creative interior life of the human being, regains the upper hand."[72] As another noted, "Only one thing is key: the inner life, the fruitful possibility of an enterprise (*Unternehmen*). For the Bauhaus, talented people will work with inner participation, honesty, and commitment. The results of this work are just a beginning . . . But there is a spirit within, that is infused with trust."[73] The Haus am Horn might yet be seen as a hopeful "house of the future," as a possible radical utopian plan of a luxurious world yet to be normalized. It is a cogent instance of the modern architectural movement's deep engagement with incipient industrial capitalism. Architects working under capitalism today continue to be seduced by the new technologies and materials it produces and the luxuries they enable. Whether this tendency supports a tethering to a more general social reality, and whether present luxuries will come to be seen as everyday necessities, remains, now as then, an open question.

# Notes

1 Gropius to Hildebrandt, undated (presumed September 1919), cited in Reginald Isaacs, *Gropius: An Illustrated Biography of the Creator of the Bauhaus* (Boston: Little, Brown, 1991), 83. Translation amended.

2 Oskar Schlemmer, "The Staatliche Bauhaus in Weimar," in Hans M. Wingler, *The Bauhaus: Weimar, Dessau, Berlin, Chicago*, trans. Wolfgang Jabs and Basil Gilbert (1923; repro, Cambridge, MA: MIT Press, 1969), 65–66.

3 For architecture at the Bauhaus, see especially Kathleen James-Chakraborty, "Henry van de Velde and Walter Gropius: Between Avoidance and Imitation," 26–42, and Wallis Miller, "Architecture, Building, and the Bauhaus," 63–89, in *Bauhaus Culture: From Weimar to the Cold War*, ed. Kathleen James-Chakraborty (Minneapolis: University of Minnesota Press, 2006); Barry Bergdoll, "Bauhaus Multiplied: Paradoxes of Architecture and Design in and after the Bauhaus," in *Bauhaus 1919–1933: Workshops for Modernity*, ed. Barry Bergdoll and Leah Dickerman (New York: The Museum of Modern Art, 2009), 40–61; Klaus-Jürgen Winkler, *Die Architektur am Bauhaus in Weimar* (Berlin: Verlag für Bauwesen, 1993); Winkler, "Das Staatliche Bauhaus und die Negation der klassischen Tradition in der Baukunst," in *Klassik und Avantgarde: Das Bauhaus in Weimar 1919–1925*, ed. Hellmut Th. Seemann and Thorsten Valk (Göttingen: Wallstein Verlag, 2009), 261–284. For the Haus am Horn see, in particular, Adolf Meyer, ed., *Ein Versuchshaus des Bauhauses in Weimar* (München: Albert Langen Verlag, 1925); "Project: Bauhaus Housing Development 'Am Horn,' Weimar," in *The Walter Gropius Archive*, ed. Winfried Nerdinger (New York: Garland Publishing, 1990), 53–55; Freundeskreis der Bauhaus-Universität Weimar e. V., ed., *Haus am Horn: Rekonstruktion einer Utopie* (Weimar: Verlag der Bauhaus-Universität Weimar, 2000).

4 For Bauhaus objects produced in this same period, see Robin Schuldenfrei, "The Irreproducibility of the Bauhaus Object," in *Bauhaus Construct: Fashioning Identity, Discourse, and Modernism*, ed. Jeffrey Saletnik and Robin Schuldenfrei (London: Routledge, 2009), 37–60.

5 Gropius, "Wohnhaus-Industrie," in *Versuchshaus*, 8–9.

6 Winkler, "Das Staatliche Bauhaus," in *Klassik und Avantgarde*, 270, 67–68.

7 Fred Forbát, "Erinnerungen eines Architekten aus vier Ländern," Fred Forbát Nachlass, Bauhaus-Archiv, Berlin (hereafter BHA), trans. in Winfried Nerdinger, *Walter Gropius* (1969; Berlin: Gebr. Mann, 1985), 58.

8 Gropius, "Wohnhaus-Industrie," 8.

9 Gropius, "Wer hat Recht? Traditionelle Baukunst oder Bauen in neuen Formen," *Uhu* 7 (April 1926): 30–40, trans. in *The Weimar Republic Sourcebook*, ed. Anton Kaes, Martin Jay, and Edward Dimendberg (Berkeley: University of California Press, 1994), 441.

10 The Bauhaus Siedlung GmbH is alternatively listed in archival documents as "Bauhaussiedlung GmbH" and "Bauhaus-Siedlungsgenossenschaft," and appears as "Bauhaus-Siedlung" on the company stamp. See "Vorbereitung und Durchführung von Arbeiten am Siedlungsgelände am Horn," July 20, 1923, Thüringisches Hauptstaatsarchiv Weimar (hereafter ThHStAW). The Bauhaus GmbH was formed in 1924 for the development of Bauhaus products, while the Bauhaus-Verlag GmbH was conceived and registered as a publishing venture, also in 1924.

11 See "Gründung und Hauptversammlungen sowie Aufsichtsrats- und Vorstandssitzungen

der Bauhaus-Siedlung e. GmbH," ThHStAW; Satzungen der Bauhaus Siedlung GmbH, April 13, 1921, 1, BHA.

12 Umlauf an die Meister, October 1, 1920 and November 11, 1920, ThHStAW.

13 Gropius to Finanzministerium, Staatsrat Palm, June 29, 1921, ThHStAW.

14 Bauhaus to Thüringische Finanzministerium Weimar, June 29, 1922, ThHStAW.

15 Ibid.

16 Forbát, "Erinnerungen," trans. in Nerdinger, *Walter Gropius*, 58.

17 Ibid. Although they encountered difficulties with the building authorities due to the flat roof designs.

18 Vorlage Nr. 537, Landtag von Thüringen, 1922, 841, ThHStAW, trans. Winkler, *Bauhaus-Alben* 4, 20. The sum was 2 million marks given on August 23, 1922 and intended for the "Produktivbetrieb" of the Bauhaus workshops. See letter, Thüringisches Ministerium für Volksbildung to Bauhaus, June 29, 1922, ThHStAW.

19 Winkler, *Bauhaus-Alben* 4, 20.

20 *Weimar Republic Sourcebook*, 60-61.

21 Gropius, "Proposed Budget for the Art Academy and the School of Arts and Crafts in Weimar 1919–1920," February 28, 1919 in Wingler, *The Bauhaus*, 26.

22 Schlemmer to Otto Meyer, December 19, 1922, *The Letters and Diaries of Oskar Schlemmer*, ed. Tut Schlemmer, trans. Krishna Winston (Evanston: Northwestern University Press, 1990), 136.

23 "Planung einer Bauhausausstellung für 1922 und Vorbereitung der Bauhausausstellung im Sommer 1923," November 23, 1922, ThHStAW.

24 Correspondence in the ThHStAW reveals that the Bauhaus paid the Reichsbahn for posters to be mounted on trains and in stations.

25 Sitzung des Meisterrates, March 24, 1922, ThHStAW, in *Die Meisterratsprotokolle des Staatlichen Bauhauses Weimar 1919–1925*, ed. Volker Wahl (Weimar: Böhlaus Nachfolger, 2001), 158.

26 Niederschrift vom September 15, 1922, ThHStAW, in Wahl, *Meisterratsprotokolle*, 235; 283.

27 These quotes were in bold in original. Advertising handout announcing exhibition, Bauhaus Ausstellung Weimar, 1923, BHA.

28 Protokoll der Sitzung – Entwurf, October 18, 1923, ThHStAW, in Wahl, *Meisterratsprotokolle*, 313.

29 Niederschrift vom September 15, 1922 als Anlage zum Protokoll, ThHStAW, in Wahl, *Meisterratsprotokolle*, 235.

30 Information sheet with statement (verso), perspective drawing, plan, and Bauhaus seal, for the Haus am Horn exhibition house, 1923, BHA.

31 See Barbara Happe, "Farbigkeit," *Haus am Horn: Rekonstruktion einer Utopie*, 36–46.

32 "Preise der Einrichtungs-Gegenstände im Wohnhaus am Horn," BHA. Following the show, efforts to swiftly sell the house and its contents failed and by default became the property of Adolf Sommerfeld who had the contents shipped to Berlin. Their whereabouts have since then been unknown. See Winkler, *Bauhaus-Alben* 4, 90.

33 Meyer, *Versuchshaus*, 49.

34 Ibid., 63.

35 "Waschanlage im Keller des Hauses am Horn," BHA.

36 "Einrichtungsgegenstände des Hauses am Horn," BHA.

37 "Haus-Telefonanlage im Hause am Horn," BHA.

38 Westheim, "Bemerkungen: Zur Quadratur des Bauhauses," Das Kunstblatt 7, no. 10 (October 1923): 320.

39 One exception to this pattern was the exterior wall construction, which utilized insulation between cinder blocks that were then uniformly plastered over, and the roof, which was made of hollow ceramic bricks in reinforced concrete; about these genuinely practical material and construction innovations, the Bauhaus announced that the 25 cm-thick wall boasted as much insulation against heat and cold as a 75 cm thick brick wall and that the central heating system accordingly saved the equivalent of 4,200 kilos of coke annually. Josef Albers, "Werkstatt-Arbeiten des Staatlichen Bauhauses zu Weimar," Neuen Frauenkleidung und Frauenkultur 21 (1925): 1–2. A period leaflet for Torfoleum, the insulation material used, in a nod to the contemporary situation noted "an urgent imperative in this time of economic need." Leaflet for Torfoleum, Firm of Eduard Dyckerhoff, 1924.

40 For costs and correspondence with the firms supplying materials and products to the Haus am Horn, see "Vorbereitung und Bau des Musterwohnhauses am Horn für die Bauhausausstellung im Sommer 1923," ThHStAW.

41 It is important to note that the goods were not donated to the Haus am Horn, but rather letters in the BHA document various firms' attempts at trying to recuperate costs and collect payment from the Bauhaus, in some cases, in a last desperate attempt, items were repossessed.

42 See "Technische Ausführung" and "Bauhaus Werkstätten" in Meyer, Versuchshaus, 25–78. Although the presentation of the wares from the Bauhaus's own workshops was in the same straightforward format as the corporate goods, the Bauhaus objects, which were mostly of wood, appear very craft-orientated and individualistic (such as Marcel Breuer's woman's firms' dressing table, pp 75–76) in comparison to the very technical-appearing outside products.

43 Weidler to the exhibition committee, May 17, 1923, ThHStAW.

44 Weimar Republic Sourcebook, 60.

45 For further discussion, see Nele Heise, "Das Bauhaus in allen Taschen," Bauhauskommunikation, 265–280.

46 See "Bauhausausstellung, Musterwohnhaus und andere Ausstellungen," ThHStAW.

47 Aktennotiz, March 19, 1923, BHA.

48 Benscheidt first committed 500,000 marks, then gave another million. Benscheidt to Gropius, January 19, 1923; April 6, 1923, ThHStAW.

49 Emil Lange to Hermann Lange, August 4, 1923, ThHStAW.

50 Cited by Winkler, Architektur am Bauhaus, 98.

51 Lange to Sommerfeld, September 4, 1923, page 4, BHA.

52 Lange, May 15, 1923, BHA.

53 Gropius to Baer (lawyer), March 6, 1923, 1–2, BHA.

54 Gropius to Baer, March 10, 1923, 3–4, BHA.

55 These were the terms for most firms; see, for example, Bauhaus to Firma B. Harrass GmbH, June 26, 1923, BHA.

56  Verkaufsbedingungen für die ausgestellten Werkstättenerzeugnisse und Bilder der Ausstellung 1923, BHA.

57  Gropius cites a letter from the Verein Deutscher Spiegelglasfabriken in Cologne to lawyer Baer, March 10, 1923, 2–3, BHA.

58  See, for example, letters from the purveyor of the house's boiler and the radiators to Gropius: J. Lastin and M. Külzow to Gropius, May 18, 1923, BHA.

59  Postcard notice, Ruberoidwerke Aktien Gesellschaft to Sommerfeld, November 10, 1923, BHA.

60  Schlemmer to Otto Meyer, December 7, 1921, *Letters and Diaries*, 114.

61  Schlemmer, Diary entry, November 1922, *Letters and Diaries*, 135.

62  Muche, "Das Versuchshaus des Bauhauses," in *Versuchshaus*, 17.

63  Gropius, "Wer hat Recht?," trans. *Weimar Republic Sourcebook*, 441.

64  Although it was not published until 1935, the manuscript dates from 1925. Walter Gropius, *The New Architecture and the Bauhaus*, trans. P. Morton Shand (1935, reprint; Cambridge, MA: MIT Press, 1965), 89–90.

65  Meyer, "Schön, neu und zweckmäßig. Zur Bauhausausstellung in Weimar im August 1923," *Fachblatt für Holzarbeiten* (1923): 165.

66  Behne, "Das Musterhaus der Bauhausausstellung," *Die Bauwelt* 14, no. 41 (October 11, 1923): 591–592. Emphasis in original.

67  Behne, "Das Bauhaus Weimar," *Die Weltbühne* 19, no. 38 (September 20, 1923), 291, Rosemarie Haag Bletter, "Introduction," in Adolf Behne, *The Modern Functional Building*, trans. Michael Robinson (Santa Monica, CA: Getty Research Center for the History of Art and the Humanities, 1996), 31. Translation amended.

68  M. [Ernst May], "Bauhaus-Ausstellung in Weimar," *Schlesisches Heim* 4, no. 8–9 (1923): 195.

69  Wilhelm Limper, *Kölnische Volkszeitung*, August 30, 1923.

70  Sommerfeld to Gropius, May 8, 1923, 2, BHA.

71  Sommerfeld to Gropius, September 17, 1923, BHA.

72  Wichert, "Ein Haus, das Sehnsucht weckt."

73  G. Fischer, "Streife nach dem Positiven, Epilog zur Weimarer Bauhauswoche," *Berliner Börsen-Courier*, August 26, 1923.

# Chapter 5

# Context: 1918–1950

The period between the world wars, split by the Great Depression, is characterized by European dependence on the American economy. Even though pre-war production figures would be reached and surpassed in most European industries by the middle of the 1920s, the percentage of the growing world market held by Europe in comparison to the US and a newly industrialized Japan declined. Exportable goods from newer industries—automobiles, radio, and film—were not enough to close the gap.

The situation for France was particularly dire. Despite being on the winning side of World War I, France's recuperation depended on reparations from Germany that stalled until 1923 with the US purchase of German bonds. Add to this France's relatively archaic economy, with small, unmechanized farms, a traditional wariness of big companies and trusts, a confidence in gold rather than stocks, and no concentration of capital, and one begins to understand the enormity of the nation's challenges in becoming a modern economy.

This "backward" trust in gold created an undervalued Franc which, while unhealthy for the general economy, was a plus for visitors who flooded into Paris to take advantage of their buying power. What Americans like Hemingway and Fitzgerald consumed was a society reinventing itself. Culturally, France was putting World War I (the der des der—the last of the last) behind it. Welcoming American culture as readily as American aid, France saw its own version of the "Roaring Twenties," including women's emancipation, jazz, and black culture. The avant-garde scene that centered in Paris—Dadaism, Surrealism, Cubism—also took full advantage of the artists displaced in World War I and the Bolshevik Revolution.

This cultural experimentation was linked to political reinvention. France, like Germany and other European countries, was deciding between two dominant political models: Russian communism—the emergent French Communist Party had, by 1921, some 140,000 members while the socialist party had only 30,000—and American Taylorism, distinguished by the management of mass-assembly techniques exploited so successfully by Henry Ford and seen

by many European technocrats as a means to social as well as economic better-
ment. As Deborah Gans shows, Le Corbusier at this time, like the government,
tried to link the economic opportunities offered by Taylorism with the social
ambitions of centralized planning.

Everything changed when the US stock market crashed in 1929.
Because France did not invest much in the market, it was spared the worst of the
depression's immediate effects. After Britain abandoned the gold standard—as a
result of pressures on its reserves after German and Austrian banks failed—France
was left to live up to the standard's demands on its own, creating an overvalued
Franc that reversed the trend that had helped it throughout the 1920s.

The economic crisis in Europe—a major cause of World War II—
started with the Great Depression in the US and was exasperated by the isola-
tionist, nationalist, and uncoordinated economic policies of European nations.
The 1930s were an era of economic devastation for all. Post-World War II politics
and economics, therefore, were not simply a result of mechanisms required to
rebuild countries devastated by war, but were a conscious reaction to the failures
of the 1930s. Central to the new world order was the Bretton Woods agreement
of July, 1944, and its embedded goal of bringing down obstacles to international
trade. This was to be enacted by the General Agreement in Tariffs and Trade
(GATT) and implemented by the newly created International Monetary Fund
(IMF) and the World Bank. The IMF sought to secure stable exchange rates, ensure
liquidity for international commercial transactions, and abolish trade restrictions.
To meet initial demands, participating nations had to fix their exchange rate to
the US dollar, not to gold, although, significantly, the dollar was keyed to the
value of gold. This adjustment allowed exchange rates to be altered in case of
persistent balance of payment difficulties.

The power dynamics following World War II were radically different
from those after World War I. Material destruction was much greater; the Soviet
Union and the US—abandoning forever its post-World War I isolationism—were
the new superpowers, with Europe acting as a buffer between; and the left—
because of the role of the USSR in defeating Germany as well as the role the
Communists played in the Resistance—experienced a resurgence in power and
popularity. In France, De Gaulle's rise and hold on power was due not merely to
his association with the Resistance, but his insistence that the government play a
strong role in the economy—equal measures USSR-inspired socialism and US-
admired capitalism.

Within this volatile and rapidly evolving French national culture, Le
Corbusier sought to define architecture's unique potential in and for "revolutionary" times.

Peggy Deamer

Chapter 5

# Big work: Le Corbusier and capitalism

## Deborah Gans

Le Corbusier's shifting affiliations between democratic capitalism, democratic socialism, communism and, most ignominiously, the fascism of and before Vichy portray but do not illuminate his thinking on capital. The shifts are symptomatic of his search for a political mechanism to bring his larger project—nothing less than the mythic-economic recalibration of man's relation to material through architecture—into the world. This recalibration entails the wresting of material from its servitude to commodity and the consideration of economy beyond profit and loss as a totalizing system of human and natural exchange. His desire for a "naked" material production—production that will simultaneously impact daily life and transcend economic and aesthetic concern—motivates his self-critique of his own plans in The Contemporary City and the l'Esprit Nouveau and delivers that critique in the form of The Radiant City and The Unité d'Habitation.

The capitalist Le Corbusier with an un-ironic attachment to capitalism is a very young man and a citizen of a world not yet racked by World War I who works as a decorator in La Chaux-de-Fonds for the enlightened, intellectual, but still bourgeois extended Schwob family, and shops for their furnishings in the capital of consumer goods, Paris. At this point, America, which he will later demonize as the world gone wrong, appears as he encounters it through the writings of Loos and others as the escape from the petit of the bourgeois and the implementation of the capitalist method at its proper scale. He writes in 1913, "I am trying to leave for America . . . I need big work."[1]

Le Corbusier immigrates not to America but rather to Paris for good in 1918, without perhaps the unadulterated faith of his early years but with his Swiss connections and ambition to leverage his work through capitalism; in other words, a man of business anxious to enter the capitalist game and excited by the rugs at Printemps ("a real bargain")[2] that he finds for his lifelong friend and Swiss client Maurice Levillan. From the start he is not just the passive consumer of the

Parisian scene but rather an experimental entrepreneur who, before actually building in Paris, attempts to reciprocally change architecture through industrial production and industrial production through architecture. He considers his Maison Dom-i-no system, which has subsequently become an ideogram of modernity, as a product for patent with potential in the housing market of war-torn Belgium. He participates in the financing and product development of the Eternity asbestos sheet in France, to be called Evervite, making overtures to the banks of his Swiss contacts such as Leopold du Bois. There is even mention in the papers of his family's collateral, which would make it the second time he had engaged them in a game of financial risk, having already bankrupted them in designing their house in La Chaux-de-Fonds. There is a brick factory venture, which also fails. With the German model of industry as the tool of nation building discredited by their warmongering and defeat, the political reform of the Third French Republic economy rendered intransigent by the polarization of the Democratic Republican Alliance and Socialist parties, and the specter of the Russian Revolution close at hand, Le Corbusier, undeterred by his own lack of skill, sees need and opportunity in the postwar Parisian milieu for architecture to assume an authoritative role. Indeed, the government acknowledged that housing and architecture were key to France's stability as it embarked on a large-scale rebuilding effort without the taxes to fund it. As Le Corbusier put it: "Architecture or Revolution. Revolution can be avoided."[3]

This first mature statement regarding capitalism, Architecture or Revolution, asserts an alternative to the avant-garde while nevertheless admitting the problematic conditions of anomie, disenfranchisement of the working class, conspicuous consumption and waste that a revolution would claim to overcome. Le Corbusier believes the tools for change can be found by the architect within the capitalist system and implemented through architecture. For him, the horror of the World War I resulted from a misalignment of technology and need rather than from capitalist production with nowhere to expend itself.

\* \* \*

The Pavillon de l'Esprit Nouveau (Pavilion of the New Spirit) for the International Exhibition of Decorative Arts in Paris 1925 presents Le Corbusier's complete thesis on capital at that time: the reconsideration of the industrial object, the reformulation of the building process as mass production, the relation of the mass-produced cell of building to the city, the reorganization of the city in terms of capital; and the relation of art to commodity. The Exhibition as a whole was dominated by a streamlined modern classicism of design that became known as Art Déco in reference to the event and catered to the decorators and collectors in Paris anxious to reassert the city's pre-eminence as a luxury good consumer marketplace after World War I. Like any good marketplace, it allowed the display of contradictory architectural goods such as the clearly confrontational pavilion of Konstantin Melnkov (which won a medal), Frederick Keisler's City in Space, and the more ambiguous l'Esprit Nouveau. L'Esprit Nouveau had two built parts: the full-size prototype of a duplex apartment, or *immeuble-villa*, furnished according to Le Corbusier's principles of standardized consumer goods, built-ins, and art, in addition to an exhibit room with a model and vistas of the imagined cities to which the apartment would belong—namely the *Plan Voisin* of Paris and The Contemporary City of Three Million Inhabitants. *The Decorative Art of Today*, the subsequent book describing the Pavilion, constitutes a third summary and a marketing component.

According to Le Corbusier, decorative art is "the totality of human limb objects,"[4] prosthetic tools, or what we might call industrial design. The singular and repetitive function of these tools in combination with the repetitive demands of industrial production together shape them over time such that their forms, once stabilized, as in the standard wine bottle, have clear and moral value and an end beyond their object-hood. As he puts it, "Utilitarian needs call for tools, brought in every respect to that degree of perfection seen in industry."[5] Thus these type abjects escape both fetishized commodification in their instrumentality, on the one hand, and, on the other hand, materialist reductionism in their perfection, which, like classical perfection, represents the act of mind. Thereby, he suggests that "the great emptiness of the machine age . . . wrongly disguised is exposed"[6] and propositionally overcome in that use value once again exceeds exchange value.

The exposure of the machine age's emptiness is identified with the exposure of the form of the object that underlies its decoration. As Francesco Passanti explains brilliantly, the lesson of the *Neu Sachlicheit* for Le Corbusier is not its utilitarianism but the "sachlich," or nakedness, found in the exposed intersection of volumes in his Purist compositions and as early as 1907 at Villa Schwob in his architecture.[7] For Le Corbusier, this compositional language communicates a larger "willingness to face naked facts" of the machine age and its economy.[8] It is notable that "nakedness" was also the term critics used to denounce the more radical pavilions of the Exposition of Decorative Arts including Melnikov's.[9] Only by facing these naked facts will society overcome alienation and discover that, in fact, industrially produced material and man's relationship to it is organic. He concludes, "This framework of a machine age which man has constructed for himself, wrested element by element from the world around us is sufficiently cogent to permit the creation of organisms performing functions similar to those of the natural world."[10]

The prototype apartment of the Pavilion and the contemporaneous houses by Le Corbusier that share its design principles are by extension "naked villas" positioned within the framework of capitalism but also in resistance to the emptiness of consumer culture. Their nakedness, in the form of their bared geometry and austerity of cladding, is their means of resistance. Irrespective of the client's economic, oftentimes extensive means, the finishes remain the same: linoleum sheet for bedrooms and reception areas, plain porcelain tile in white for the "clean spaces" of the kitchen and bathroom and in black for others with occasional black and white tribal rugs, rubber carpet for ramps, bare light bulb fixtures, and walls painted with distemper or oil paint rather than papered.[11] The standard furnishings were Thonet chairs, Maples armchairs and then subsequently the tubular steel prototypes that Le Corbusier designed with Charlotte Perriand in anticipation of their eventual mass production. Industrial stairs and ship ladders gave access to desirable roof gardens. Bathrooms and bedrooms were often exposed to the rest of the house on balconies or behind half walls. Wash-basins and toilets could be identified from behind their curved enclosures. The scale of the work, like the materials, related to an ideal of restraint rather than budget, as directly expressed in the typical ceiling height of 2.2 meters, even when, as in Villa Stein at Garches, the extent of the total building program produced a more monumental whole. The luxury available to every citizen, whether an inhabitant of a gracious *immeuble-villa* or a modest flat in the houses Le Corbusier designed for the working community of Pessac, was to be the same: an experience of space, light, and greenery amplified through sculptural means and the painterly use of color.

The artwork by Le Corbusier, Lipschitz, and Leger displayed in the Pavilion similarly presents a world of simple material in clarified form; but it also communicates the limits of Le Corbusier's critique of capitalist culture. The mere presence of conventional forms of painting and sculpture asserted the continued status of art in the face of its ideological dismissal—by other more anti-capitalist artistic movements of the day such Dada and early Surrealism—as a consumerist fetish object. Le Corbusier's Purist paintings reclaim the bottle from its Cubist fragmentation, restoring it to its identifiable form and function and its potential economic role. In this compositional "return to order" (*rappel a l'ordre*, as Jean Cocteau puts it), the erotic potential of the painting's limb objects and its bottle tops that appear like navels is sublimated without the violent frisson of the surrealist dream image of a dismembered body.

In *The Decorative Arts of Today*, Le Corbusier further reclaims the human limb object from the Dadaists. The chapter, "Other Icons—The Museums," begins with the image of a douche, in direct confrontation with Duchamp's urinal, that seminal critique of the museum as a consumer of fetish. Le Corbusier asserts rather that the douche is *not* art, but rather an object with ambiguous status as a thing perfected. It belongs in a museum, just not an art museum; rather, it belongs in an anthropological museum of Le Corbusier's invention, The Museum of Unlimited Growth or Infinite Museum that he returns to as a building type repeatedly throughout his lifetime.

In its dual conceptual context of Paris and Exhibition of Decorative Arts, the propositional Infinite Museum is in part an Enlightenment project and in part critical simulacrum of the department store. It is an ever-expanding encyclopedic collection in the tradition of Diderot organized on the basis of reason with limited curation. It is also a corrective to the museum of pre-industrial and capitalist cultures alike, which, like Duchamp, Le Corbusier considers a false value system, but one that pertains to pre-industrial and capitalist culture alike based on the "sanctification of the collectible." He asserts, "The museum reveals the full story and is therefore good. It allows one to choose; to accept or reject,"[12] as if to shop without the takeaway, or as if to visit the display of the *Pavillon de l'Esprit*

*Nouveau*. Indeed, Le Corbusier's description of the objects in the museum overlaps conspicuously with the furnishings of the Pavilion, "a radiator, a table cloth of fine white linen, everyday drinking glasses and bottles of various shapes," as well as Berber rugs and laboratory flasks. This curated collection displays what Arthur Rüegg describes as "the natural relation of society and its artifacts expressed through vernacular,"[13] a concept clearly indebted to Adolf Loos. This vernacularization of the industrial likewise rescues it from pure commodity by suggesting its organic, naturally evolving, and "naked" relationship to the user.

Established in concert with the flowering of the bourgeoisie within Baron von Haussman's plan for the Place de l'Opera, the new building type of the great department store was fundamental to Paris's identity and functioning as a capitalist capital city. The department store and arcade were, as Manfredo Tafuri puts it, instruments in the coordination of the production-distribution-consumption cycle and also the places in which the crowd found means for self-education from the point of view of capital.[14] Le Corbusier, shopping in the great department stores for his clients, starts his life in Paris as such a Tafurian subject.[15] It is therefore of great significance that the department store, not to mention the Infinite Museum, are absent from Le Corbusier's *de l'Esprit Nouveau* city plans that make up the second half of the Pavilion.

Displayed in a curved pavilion attached to the prototype dwelling of *l'Esprit Nouveau*, The Contemporary City of Three Million Inhabitants identifies in spatial terms the key players in Le Corbusier's mediated cycle of production and profit: the factory, the center of finance, and the housing of the populace. In addition to the department store, the opera house, parliament, and arcade are not specifically located let alone designed, although there is mention of luxury shopping in the one grand *Place Central*. At the center stand twenty-four, sixty-storey glass cruciform office towers envisioned as the headquarters of international capitalism, surrounded by housing blocks for a population of 60,000 equipped with a panoply of hotel-like kitchens and laundry services for the intelligentsia and captains of industry who resembled Le Corbusier's architectural clients. The entirety stands within verdant and continuous grounds freed from the car by virtue of a raised system of highways. To the east is the industrial sector; to the south and west are garden city settlements for the working class. It is a capitalist city that attacks the "emptiness of capitalism" through an emptiness of ground in that its park is not a romantic stand-in for a lost pre-industrial, pre-capitalist landscape but a defense against a petit bourgeois city fabric.[16] The towers of finance concentrate business in such a way that they remove the rest of the city from the infection of consumption. The ability of the housing to accommodate the full population of the completed city eviscerates speculation.

* * *

The components of housing blocks, high-rise towers of business, factory zones, vehicular routes, a verdant ground and its concomitant light and air—as well as a postulated AUTHORITY (Le Corbusier's capitals) of unspecified politics needed to implement The Plan, which is the ultimate authority—remain so constant among Le Corbusier's urban projects that these cities are together often misconstrued as a singular Radiant City. But The Radiant City is a distinct statement that emerges as a critique of The Contemporary City in 1930 as Le Corbusier's response to direct encounters with Soviet Russia and to the worsening economic and political situation in France. His Soviet experience begins positively with the construction of his design for a large office complex, the Centrosoyus, his encounter with the architecture of Ginsburg (whose Narkomfin housing is a precedent for his later Unité), and with planners such as Nikolay Milyutin who are looking seriously at linear industrial cities that decentralize production in relation to denser rural populations. Meanwhile, the fall of the German Mark, the lack of real capital investment throughout France, the inflation, poverty, and unrest that are its consequences, and American protectionism all undermine the stable currency and open markets that are required to restore European trade and real economic growth. Together these experiences shake his belief, despite his work on the international organ of the *Congrès International de l'Architecture Modern* (CIAM), in the power of democratic capitalism and architecture to reorganize the city and to restore man to himself. In addition to his new admission that "revolution might be required,"[17] he specifically proposes economic programs such as a governmental review of consumer goods to curtail the production of useless commodities, and a partial redistribution of property by eminent domain according to his "law of recuperation of enhanced value" whereby the original owner of land and the authority that improves it split its increased value.[18]

These policies jibe with the goals of the French *Planiste* group and the larger Syndicalist movement in which he participated (as well as with the Calvinist traditions of his family). Syndicalism, or trade unionism, had mid-nineteenth-century roots in the Jura Federation, a federalist and anarchistic movement among the egalitarian and independent-minded Swiss watchmakers of Le Corbusier's youth. It flowered in Paris at the turn of the century with a platform advocating direct action by the working class to abolish capitalism and ultimately the state through free organizations of workers called "syndicates." The elected representatives of a bourse—a labor exchange that would function as an economic planning and employment agency—would coordinate production to serve the needs of the region. Eschewing political affiliations that were unavoidably linked to the state, syndicalists argued they would be organized from the bottom up through solidarity, sentiment, and "social myth," to use the term of Georges Sorel, philosopher of syndicalism. Communists interested in its trade unions and Fascists compelled by the idea of social myth both adopted syndicalist tenants. It was through Parisian syndicalists with an increasingly fascist tilt that Le Corbusier later became involved with Vichy.

The *Planistes* of the early 1930s—in particular the group now known as the Young Nonconformists and including the surrealist Robert Aron, Phillipe Lamour, and Georges Bataille—viewed the syndicalist goals in the largest sense as a recuperation of subjectivity from the limited materialism of capitalism and communism both. Skeptical of all political solutions, *Planistes* proposed a "plan of structural economic reform" involving a mixture of socialist strategies within a capitalist framework including the nationalization of credit and of some industries. But their ultimate goal was to displace the economic protagonists of machine civilization whom they viewed with disgust, or with "nausea," as Malraux put it.[19] In lieu of the anonymous citizen of the Third French Republic who could be all too easily neutered by the political system, they proposed l'homme réel, a naked man of action with a metaphysical rather than political purpose. They relied on the lenses of anthropology, sociology, and phenomenology and the work of Emile Durkheim, Marcel Mauss, Henri Bergson, and Sigmund Freud to make their arguments. The Planistes suggest that underlying all economic exchange, including that of capitalist commodity culture, is a desire for expenditure as an act of power and also of philanthropy akin, as described by Mauss in his The Gift (1924), to the role of the potlatch in tribal culture.[20] Planisme embraced the productive force of these theories of expenditure, celebrating equity in the distribution of wealth and the maximization of all energy, as exemplified by Le Corbusier's regulation of useless commodity. It tried to release capitalist expenditure from the abstraction of international wealth by returning it to land-based goods, as promoted by Le Corbusier in his use of eminent domain to harness fallow property.[21] The goal of this economic reorganization was happiness and force, or as Le Corbusier put it, "pleasure," consisting of "satisfaction of psycho-physiological needs, collective participation, freedom of the individual in that order."[22]

The Radiant City is an ecology in keeping with the organicism of the Planistes that maximizes growth and also minimizes waste. It is not a plan of limited dimensions like The Contemporary City, which has the geometric boundaries of the golden section commensurate with its population limit of three million. Rather, it is a matrix of expansion constructed of striations or zones of housing, industry, and culture along a vertical spine of circulation on top of which is overlaid a biomorphic hierarchy of business head, circulatory spine, and central organs of culture within a body of housing. This biomorphic figure of growth is a diagram intended to take a great variety of forms as illustrated in Le Corbusier's global case cities—Zlin, Bogata, Algiers, and Stockholm—that compose the majority of the book The Radiant City. Le Corbusier takes the syndicalist position that these cities should have boundaries determined by nature and economic region, rather than by politics and nationality, in ways that will ultimately link them in a cross-continental development along perpendicular north–south and east–west axes between the capitals Paris, Rome, Stockholm, and Algiers. The individual inhabitant of this radiant world, like the syndicalist l'homme reel, is stateless, in direct communication with nature, and organized communally by a reinvigorated and humanized form of labor. In the subsequent texts of The Three Human Establishments (1943) and Four Routes (1947), the zones of The Radiant City become settlements in themselves that carpet the continent with radial cities of exchange, linear industrial cities, and a tiled landscape of large-scale and communal radiant farms. In consonance with the synthesis of town and country found in the precedents of both Tony Garnier's socialist proposal for the Industrial City and Milutin's Soviet linear industrial city, Le Corbusier's symbiotic figure-ground of agrarian and urban production is intended to counteract the profit-driven capitalism that has infected both the urban and the rural vernacular. He writes, "The country today is harsh unattractive tyrannical: the money civilization by which modern society has been blackened and deflowered has extended its grip to the peasant and made his life a barren sooty thing . . . The plan must extend to the countryside given the highway and dispersion."[23]

In The Radiant City, Le Corbusier also depicts a newly articulated position on leisure. One of the objectives of Syndicalism, and really all avant-garde movements of the 1930s, was the reduction of work in hand towards the elimination of a permanent working class, which the Syndicalists thought could be accomplished if everyone were willing to donate a few years of industrial labor. But for Le Corbusier, leisure is problematic, indeed a "social danger" and an "imminent threat" if it is to occur within the existing city where "millions of men, women and young people, will spend seven or eight hours a day in the streets at a loss of expenditure"[24]—or perhaps recreationally shopping. To counter its destructive power, "Leisure has to be made into a function";[25] and as a function, it can become part of the plan like housing and factories. The void of The Contemporary City's landscape emptied of commerce is now to be filled with healthful activity—playing fields and such. Unlike The Contemporary City, where housing for the 60,000 elite surrounding the towers of business shared parks and cafés with the towers of finance, The Radiant City has a single and separate class-less zone of housing and leisure, "in immediate proximity of people's homes," for the ostensibly pragmatic elimination of the long commute and the nervous fatigue that Le Corbusier and medical journals of the time associated with urban life. In contrast to the Soviet model of disurbanization, he proposed decentralized production in proximity to housing in order to tap into local markets, avoid standardization of goods, and unite work and leisure. Le Corbusier said that the purpose of leisure is to free the mind and body of the individual, to create a platform for the bottom-up delineation of local community, and to physically separate man from the servitude of work. Like other Planistes, Le Corbusier seeks a holistic world context and a symbolically charged language derived from syndicalism to apply to his principles of work and leisure.

The Authority of Le Corbusier's Radiant City who bifurcates work and life, sets the rhythms of existence, and controls the distances between zones and the places of leisure is no less than the Sun. This gendered male sun, with its feminine complement of water and her tugging moon, participates in a cycle of evaporation and precipitation that animates the earth.[26] Within the economy of The Radiant City, the law of money is a small analogical subset of this larger solar law. Expenditure is an organic process in which growth, death, consumption, and waste are in dynamic equilibrium. As Le Corbusier explains, "Money is simply an economic relationship between production and consumption. Credit is a levy on work to be done. It is therefore the work that is needed and subject to the hardest and severest law of all—the law of nature itself."[27] Because money is a symbol of fundamental exchange, he has no fundamental objection to the idea that "city planning is a way of making money."

The sun is a similarly powerful force for *Mediterraneanistes* such as Albert Camus and André Gide, but Le Corbusier's economy of solar transaction is particularly related to the symbolically charged idea of general economy framed by Bataille, the *Planiste* whose ideas Le Corbusier absorbed and whose inscribed copy of *The Accursed Share* he later received, in 1953, from the author. For Bataille, the sun is the sovereign power in an ecology that joins human production and nature. As he describes it:

> Solar energy is the source of life's exuberant development. The sun gives without receiving . . . Living matter receives this energy and accumulates it within the limits given by the space that is available to it and then radiates or squanders it, after it makes maximum use of it for growth. The excess energy (wealth) can be used for the growth of the system (e.g. an organism). Only the impossibility of continuing growth makes way for squander.[28]

Bataille, among many others, perceived that the catastrophic expenditure of excess energy was war, unless alternative economic engines provided peaceful alternatives to the need for capital to grow. Following the projected calamity of World War II, he placed his hope in the Marshall Plan as an excessive and seemingly profitless gift in the rebuilding of Europe that would ultimately yield a global network of opportunities for capitalistic growth.[29]

For Le Corbusier as well as Bataille, then, the sun is the literal comptroller of all exchange at the largest scale, transmuting energy into life; and, as a consequence, structuring the linguistic exchange of meaning. This symbolic portion of exchange is a kind of excess but an excess that is necessary to the fulfillment of *l'homme réel* as a conscious being. In Le Corbusier's words, the pursuit of society is "radiance, a consciousness exceeding function." This excess might be described as poetic and traced in Le Corbusier's "Poem of the Right Angle" written between 1947 and 1953, during the construction of the *Unité d'Habitation*, where he symbolically encodes The Radiant City's economy as a series of analogical and ecological exchanges between sun and moon, earth and water, male and female, vertical and perpendicular, the meander and the straight line, tools and environment, and spirit and flesh with their synthesis or "fusion" as the centerpiece.

The implementation of Le Corbusier's *Planisme* ultimately occurs indirectly in diluted form in other projects. After three years of promoting his plans for Algiers at Vichy with some success, Le Corbusier is dismissed by the regime and rejected by the Mayor of Algiers who judges his proposal to destroy 200,000 homes (though he preserves the Casbah) as distastefully authoritarian in its methods and utopian, if not naive, in its economic claims. Rather, Le Corbusier's pronouncement that to renovate (*aménager*) the cities, you first must reorganize (*aménager*) the countryside, entered the world indirectly through Michel Ecochard, the director of urban services in Morocco until 1946, whose reformist platform, admittedly indebted to Le Corbusier, called for decentralization of industry and the establishment of rural market centers and mid-size cities with mass social housing (*habitat du plus grand nombre*). The belief was that these spatial reorganizations would engender changes in patterns of work and consumption and control the speculative arm of development in Morocco. The failure of Echouard's reforms is credited as one cause of the violent struggle to overthrow the French colony in Algiers.

Similarly, The Radiant City's zoned matrix of housing, circulation, labor, and leisure—to which Le Corbusier subsequently added historical culture—likewise entered the world indirectly through the mechanism of the Athens Charter, the document produced by the CIAM meeting of 1937 but subsequently published by Le Corbusier under his own name. In the early post-World War II years, the French Ministry of Reconstruction and Urban Planning (MRU) made frequent references to The Charter of Athens, but in terms narrowly addressed to the great need for mass-housing and city building, which they approached through standardized mass-produced units on the one hand and Beaux Arts urban design on the other. Architects of the French Union of Modern Architects denounced the MRU's unintegrated strategy for its narrow functionalism, inattention to human spirit, and, in the words of George Henri Pingusson, "ugliness of our public buildings, the misery of our suburbs and our villages," concluding, as could have been uttered by Le Corbusier himself, that "without urbanism, there cannot really be any such thing as architecture."[30]

\* \* \*

While one of the many attacks on MRU singled out their programs of prefabrication as reductively materialist, Le Corbusier continuously argues for this aspect of his program, from his initial argument for the *objet type* in relation to the *Pavilion de l'Esprit Nouveau*, to his embrace of Fordism and Taylorization in his construction of the Salvation Army Building, to the arguments of The Radiant City. What distinguishes the prefabricated standardization of Radiance from MRU and also Le Corbusier's earlier thinking is The Modulor. The Modulor is Le Corbusier's alternately rational and obscure attempt to create universal anthropometric dimensions with systematic geometrical proportions understood to be, in the classical sense that they structure nature, harmonious. Two interpolated spirals of numbers, one red and one blue, provide dimensions for construction that descend from man to the size of the tool and smaller, and rise up from his outstretched arm to the infinitely large. It borrows heavily from many sources, including Matila Ghyka's work on harmony and human dimension from the 1920s and the anthropometrics of Jay Hambridge who linked his design principles to Greek dynamic symmetry and the Fibonacci series.[31] It gains legitimacy from the post-war resurgent interest in earlier humanism as a way to recuperate man's moral standing, including works such as *Architectural Principles in the Age of Humanism* by Rudolph Wittkower that describe the Renaissance relation of geometry, nature, man, and cosmos. While Le Corbusier began to develop The Modulor as early as 1941, he promotes it as a challenge to component dimensions proposed by AFNOR, the French Association for Standardization of the Vichy government (with which he was no longer associated) and simultaneously as an opening to establish relations with the Resistance, who shared Vichy's concerns over the need to produce mass housing after the war. He likewise establishes a research group in counterpoint to AFNOR called ASCORAL (*Assemblée de Constructeurs pour une Rénovation Architecturale*) that acts as a kind of syndicalist guild of interdisciplinary arts and trades. Together ASCORAL and The Modulor will be his platform for addressing reconstruction from a war he considers to have begun not in 1939, but a hundred years prior with the Industrial Revolution. As he puts it, "The men of those hundred frantic years have strewn the earth with the refuge of their action . . . we have destroyed the relation between material progress and natural elements of a spiritual life."[32] The Modulor will imbed the answers to the spiritual as well as physical needs of *l'homme réel* into the production process itself.

The first and seminal statement of The Modulor rises from the ashes of postwar Marseille in the apartment building of the Unité d'Habitation—*de grandeur conforme*, or a unified dwelling of proper size. While Le Corbusier would have liked to build it as part of a larger fragment of The Radiant City, as he inevitably proposed time and time again, his postwar studio managed to secure commissions for a series of single Unités in various cities to which, for a time, he devoted the entire production of his architecture studio and a linked development and research Studio of Builders (*Ateliers des Batisseurs*, or AtBat) led by the aviation and prefabrication engineer Vladimir Bodiansky. Additionally, the Unité d'Habitation project architect, Georges Candilis, was a founding member of ASCORAL. Le Corbusier understands the Unité as a grand experiment, not just as a Modulor building but as a modulor building process with economic implications. It is:

> to call for the creation of a new body in the building industry: that of the "Nomenclators" (or classifiers) . . . The Nomenclator would break down plans into elements of all kinds: wood, iron, miscellaneous material, etc. He would possess full information on the productive capacities of the country (workshops, factories, plants, etc.) and would therefore be able to distribute orders according to "classified order lists." Assembly orders drawn up parallel with these order lists would help to guide the construction work on the building site itself.[33]

In place of the Authority of The Plan who organizes the landscape of work and leisure, here Le Corbusier offers an analogous structure at the scale of the building, the Authority of the "Nomenclator" who organizes the guilds of producers and assemblers.

The Modulor that facilitates this quasi-syndicalist reorganization is not only "a harmonious measure, both human and mathematical" but also a means to standardize and economize material production and the organization of manufacturing.[34] The designer and the maker, split into warring factions by the

Industrial Revolution, will reconnect here within the larger class of "technicians [who] will be architects or plastic artists, makers of domestic equipment, mechanics, family planners."[35] This synthesis of all the producers of modern society into a single and harmonious workforce will insure a similar coordination and synthesis among the things produced. From the domestic hearth to the entire city and country, there will be no break, and each thing will react and respond one upon the other.[36] The oppression of l'*homme réel* and Le Corbusier's defensive split of work and leisure can be overcome with the tool of The Modulor. As Le Corbusier concludes, "The economy of the country can henceforth benefit from the laboratory set up at Marseilles." And indeed, the entirety of the building was designed and executed according to fifteen Modulor measurements using prefabricated parts within its concrete frame and an array of materials from wood to bent aluminum and steel to fiberglass that were coordinated through the collaboration of AtBat and *Atelier Le Corbusier*, together producing over 2,785 drawings.[37]

In a rare example of consonance between Le Corbusier's agenda and realpolitik, his ambitions to create in the Unité a pivotal point in that expanding sequence from the hearth to the city had the unwavering support of two Ministers of Reconstruction, Raoul Dautry and Eugene-Claudius Petit, and six successive mayors of the then communist city of Marseille. As a community, the Unité houses 1,600 inhabitants—not, incidentally, the same number proposed by Charles Fourier for his social utopian phalanstery—with twenty-three types of accommodations ranging from bachelor pads to eight-bedroom apartments "extended" (*prolongé*) through the provision of collective services. The collective realm was constituted physically by the interior streets articulated with apartment mailboxes, a mid-block two-storey shopping street, and a rooftop kindergarten; and socio-economically by the cooperative governance of the building by owner residents, each of whom received votes proportional to the size of their units, in league with the city officials who represented the publicly held portion of apartments. The *Unité d'Habitation* as well as the other *Unités* are then the fundamental constituent piece of a Radiant City that was never fully realized. Sited outside or off the city grid, poised on muscular piloti like colossi, each of the Unités gives a visceral impression of belonging to some other order of living that is yet to be fully implemented. They each experiment in slightly different ways with new forms of modulor standardization, a guild-like structure of design and fabrication, and an internal social organization. Indeed, the Unité at Nantes and at Briey-en-Forêt were commissioned by workers' cooperatives.

They also, almost particularly at Marseille, begin to acknowledge the grand general economy of the radiance law of the sun. By virtue of the skip-stop section of the building, almost all of the apartments face both east and west so that they capture the rising and setting of the sun from their deep loggias, "such as Socrates advocated," in Le Corbusier's words, to provide "coolness in summer and warmth in winter."[38] At the scale of the individual dwelling, the sun operates as a rather benign ruler in support of a new kind of folkloric existence for l'*homme réel et concret*. The *beton brut*—literally "naked concrete"—of the loggia is imprinted with sea shells and an actual sundial while the entire depth of the screened loggia acts as an informal clock of sun and shadow throughout the day. The apartments open on a kitchen hearth overlooking an open living space suspended in a new vertical garden. On the roof, a more brutal Mediterraneanisme that Le Corbusier called "Homeric" appears. Platforms and steps beneath totemic smoke stacks and blank screens suggest sacrificial alters—perhaps to the sun?—before a landscape reduced to mountain, sky, and sea by the blinding height of the parapet walls.

It is unclear if Le Corbusier had read the inscribed copy of *The Accursed Share* he received from Bataille before the completion of the Unité since he notes that he finishes it in 1953,[39] but, again, their shared sympathetic understanding of the sun is evident. The economic ambition of the Unité is likewise a form of fusion between the symbolic excess of the roof and the working of the social cooperative beneath, between standardization and the proportion of The Modulor. Its goal is nothing less than the renegotiation of man's relation to material through architecture.

## Big work

The Unité is a single building that takes on the burden of the Big Work which the youthful Le Corbusier first dreamed of in relation to New York. Its material production becomes a model for building the entire democratic socialist nation in the capital city of Chandigarh, where the construction of the raw concrete known as *beton brut* employed thousands of peons, and the Unité sun break wall known as *brise soleil*, together with vast gutters, manage the seasonal sun and monsoon rain. This *beton brut* is not a fetish, but a grand organic language of production tied to an organization of labor, which Le Corbusier rationally puts aside in the context of a developed industrial nation, as, for example, at the Carpenter Center in Cambridge where the availability of plywood formwork made a smooth finish possible and rough pine boards unnecessary. Indeed the Unité at Marseille was built of concrete only because the initial idea of steel proved untenable in the context of immediate postwar shortages. Its typology as a building and a community was geared towards the emergent global capitalist economy as a replacement for the proliferating suburb. Le Corbusier proudly writes of the Unité at Rezé-lès-Nantes (also known as *La Maison Familiale*, with its Syndicalist ring) that it replaces the roadwork infrastructure for 1400 inhabitants with a small bridge that crosses a small lake into the building. But it is the building at Marseille that establishes the Unité's mythic stature. A complete, yet headless, figure of naked concrete astride the splayed monumental legs of pilotis that lifts up and shelters its inhabitants, the Unité presents the aspiration of a self-regulating, totalizing system of human and natural exchange lodged in a single body.[40]

## Notes

1 Le Corbusier quoted by Francesco Passanti in *Le Corbusier Before Le Corbusier: Architectural Studies, Interiors, Painting and Photography, 1907–1922,* ed. Stanislaus von Moos and Arthur Rüegg (New Haven: Yale University Press, 2002), 89.

2   Le Corbusier quoted by Arthur Rüegg in *Le Corbusier Before Le Corbusier*, 127.

3   Le Corbusier, *Towards an Architecture*, trans. John Goodman (Los Angeles: Getty Research Institute, 2007).

4   Ibid., xxiii.

5   Ibid.

6   Ibid.

7   Passanti, *Le Corbusier Before Le Corbusier*.

8   Le Corbusier, *The Decorative Art of Today*, trans. James Dunnett (Cambridge, MA: The MIT Press, 1987).

9   Catherine Cooke, *Russian Avant-Garde: Theories of Art, Architecture, and the City* (London: Academy Editions, 1995), 143.

10  Le Corbusier, *The Decorative Art of Today*, xxiv.

11  Tim Benton, *The Villas of Le Corbusier: 1920–1930* (New Haven: Yale University Press, 1987), 10.

12  Le Corbusier, *The Decorative Art of Today*, 26.

13  Rüegg, *Le Corbusier Before Le Corbusier*.

14  Manfredo Tafuri, *Architecture and Utopia: Design and Capitalist Development* (Cambridge, MA: The MIT Press, 1979), 83–84.

15  He writes to Fritz Ernst Jecker, who had purchased his parents' house in Switzerland, "One question quite rightly concerns you: that of the minor objects, vases paintings, drawings, prints, *bibelots*. . . Have no anxieties on this score. . . This is easy for me to do in a city like PARIS where anything can be found if one knows where to look, and at some astounding prices too." Le Corbusier quoted by Rüegg in *Le Corbusier Before Le Corbusier*, 127.

16  Tafuri makes a related point in *Architecture and Utopia*, 89.

17  Le Corbusier, *The Radiant City* (New York: The Orion Press, 1964).

18  *Radiant City*, 24.

19  Julian Jackson, *France: The Dark Years, 1940–1944* (London, Oxford University Press), ch. 2.

20  In his most renowned work, *The Gift* (1924), Marcel Mauss argues that gifts are not simply bestowed but form a complex system of reciprocal exchange that involves competition for rank and forms the basis of a commodity economy. He was a collaborator of Durkheim among others (including George Sorel) on the newspaper *The Socialist Movement*.

21  For an excellent treatment of these ideas see A. Stoekl, "Truman's Apotheosis: Bataille, 'Planisme,' and Headlessness," in ed. A. Stoekl, *Yale French Studies 78: On Bataille* (1990): 185–187.

22  *The Radiant City*, 24.

23  Ibid., 115.

24  Ibid., 60.

25  Ibid.

26  Ibid., 75.

27  Ibid., 72.

28  Georges Bataille, *The Accursed Share: An Essay on General Economy, Vol. 1: Consumption* (New York: Zone Books, 1991).

29  Bataille's solution is the Marshall Plan.

30  Catherine Blain, *Team 10: The French Context*, www.teamtenonline.org, 74.

31  Jodi Loach, *Le Corbusier and Mathematics*, British Journal of the History of Science 31, 1998, 201.

32  Le Corbusier, *Talks with Students* (Princeton, NJ: Princeton Architectural Press, 1999), 13, 15.

33  Le Corbusier, *The Modulor I and II* (Cambridge, MA: Harvard University Press, 1986), 160.

34  Ibid.

35  Ibid., 162.

36  Ibid.

37  Deborah Gans, *The Le Corbusier Guide* (Princeton, NJ: Princeton Architectural Press, 2004).

38  *Modulor*, 304.

39  Nadir Lahiji, "The Gift of the Open Hand: Le Corbusier Reading George Bataille's *Le Part Maudit*," JAE 50, no. 1 (September 1996), 50–56.

40  *Acéphale*, or the "headless man," was the name of a secret society and journal founded by George Bataille between 1936 and 1939. The headless man represents, among other things, anti-sovereignty—as in the headless crowd that rose up in reaction to, and decapitated, the French monarchy—and as in his own intellectual resistance to fascism.

# Chapter 6

# Context: 1943–1975

From the end of World War II to the oil crisis of the early 1970s, both America and France experienced a world shaped by new global co-dependencies. The Marshall Plan; the departure of US forces from Europe; the undoing of Bretton Woods; the shared failures in Vietnam; positioning vis-à-vis the USSR; membership in NATO—all linked the two countries and caused a mutual anxiety over the nature of state governance. The concern in both countries was less about the forceful role government would play in the economy than the role it would play in the lives of its citizens. Not surprisingly, critical movements in American and French architecture in this period can be discussed together.

In the thirty years between 1943 and 1973, France's economy grew by approximately 4.5 percent. The average income in France in 1950 was 55 percent of a comparable American; in 1973, it was 80 percent. De Gaulle's "indicative planning," in contrast to mandatory planning, combined informal agreements between high-level officials educated at the École Nationale d'Adminstration with leaders in industry trained at the École Polytechnique, and leaders of financial institutions. As Simon Sadler points out, this move was understood to be the correct middle path between American laissez-faire policies and Soviet state control.

However, France's productivity lagged behind West Germany. Germany invested more heavily in research and development and, singularly, never sought governmental economic control. Despite encouraging large mergers, France had a relatively small financial sector, and farmers remained unmerged, unorganized, and unambitious in regards to productivity. Likewise, the mixed nature of government coalitions and the lack of agreement over colonial wars in Vietnam and Algeria yielded cabinet changes and general unease.

The events of the late 1960s—North Vietnam's successful Tet offensive, the USSR's suppression of the Prague Spring, the growing influence of Maoism in China after the Sino-Soviet split, the expansion of communist parties across Europe—led to the political and intellectual crisis of May 1968. Student protest that began at the University of Paris at Nanterre spread to the Sorbonne and to labor groups, resulting in popular criticism of the patriarchal De Gaulle presidency and, in 1969, his resignation. Likewise, orthodox Marxism, the traditional heart of French intellectual currents since the Russian Revolution, was rejected. The Left—splintered between Maoism, anti-party individualism, and diffused anti-liberalism—failed to galvanize around a critical intellectual and/or political platform, explaining in part the success of the French Right until the election of a Socialist president Francois Mitterand in 1981.

In America, these same three decades marked the era of faith in Keynesian economics and the bias toward regulation, inflation-in-support-of-employment, and deficit spending. Harry Truman's "Fair Deal" supporting returning soldiers of World War II increased social security benefits, higher minimum wage, federal subsidies for housing, and compulsory federal health insurance. Eisenhower's "less government in business and more business in government" actually endorsed the expansion of many benefits and fought the slumps of 1953–1954 and 1957–1958 with prodigious spending and large deficits; Kennedy's "New Frontier" mimicked Truman's "Fair Deal"; Johnson's "Great Society" launched the "War on Poverty," civil rights, public broadcasting, Medicare, Medicaid, environmental protection, and aid to education; Nixon's use of strong government opened relations with China and initiated detent with the USSR.

However, Nixon also initiated the end of the Keynsian era by terminating the Bretton Woods agreement decoupling the dollar from gold and effectively allowed international monetary values to float freely. Jimmy Carter's presidency, marked by "stagflation" (high inflation coupled with high unemployment), further diminished the belief in strong governmental regulation. Its death-knell was then tolled four years later with the election of Ronald Reagan, the rise of the Chicago School of economics, and subsequent "supply-side" economic policies.

In the midst of this shift from left to right, America was alone in the western world in not pursuing aggressive industrialization. In 1950, industry accounted for 28 percent GDP; in 2007, 12 percent. In 1950, 25 percent of labor was in manufacturing; in 2007, 10 percent. The "moral awakening" ushered in by Johnson in the 1960s changed the labor market, with women entering the now largely service-oriented workforce. As a consequence, labor unions declined and never recovered. Likewise, the rise of the Sun Belt in the 1970s and 1980s moved American politics further to the right, as did white flight in northern cities.

In the US as in France, the relationship between politics and culture was tightly knit in the late 1960s. While there has never been the same intellectual interest in Marxism in the US as in Europe, nor governmental support for culture, the same world events shook the prevalent faith in western hegemony and American bombast. As Sadler explains, protests against the war in Vietnam and its seemingly overt imperialism were matched by a fascination with eastern mysticism. In the concrete world of architecture, the body/mind as much as the building was seen as the temple of power and resistance.

Peggy Deamer

Chapter 6

# The varieties of capitalist experience

## Simon Sadler

During the formative years of today's senior architects and educators in the late 1960s and early 1970s, the architectural discipline faced seismic developments in political economy and culture. The global west's post-war boom—that Golden Era of Capitalism, as it is sometimes called in the United States or, as it is has since been recalled in France, the *Trente Glorieuses*[1]—was met by its rejoinder from the New Left and the counterculture. Architectural education was drawn to the way that the New Left and counterculture habitually located political consciousness close to architecture's disciplinary heart in design, aesthetics, and everyday life. The situationists, based in Paris, and the hippies, congregating in the West/Southwest of the US, advanced analyses of the political economy of space and suggested tactics for its transformation. Their theses intrigued the architectural discipline to the same extent as they threatened the discipline's extinction.

After 1968, partly in response to counterculture, the architectural discipline did indeed de-emphasize rote technical training and service to the booming post-war military industrial complex. Architecture schools reconsidered the making of the architect and architectural culture. But the discipline also prevented design from becoming the instrument of total revolution that the counterculture demanded. Rather, the cleft between capitalism and counter-culture, in which architecture was wedged by the late 1960s, prompted the discipline to reassert its relative autonomy from political economy. It was a sort of non-alignment that allowed architecture to pose as a "third way" out of the impasse between capitalism and counterculture, much as counterculture earlier suggested a way out of the Cold War impasse between capitalism and commu-nism. This shared historical calling—as a sort of Hegelian play of contradictions—points to architecture and counterculture's shared ambition to open up "spaces" for critical consciousness in the commune, studio, and seminar room. Even as counterculture waned, the assumption that architecture is a means of forging its students' and clients' consciousness became central to pedagogy.

## Capitalism and counterculture: two world views of plenty

These world views were founded on high, stable, and sustained economic growth throughout a US-led bloc bound by gifts, loans, and transnational agreements. Most important of these were the legendary Marshall Plan, administered from France by the Organization for European Economic Co-operation which pumped over $12 billion to rebuild and modernize Western Europe from 1947–1952, and the Bretton Woods system, established by the victorious Allies to ensure stability in the world economy and promote free trade. The effect was to lock western countries into largely Keynesian economies that allowed regional variations of state intervention and cultural preference. The bloc's members partnered government-funded fiscal stimulus with private enterprise. As General Motors president Charles Erwin Wilson told the Senate Armed Services Committee in 1953 when asked about any potential conflict of interest in his role as Secretary of Defense, "For years I thought that what was good for the country was good for General Motors and vice versa."[2] The system provided a framework for economic growth while feigning the appearance of the market's fabled hidden hand. Indeed, the US government oversaw something like a permanent war economy, ballasted with lavish military spending and infrastructural investment, such as the new freeway system, across which ran that quintessential post-war consumer product, the car, reshaping the built environment through which it sped.

In France, the role of technocratic central planning was more explicit, fixing war damage (which included well over one million buildings) and reconstructing Paris: in the 1950s and 1960s, the city witnessed its largest building campaigns since Haussmann, drawing comparison between the Trente Glorieuses and the France of the Second Empire.[3] Nationalization of France's key economic sectors had the effect of unifying a capitalist economic system relatively fragmented before the Second World War and yielded a planned economy that was Soviet as well as American in inspiration. Beginning with Charles de Gaulle's provisional government of 1945, which included communists and socialists alongside Gaullists, the mainstream left was embraced by the state through workers' councils and trades unions, and buffered by social security.

Near full employment and rising standards of living in the US and France grew the middle class, served by the expansion of education financed at the university level by the G.I. Bill in the US, and spurred in France by the development of a French dirigisme (government direction) which demanded the training of a meritocratic technocratic cadre to lead government and industry. As low-income rural labor flowed into better paying urban jobs in the towns and cities, the US and France both continued their conversion from agrarian to urbanized and suburbanized societies.

The comprehensiveness of the economic, ideological, social, and spatial modernization upon which a post-war consensus was founded served the vast majority of architects well. Architecture reified the Pax Americana as the sort of repetitive abstraction typified by Raymond Lopez in France or Skidmore Owings and Merrill in the US. Mass-employed by an animated construction industry, professional architects in the 1950s and 1960s had little motivation to explore alternative aesthetics and politics. There was, rather, the sense of a utopia in the here-and-now, with modernism's reformist mandate somewhat satisfied by western liberal democracy's basic guarantees of post-fascist civil liberties, ample affordance for large-scale modernizing projects—including potentially progressive housing programs—and its enthusiasm for technocratic and "avant-garde" solutions. However far western liberalism fell short of leftist ambitions, the authoritarian eastern bloc exerted little appeal following its occlusion of modernism with Socialist Realism, and was, in any case, closed off geopolitically.

If the profession was pleased and appeased by modernism's benefits, the New Left and counterculture were not. Indeed, it was the *transformative* capacities of western modernization that caught their attention. The long boom, both noted, was reorganizing physical space and spatial consciousness. An increasing dependence on cars, telecommunications, and television attended a decline in face-to-face interactions in public space. Social relations were increasingly mediated, it was seen, through technology and consumerism—as the core market for commodities became the proletariat itself, pursuing fashionable clothes, gadgets, and entertainment to amplify the leisure time freed by increased GDP. Guy Debord, the leading situationist organizer and theorist, described how, at this new advanced stage of capitalism, representation itself, dislocated from its material bases and floating through advertisements and across screens, became another form of exchange. France and all other advanced capitalist countries had entered the era of the "spectacle," he explained, in which social relations are mediated not simply by commodities, as Marx had shown in his description of alienation, but by the imagery of commodities, by the language used to describe them, and by the news events packaged by commercial and state media.[4] And so the spectacle of late capitalism—the very means of enforcing the alienation of things in the world—also concealed those separations, effecting the illusion that capitalist organization was so seamless, so organic, as to be literally cyclical, as fiscal stimulus offset business downturns and as workers purchased the products of their own labor.

Yet communism and capitalism alike, to degrees of greater or lesser freedom or oppression, separated the world with ever greater violence, from the micro-scale of everyday life to the meta-scales of gender, race, and nation. The eastern and western blocs' suppression of dissent, the defeats of the 1956 Hungarian Uprising and of the Prague Spring of 1968, and the escalation of military intervention in Algeria in the 1950s and Vietnam in the early 1960s made this evident. Domestically the incapacity of the American state to ensure Civil Rights or to stem "White Flight" to the suburbs shredded the nation racially; the modernist *projets* ringing French cities were emerging as the new ghettos. More abstractly, neither communism nor capitalism presented viable models of the natural commonwealth and human subjectivity upon which political economy is founded.[5] The golden age, it was apparent, was based on the odd combination of instrumentality—so apparent in France's technocratic turn—and surrealism— so insidious in the push for consumption which isolated life on the domestic front from the horror of the foreign front.[6]

Architecture served the Cold War political economy with a stark dutifulness all too apparent in the repetitive slab blocks of apartments and offices on both sides of the Iron Curtain, the suburban "ticky-tacky" tracts, the strip mall sprawl, and the widened streets and parking lots of an urban renewal guided by increased car ownership—all isolating humans from one another and from their environments. Tall buildings, plazas, social housing, comprehensive education and medical care, cars, fitted kitchens, package holidays, televisions, and the opening frontiers of computing and outer space were deepening anomie, not mitigating it.[7]

In contrast to this, the New Left and counterculture theorized a day- to-day, individually experienced space, one that was bottom-up, socially engaged, environmentally attuned. And the events of 1968 in both countries turned theory into reality. The protests around the Democratic National Convention in Chicago and the revolutionary Events of May centered in Paris coalesced into a larger— more immediate, more demanding, and more shared—program; a praxis seced- ing, as best they could, from Stalinism, consumerism, liberal democracy, and bourgeois mores; from the very game of electoral politics itself. Counterculture— seemingly a "third way" out of the Cold War impasse of capitalist/communist, left/right, domestic/overseas—sought a renewed plenitude in the relationships between people and the world.

The programs of the hippies and situationists are strikingly parallel: their gestation and peak influence roughly coincide; they both sprang from comparable frustrations in the remaking of the Cold War landscape; they both grew from tiny, ultra-vanguard, cross-disciplinary cadres gathering around charismatic figures such as Ken Kesey in the US and Guy Debord in France to proto-mass movements during the Summer of Love of 1967 and the May Events of 1968.

But there were significant distinctions. Situationism suggested a hyper-French vision of alternative society, and the hippies a hyper-American one. The situationists were principally inspired by Franco-German revolutionary Romanticism from anarchism through Marx to surrealism. Particularly reverential of the Paris Commune of 1871, the situationists demanded an assault on political economy through culture, principally architecture and urbanism.[8] By contrast the hippies—cherishing typical Yankee values such as free speech, civil liberty, and civil disobedience over any party line—were inspired more by the heterodox communal models hailing from religious dissent and founded in love; they were much more numerous, less centralized, and less doctrinaire than the situationists.[9] US counterculture required the abundant space of the US subcontinent, first when it went "on the road" in the sorts of peregrinations inspired by Kesey, and then when large numbers of its denizens decided to move off the grid in self-imposed exile from the military-industrial complex. Situationism was by comparison avowedly urban, based in the traditional locale of revolution. Situationist collage, including cut city maps, augured a violent readjustment of the class relations of the city, whereas hippiedom proposed a more pastoral, more pragmatic adjustment in ecological relations. The former was a form of insurgency, the latter of bootstrapping dissent. The epistemological traditions that the hippies looked back to were Pragmatism, with its acceptance of plural and practical outcomes over any singular epistemology, and Transcendentalism, with its aversion to the corrupting influence of organized religion and politics and adherence to the inherent good of man and nature. Situationism was embedded in an epistemology that combined the European avant-garde inheritances of futurism, expressionism, Dadaism, constructivism, and surrealism with the continental philosophy of existentialism and revisionist Marxism.

Nevertheless, hippies and situationists both recognized the difficulty of initiating rebellion in liberal and capitalist democracies. They posited a sort of "non-cooperation" with capitalism, the hippies often pursuing a self-abnegation with strong affinities to eastern religions, such that the transcendental, self-organizing properties of the universe could be finally perceived and the trivial relations of capitalism relegated. As far as possible the situationists declined to work or consume, reputedly "drifting" through the cities they idly contemplated, but thus remaining absolutely engaged with capitalism, as though trying to exhaust or outflank it. Hippies combined the altered consciousness stemming from pharmaceutical and philosophical experiment with the techno-science of cybernetics, design science, and ecology. Situationists synthesized Marxist and surrealist critiques of the bourgeois lifeworld. Hippies and situationists believed in a restored, visceral response to the world, provided a new understanding of totality that profoundly overturned bourgeois order—its state, its ideology, and its political economy.

The spatio-temporal world that the counterculture envisioned was continuous and scaleless. All upheavals of the 1960s could be seen as a continuum, from the Watts riot to the Vietnam and Arab-Israel wars, from the Prague Spring to the Chinese Cultural Revolution. Aesthetic senses of the world would be derived from overlooked indices across extreme scales: hippies could find the world in a grain of sand, in a chance encounter, or in a photograph of the world taken from space; situationists would see the world in composite aerial photos taken from surveillance aircraft, in a trace of graffiti, or in an ad torn from a magazine. Representation had to be de-naturalized before it could yield information about the fabric of reality: film, say, could slow down or speed up reality, edit it, stop it, so that its gestures, conventions, and performance could be better perceived. In the classic formula of the avant-garde—perhaps never better represented than by the program of the situationists—the solution to the modern crisis of consciousness was the living of life as a work of art, moment to moment, in a voluntarist or anarchist gift economy. Rather than depict reality, reality was the medium—the medium for making "situations," as the situationists identified their project, or the "be-in," to invoke the notorious hippie gathering. The party, the happening, the situation: these moments of transcendence of the alienated relations of everyday life under capitalism were the proper site of creativity after the work of art and after the gallery. So it was that the most iconic mode of hippie building, the geodesic dome, was emphatically resistant to subdivision.

And so counterculture demanded limitless space for the new human being. The Parisian situationists favored what they called a "unitary urbanism," in which humanity's destiny would be negotiated en masse through revisions to the metropolis, that locus of modernization; the hippies tended toward what we might call a "new homesteading."[10] The whole earth was perceived as but a single spaceship (as the hippies read Richard Buckminster Fuller);[11] in his epic New Babylon project, the situationist Constant Nieuwenhuys proposed that all cities be united into a continuous network. Threading these scales were newly exploratory human subjects, freed from their dependence on commercial and governmental hype for their information about reality and unencumbered by private property, subdivisions, and zoning. These new subjects would work collectively, it was imagined, to create social space, on the move. As depicted in the Guy Debord and Asger Jorn 1957 collage the Naked City, where Paris's neighborhoods float one against the other, or in the diagrammatic representations of space shown in the drawings submitted in 1971 to Architectural Design by the southwestern US commune of Lama,[12] space was an ecological continuum.

But in the effort to reconvene humans as a tribe, to make space unitary, the counterculture—staffed as it so often was by the enfants terribles of the bourgeoisie—re-deployed the bourgeois strategy of colonization.[13] Working-class neighborhoods, rural towns, ranches, minority cultures, technology, arcane knowledge all provided domicile to the new culture. It learned to "recycle" or "divert" the baubles of the bourgeois manifold: philosophy, science, markets— capitalism itself being reinvented by the bottom-up models of exchange exemplified by the Whole Earth Catalog, first published in 1968. In its very nostalgie de la boue and repugnance at the profligacy of consumerism, the counterculture encouraged an extraordinary connoisseurship around street markets, good food and drink, music, craft, and traditional architecture. Conversely, it exploited advanced technologies—drugs and computers—as tools for the making whole of consciousness through knowledge and experience, reversing instrumentalism.

It is as though these movements of liberation—as steeped as they were in a history of self-management drawn from American rural life and European workers' councils—had no great need, after all, to exert a claim to be authentic subaltern movements. They were vanguards, and as such were alluring to another branch of the intelligentsia enthralled by utopianism, universalism, innovation: the architectural discipline.

## Architecture and counterculture

Full cognizance of points of doctrinal variance within the counterculture were surely tricky for architects to ascertain.[14] They might have learned about the hippies of Drop City, retreating in 1965 to rural Colorado to paint, to live off food stamps and recycled materials and build geodesic and quasi-geodesic domes; or they might have encountered the situationists' unwatchable films and inscrutable maps of cities existing and projected. Aside from the specifics, though, there was an uncanny semblance between architecture and the counterculture. Both sought a more perfect union of mind, body, nature, and economy than was present in the existing political and built environment.

Counterculture shared architecture's objective of sublimating art into life in the tradition of the historical avant-gardes, concurring that architecture took precedence over gallery art in the changing of being. Counterculture enthused that massive social change could be, to a very considerable degree, *designed*; and counterculture subscribed to the profession's faith in individual and collective agency.

In counterculture, architects reciprocally saw a system in which building was complicit in organizing productive and social relations. As a politics, counterculture kept humanism and aesthetics intact, so its importation into architecture had the effect of shoring up the traditions of architecture against the ingress of functionalism. Successfully negotiated, the translation of counterculture into architecture might allow architects to act as active political subjects by practicing as architects. Guilt about the proximity of design to money would be offset by architecture's increasingly assured claims that it had become "critical," putting to rest the discipline's proletarian lack. Progressives in the profession of the 1950s and 1960s had long questioned the direction of modern architecture, in any case; CIAM collapsed from the inside, increasingly tortured during its last meetings by the problem of the found city, of functionalism, and the existential soul-searching of Team 10. The encounter with counterculture was presaged by vanguard architects' wide-ranging search for "bottom-up," "organic," and "systemic" alternatives to determinist planning of the sorts found variously in the work of Paul and Percival Goodman, Karl Popper, Norbert Weiner, Geörgy Kepes, Bernard Rudofsky, Herbert Gans, and Paul Davidoff. Some architectural dissent was properly politically informed—one thinks of figures like libertarian socialist Giancarlo di Carlo, or Aldo van Eyck, a correspondent with the situationist Constant Niewuwenhuys—or of the anarchic sympathies of Georges Candilis, and the milestone in the secession from mainstream modern architecture marked by the foundation of the Candilis/Josic/Woods atelier in 1964. In California in the mid-1960s, architects like Sim van der Ryn and Charles Moore (moving to a turbulent Yale from 1965–1970) began to explore user participation, gestalt psychology, phenomenology and design/build, in which students took part in actual construction in direct contact with the community.[15]

New Left and counterculture tendencies mingled in the projects, posters and agitations spilling from architecture schools from 1968 to 1973.[16] Because the counterculture regarded vocational architecture as a mechanism of hegemony, its reception by students and faculty prompted both soul-searching and exhilaration. The US witnessed a wave of refusal and disciplinary rethinking centered, for example, around the Architects' Resistance group in northeastern schools, which circa 1969–1970 petitioned the profession's "moral and social conscience" and demonstrated against SOM's work in South Africa.[17] In 1968 there were occupations of the schools of architecture at Columbia, Yale, and Berkeley. In France, the active participation of architecture students in the May

Events in Paris in 1968 led to the dismantling of the Beaux-Arts—the school whose name was literally synonymous with rigorous bourgeois architectural education—and of the Prix de Rome, awarded to architects since 1722 to designate France's *maîtres*. The crisis continued when 80 staff and 1200 students defied the French Ministry of Cultural Affairs' reorganization of the Ecolé des Beaux Arts as five new Unités pédagogiques. They gathered as UP6 and dedicated themselves "to returning to the people the right to manage their own affairs," denouncing "the class segregation perpetuated and augmented by present bourgeois urbanism."[18]

UP6's radical working methods included the adoption of the situationist-derived technique of *détournement* (the tactic of "diversion" or "hijacking"). UP6's most charismatic achievement was the *détournement* of a building exercise to provide a roof for an improvised community center in the Parisian Bidonville of Villeneuve-la-Garenne. Something similar was tried at Berkeley, where in 1969 Sim van der Ryn led architecture students to join their UC Berkeley colleagues and other sympathizers who were turning a block of empty land awaiting development by the University of California into the infamous experiment in anarchic social ecology known as the People's Park. The spectacle itself was *détourned* when the media spotlit the violent state suppression of the experiments at the People's Park and the Bidonville community center, which was demolished by local authorities in full view of the press and television cameras.

## Denoument: architecture as counterculture

In Martin Pawley and Bernard Tschumi's 1971 article in *Architectural Design* entitled "The Beaux-Arts since 1968," they concluded that détournement in France was briefly effective because of its shock value. But that shock, they indicated, gave way to architectural custom (UP6's more militant students following the example at Yale in 1968[19] by burning down the school office in 1971 in a last-ditch attempt to prevent the unit from awarding diplomas).[20] With mixed results, UP6's strike in the winter of 1969–1970 took teaching to the streets and into the decision-making institutions of building production, and the summer of 1971 brought with it encouraging signs of coordination with ordinary residents via the local Action Committees established in 1968.[21] But as UP6 students strenuously fraternized with locals in Belleville, a Parisian neighborhood subject to redevelopment, "The attitude of people in the market was at first one of resignation and sympathy tinged with a patronizing concern for the 'Daddies boys.'"[22] Clearly, perceptions of class difference had survived the May Events.[23] UP6's revolutionary paper, *La Maison du Peuple* (a skit on *La Maison de Marie-Claire*) was, in the opinion of Marxist architect Anatole Kopp, a sign of the desperation of those who "attempted to reignite the events of May every morning since," and an editor of the paper conceded in 1971, "It is impossible to stop capitalism . . . we should concentrate on marginal production, by people for themselves."[24]

After 1968, then, the architectural discipline largely reverted to its historical role as a form of *indirect* action. Architectural education was restored, even in France, alongside the rest of the French higher education system and indeed the French state itself—if in significantly altered form, notably decentralized and notably no longer dependent upon a core functionalist technocratic syllabus. The destruction of the Prix de Rome system and introduction in 1973 of open PAN (*Programme d'Architecture Nouvelle*) architectural competitions in France prompted the blooming of a generation of architects previously disillusioned by architecture but now discovering the possibility of working on progressive urban-scale projects.[25] Moreover, the architectural discipline post-1968 became somewhat fascinated with, and defiant of, the near-death experience it survived.[26] By 1972, Tschumi explains, the situationists "already seemed like distant history,"[27] becoming the latest addition to the ever-accumulating stock of experimental art, cinema, and literature available as a formal and theoretical resource to the progressive architect. The revised architectural syllabus was marked by the adaptation of revisionist Marxist, existential, phenomenological, and psychoanalytic theory, previously explored by the New Left, not now toward a general political praxis but to a general *architectural* praxis destabilizing preconceptions about architecture. With both modernist universalism and the revolutionary *Événements* of 1968 now apparently failed, theories once associated with the New Left amalgamated in the 1970s with the debates taking place internally to architecture since the 1950s to form the larger epistemological turn to postmodernism. As a further component of that turn, poststructuralism maintained the potential for the destabilization of the systems and languages of power; but as the 1970s wore on talk of power as radically decentered, atomized, and competing began to undermine notions of solidarity, and of the possibility of an organic non-alienation just the other side of spectacle. Though community activist architecture nobly remained in some schools, any correlation with revolution disappeared.[28]

Pawley and Tschumi dated the beginning of "La récuperation" to the Fall of 1969.[29] A new *unité*, UP8, splintered from UP6, taking with it staff and students increasingly frustrated by the lack of a coherent political framework and by their desire to actually make architecture rather than talk about it, a skepticism echoed in the American criticisms of Berkeley "talkitecture."[30] Among even radicalized architects, respect for the vocation of architecture tended to be more enduring than the call for absolute resistance to bourgeois spectacular-commodity society. Bernard Huet explained UP8's position: "We say that space has a certain influence on social behavior, it does not transform it, but it does act upon it in such a way that we as architects can perhaps make possible certain unspecified and unexpected possibilities through the space we design."[31] Much as architectural reformism moved upstream into boardrooms and government ministries after the Second World War, after 1968 it moved into virtuosity. UP6 dismissed the adjustment as "an old modernism, but more snobbish for an elite of the Left."[32] The situationist-inspired Utopie group seemed to dismiss UP6 and UP8 alike: "To imagine," commented its member and faculty member at the new Experimental University at Vincennes, Herbert Tonka, ". . . as do some at the Beaux-Arts—that it is possible to act politically through urbanism, architecture, or the *détournement* of either is a dream."[33]

Tschumi had been a student with Candilis/Josic/Woods, a practice which joined the student protests at the École, but by the early 1970s his teaching unit at the Architectural Association, too, was at pains to explain that, despite its immersion in the work of the situationists, their fellow-traveler Henri Lefebvre, and the Frankfurt school, its interest in politics was not in "politics in the institutional sense . . . nor politics in the ideological sense . . . but [in] politics in a sense that has not yet been defined," that is, the politics of "the elaboration of subjective spaces and social playgrounds."[34] Tschumi's interests had been amongst the most radical ever to enter the architectural syllabus—he used IRA contacts to garner information on insurgency (a project eventually dropped after bomb threats against the AA)[35] and explored the idea of the so-called autonomous zone, then exemplified by the Irish Republican enclave of Free Derry.[36] But he now looked instead toward what was called the *environmental* trigger, rather than the trigger of a gun, for a "violence" that would be metaphorical rather than literal, with a new concern for the qualities of social space, heterogeneity, nomadism, and the urban event.

Ecology initially suggested another countercultural negation of architecture, though it tempered within architecture schools into another reform movement, apparently "sustaining" capitalist political economy as much as opposing it. Like many of the other countercultural spheres of direct protest, it became a "relevant" issue for architecture to address.

It would seem easy, then, to lament architecture's absorption and neutering of counterculture as crass self-interest. But it is more interesting to conclude by exploring the odd particularity of their relationship. While intimately related to counterculture in its desire to change consciousness and rationally distribute resources, architecture is an antinomy of counterculture insofar as it is founded on the alienations that counterculture tries to overcome. In its ambition to end alienation, complete the whole, and terminate history, counterculture had been an extraordinary *threat* to architecture. While architecture assumed a central importance to counterculture, by the same token, counterculture deprived architecture of its independence as a discipline and vocation. Professionalized in the west since Vitruvius, architecture had to remain *counter* to counterculture—urbane, instrumental, capitalized, committed to service. Architects' roles as individual, private political beings would remain ultimately bracketed off by definition, by their practice and teaching. "Whether it expresses bourgeois or proletarian interests architecture has always been linked to social repression because it remains external to the quotidian experience of people,"[37] noted Tonka brusquely. The notion of a countercultural architect, meanwhile, was practically a contradiction in terms.[38]

Nor should the political superiority of counterculture be assumed without scrutiny. Counterculturalists' exhortations to live transformative "situations" were always a little overbearing, and their claims to be able to transform political economy were more crudely behaviorist than those sometimes indulged by architects. Architecture at least allowed one thing to *represent* another—as language, as symbol, as art—in contrast to the 1:1 correlation between political economy and political culture offered by the counterculture. Architecture's revival of symbolic thought after 1968 allowed it to once more abstract function, thought, meaning, behavior, and beauty and restore moral judgments, including those concerning political economy, that aesthetics was meant to embrace. Architecture could, in other words, represent counterculture.

The difficult dance between counterculture and architecture is paralleled by that of counterculture and the academy. Counterculture vastly expanded the public sphere but it was nonetheless lodged in its most traditional hub: the university, expanding under the era's subsidized provision of higher education. The Free Speech movement fanned out from UC Berkeley; the situationists antagonistically tested their ideas on the student-dominated Left Bank and at the University of Strasbourg in 1966, then at Nantes and Lyon (developing their ideas with Lefebvre, Nanterre University's professor of sociology), and finally occupying the Sorbonne. And the intellectual gurus of the time were largely sometime academics: Leary, Marcuse, Dass, Chomsky, Lefebvre, Foucault.

But the counterculture often tried to escape the gravitational pull of this bourgeois locus, as if trapped in an Oedipal relationship with the academy. "'Destroy the University' was a popular slogan both during and after the May events," Pawley and Tschumi reported in 1971. "But," they concluded, "to close the school utterly and completely was to destroy any real possibility of systematic analysis and critique."[39] Indeed, Beaux-Arts students in 1968 had demanded their incorporation into a full university system that they believed would be "objective" and "relevant."[40] In the late 1960s and 1970s, universities suggested a "heterotopic"[41] space relatively autonomous from the spectacular-commodity city at large, capitalist labor superseded by pure learning, its refectories a sort of countercultural "be-in" replacing city cafés driven out by escalating rents.

The model of the university as a locus for criticism within the dense relations of capitalism depends on the possibility of immanent critique—on locating the contradictions in the rules and systems necessary to production. Nested within the bourgeois institutions of higher learning, notably in elite private institutions, architectural educators post-1968 undertook to analyze the world more thoroughly than its countercultural counterparts that opposed capitalism from without. The very possibility of immanent critique surely functioned to *reconcile* the apparent contradiction of leftist educators pursuing careers in universities and private schools of architecture, often with great success; the discipline's ideology became Gramscian by default, its faculty apparently hoping that the ideological superstructure can affect the economic substructure.

The contradiction internal to architecture of serving two masters, hegemonic and counter-hegemonic (tacitly registered in the long-running tensions between the profession and the schools), has been played out from the most arcane corners of education to the highest levels of pedagogy. To be clear, the contradiction became *central* to advanced pedagogy. Something more than counter-revolutionary parody or post-revolutionary melancholia was immediately registered in the appearance of hippies in the 1969 Superstudio collages depicting an ultra-spectacular, ultra-technological, ultra-commodified future, for instance, or when depicting the vestiges of New Babylon in the equally iconic collages of Elia Zenghelis and Rem Koolhaas's *Involuntary Prisoners of Architecture*, a 1972 AA thesis extended 23 years later into the opening pages of S,M,L,XL.[42] Certainly, architectural interventions like these have an air of *forgetting* the larger, totalizing euphoria of 1968 (many architects, notably Koolhaas—observing the May Events as a journalist—were never much convinced about counterculture),[43] preferring to play a postmodern language game or search for form. The reappearances of countercultural utopia in architecture since 1968 have always been a little uncanny, shorn as they are from a comprehensive revolutionary political agenda.

But they have also had the effect of *remembering* the countercultural dream of the "lived situation." The ascent of architectural theory, registered in these surrealistic collages, can be fairly attacked as promoting the most haute-bourgeois forms of autonomy, of course. But they also herald a new era of pragmatism after the "certainties" of modernism and counterculture alike. The collages by Superstudio, Zenghelis and Koolhaas were memoranda on the inevitable, unending, irreconcilable contradictions of the architectural discipline, ever wanting to alter reality, yet complicit in its concretization. As if to underscore the difference between architecture and counterculture, then, those collages acted as perpetual missives that architecture imprisons as it frees, shores up the subject only by shoring up the territory.

Architecture is an unlikely savior of counterculture, then; counterculture is now an architectural work, a theme in architecture's studio and literature. Architectural education started curating the counterculture at the same time that it began archiving counterculture's revolutionary forerunner in Russian Constructivism—at the same time, indeed, that it was completing its long post-war taxonomy of *all* sources of environmental organization outside the main models of political economy: phenomenology, structuralism, post-structuralism, the vernacular, eco-cybernetics, rationalism, typology, the psychoanalytic. The title of this chapter, a play on *The Varieties of Religious Experience*, alludes to the way that William James, the philosopher and psychologist of Pragmatism, elaborated a pluralistic framework in which "the divine can mean no single quality . . . it must mean a group of qualities, by being champions of which in alternation, different men may all find worthy missions."[44] James argued that universal conceptions have practical applications only through a messy reality, and that it was this *applicability* that prevents idealism from running amok in everyday life. If the immanent relationship of architecture to capitalist oppression gnawed at the possibility of a "critical" architecture after 1968, the very *pursuit* of architecture was an anti-nihilism—a relentless making do, a mixing and matching of ontologies with design tasks and economy, a hunt for a *juste milieu* with disputes to the left and right adjudicated by intellectuals.

"*Sous le pavé, la plage* (under the pavement, the beach)," Koolhaas wrote in S,M,L,XL, recalling the famous situationist-inspired graffiti: "initially, May '68 launched the idea for a new beginning for the city."[45] He then offered architecture as a proxy for the collective action that was superseded after 1968 by pluralism, historicism, and development, and left bereft of Golden Era plenitude following the Energy Crisis and collapse of Bretton Woods in 1973. Architecture could be imagined as a holding operation awaiting the next cultural coda, the next 68 or Occupy, the next appeal to unalloyed partisanship, standing off against the new entropic threat to design embodied in neoliberalism.

## Notes

1 See Jean Fourastié, *Les Trente Glorieuses, ou la révolution invisible de 1946 à 1975* (Paris: Fayard, 1979).
2 Quoted in James McConaughy, "Ike Battles for the Party," *Life*, October 29, 1956, 131.
3 See, for instance, Louis Chevalier, *L'assassinat de Paris* in *The Assassination of Paris*, trans. David P. Jordan (1977; Chicago: University of Chicago Press, 1994); Rosemary Wakeman, *The Heroic City: Paris, 1945–1958* (Chicago: University of Chicago Press, 2009).
4 See Guy Debord, *La société du spectacle* (Paris, 1967), trans. *The Society of the Spectacle* (London: Rebel Press and Aim Publications, 1987).
5 See Max Horkheimer and Theodor Adorno, *Dialectic of Enlightenment: Philosophical Fragments* (1944; Stanford: Stanford University Press, 2002).
6 See Kristin Ross, *Fast Cars, Clean Bodies: Decolonization and the Reordering of French Culture* (Cambridge, Mass.: MIT Press, 1995).
7 See, for instance, See Henri Lefebvre, *La production de l'espace* in *The Production of Space*, trans. Donald Nicholson-Smith (1974, Paris; Oxford: Blackwell, 1991).
8 For readings on situationism, see *Internationale situationniste* (1958–1969), reprinted (Paris: Fayard, 1997); important secondary sources include Anselm Jappe, *Guy Debord*, trans. Donald Nicholson-Smith (Berkeley: University of California Press, 1999); and Sadie Plant, *The Most Radical Gesture: The Situationist International in a Postmodern Age* (London: Routledge, 1992).
9 For readings on American counterculture, see, for instance, Peter Braunstein and Michael William Doyle, eds, *Imagine Nation: The American Counterculture of the 1960s and '70s* (New York: Routledge, 2002).
10 See, for instance, Iain Boal, Janferie Stone, Michael Watts, Cal Winslow, eds, *West of Eden: Communes and Utopia in Northern California* (Oakland: PM Press / Retort, 2012).
11 See Richard Buckminster Fuller, *Operating Manual for Spaceship Earth* (Carbondale: Southern Illinois University Press, 1969).
12 See "Lama Foundation," *Architectural Design* 42 (December 1971): 743–752.
13 The counterculturalist typically posed as a figure transcending allegiance to corporation, nation, class, race, and gender. Counterculture was therefore a legatee of Enlightenment universality diverted through Romantic individualism. The life and work arrangements of counterculture do not in practice always bear out its egalitarian claims, and one of the most ridiculed aspects of counterculture, then and since, was the assumption by its participants, who were primarily white, bourgeois, and highly educated, of déclassé identity with peasants, workers, and minorities. But one corruption of Enlightenment rationality had been its management of difference and crisis through separation. The transcendence of difference (of class, race, etc.) located political struggle not in the factory but in the everyday life of the subject—including the bourgeois subject.

14  For accounts of the intersections of architecture and counterculture, see, for instance, Margaret Crawford, "Alternative Shelter: Counterculture Architecture in Northern California," in *Reading California: Art, Image, and Identity*, Stephanie Barron, Sheri Bernstein, Ilene Susan Fort, eds (Berkeley: University of California Press, 2000); Caroline Maniaque-Benton, *French Encounters with the American Counterculture, 1960–1980* (London: Ashgate, 2011); Felicity D. Scott, *Architecture or Techno-utopia: Politics after Modernism* (Cambridge, Mass.: MIT Press, 2007); Martin van Schaik and Otakar Máãel, eds, *Exit Utopia—Architectural Provocations 1956–76* (Munich: Prestel, 2005); Simon Sadler, "An Architecture of the Whole," *Journal of Architectural Education* 61, 4 (2008); Simon Sadler, "Drop City Revisited," *Journal of Architectural Education* 58, 1 (2006); Simon Sadler, *The Situationist City* (Cambridge, Mass.: MIT Press, 1998); Jean-Louis Violeau, *Les Architectes et Mai 68* (Paris: Éditions Recherches, 2005).

15  See Anthony W. Schuman, "Community Engagement: Architecture's Evolving Social Vocation," in *Architecture School: Three Centuries of Educating Architects in North America*, Joan Ockman, ed. (Cambridge, MA: ACSA / MIT Press, 2012); Richard W. Hayes, *The Yale Building Project: The First Forty Years* (New Haven, Yale, 2007).

16  See the key account on education in America by Mary McLeod, "The End of Innocence: From Political Activism to Postmodernism," and sections of Joan Ockman and Avigail Sachs, "Modernism Takes Command," in *Architecture School*, ed. Ockman, Joan.

17  The Architects Resistance, "Architecture and Racism," n.d. (1969), quoted in Schuman, "Community Engagement," 255.

18  Manifesto of the group *Environnement Mai 68*, in Martin Pawley and Bernard Tschumi, "The Beaux-Arts since 1968," *Architectural Design* 41 (September 1971): 533–566, 553.

19  See George Baird, "1968 and its aftermath: the loss of moral confidence in architectural practice and education," in *Reflections on Architectural Practices in the Nineties*, William S. Sanders, ed. (New York: Princeton Architectural Press, 1996), 64.

20  See Pawley and Tschumi, "The Beaux-Arts since 1968," 562.

21  Pawley and Tschumi, "The Beaux-Arts since 1968," 554–555, 566.

22  Ibid., 559.

23  On the persistence of this class problem in community architecture, see Schuman, "Community Engagement."

24  Pawley and Tschumi, "The Beaux-Arts since 1968," 565.

25  See Jacques Lucan, *France, Architecture 1965–1988* (Paris: Electa, 1989). My thanks to Caroline Maniaque for drawing my attention to the PAN.

26  An expression I borrow from Kazys Varnelis.

27  Bernard Tschumi, *Architecture and Disjunction* (Cambridge, Mass: MIT Press, 1996), 15.

28  See Schuman, "Community Engagement."

29  Pawley and Tschumi, "The Beaux-Arts since 1968," 561.

30  McLeod, "The End of Innocence," 163.

31  Pawley and Tschumi, "The Beaux-Arts since 1968," 566.

32  Pawley and Tschumi, "The Beaux-Arts since 1968," 561.

33  Pawley and Tschumi, "The Beaux-Arts since 1968," 566. See also Craig Buckley and Jean-Louis Violeau, eds, *Utopie: Texts and Projects, 1967–1978* (Cambridge, Mass: MIT Press, 2011).

34  Tschumi, *Architecture and Disjunction*, 19.

35 Tschumi, *Architecture and Disjunction*, 7.

36 See Bernard Tschumi, "The Environmental Trigger," in *A Continuing Experiment: Learning and Teaching at the Architectural Association*, James Gowan, ed. (London: Architectural Press, 1975).

37 Pawley and Tschumi, "The Beaux-Arts since 1968," 566.

38 Certainly, there are counterculture figures of interest to architectural historians—Steve Baer, say, or Lloyd Kahn or Constant—but Baer, Kahn, and Constant had no formal training in architecture, and their concentration on design removed them somewhat from the larger political projects with which they were associated. For counterculture, architecture was a key *medium*—a means of knowledge and a means of action (as the situationists once put it), but categorically not an end.

39 Pawley and Tschumi, "The Beaux-Arts since 1968," 564–565.

40 Pawley and Tschumi, "The Beaux-Arts since 1968," 549.

41 On heterotopia see Michel Foucault, "Des Espace Autres," in *Architecture/Mouvement/Continuité*, October, 1984, based on a lecture of March, 1967.

42 See Rem Koolhaas, *S,M,L,XL* (New York: Monacelli, 1995). At a conference on New Babylon in Delft in 2000, Constant himself, apparently unfamiliar with the "Voluntary Prisoners" project being revisited by Zenghelis, looked at it with an expression at once of recognition and dismay.

43 See Ellen Dunham-Jones, "The Generation of '68–Today: Bernard Tschumi, Rem Koolhaas and the Institutionalization of Critique," *Proceedings of the 86th ACSA Annual Meeting and Technology Conference*, 1998, 527–533.

44 William James, Lecture XX, *The Varieties of Religious Experience: A Study in Human Nature* (1902; Hazleton: Pennsylvania State University, Electronic Classics Series), 469.

45 Rem Koolhaas, "What Ever Happened to Urbanism?" (1994), in *S,M,L,XL*, 959–971.

# Chapter 7

# Context: 1943–1975

After World War II, Italy, like other European nations, hoped to navigate the line between USSR-modeled government control of the economy and US-modeled *laissez-faire* economics. But its economic, political, and cultural evolution was shaped by its particular circumstances, not the least of which was being on the losing side of the war. Under the Fascist regime, Italy had joined Germany against the Western Allies, but defeats in Greece and North Africa along with the Allied invasion of Sicily toppled the regime in July 1943. By the end of the war, Italy was fractured and impoverished. The new constitution of 1947 after Italy became a republic instituted extensive parliamentary control of the government and guaranteed against the centralization of power represented by Mussolini. This spread of power has since been the cause of frequent crises and changes; sixty-three governments have ruled in Italy since 1943.

Under the Paris Peace Treaty of February 1947, Italy was required to pay reparations to the USSR, Yugoslavia, Greece, Ethiopia, and Albania. With its economy in disarray, Italy accepted $1.5 million of aid offered by the Marshall Plan to fuel its economy and stimulate industry in the north. By 1950, Italy's economy had recovered to its pre-war status and subsequently experienced unprecedented development through the 1960s, transforming from an agrarian to an industrial society. Demand for Italian metal and manufactured products by the US during the Korean War softened the impact of the end of US aid, as did increased private US investment in Italy, the largest in Western Europe. By joining the IMF in 1947 and the OEEC in 1948, Italy internationalized its economy and ended seventy-five years of protectionism. The creation of the European Common Market in 1957—with Italy as a founding member—provided more investment and eased exports. Other factors contributing to Italy's growth include a large, cheap labor force, and a unique combination of "industrial clusters" consisting of small-to-medium-sized enterprises, and large, industry-dominating monopolies such as Fiat, Pirelli, and Olivetti.

The latter is a particular example of Italy's interest in combining Socialism with Taylorism, and both models with an uniquely Italian aesthetic aspiration. Adriano Olivetti, having travelled to the US and been impressed by the Remington Corporation, combined his management skills with his commitment to the utopian Community Movement. This movement identified the benevolent company, which supported and housed its workers, as the essential locus of government. He was equally committed to aesthetics, not only hiring architects to design Olivetti typewriters (which became a significant part of its industry domination) but also his factory and the town it occupied—Ivrea. His example and his influence continued to shape Italian design, even the radical utopian visions of Archizoom and Superstudio, as Pier Vittorio Aureli discusses here.

Behind these radical designs is a strain of intellectualism also particular to Italy. More than in any other western nation, the relationship in Italy between Marxist theorists and Left politicians has been consistently strong, Antonio Gramsci, Mario Tronti, and Antonio Negri being prime examples of this alliance. The intellectual Left's dominant desire was to steer the Communist Party— singularly strong after World War II given its role in the resistance and lack of competition from any other pre-Fascist parties—away from the liberalism that accompanied economic expansion and toward a more radical, pro-worker agenda. Growing wage pressure in the mid 1960s and the eventual stalled growth leading to the massive strikes of the "Hot Autumn" of 1969, gave the Left its opportunity to pounce. As documented by Aureli, the architectural community saw itself as integral to this political work.

Peggy Deamer

Chapter 7

# Manfredo Tafuri, Archizoom, Superstudio, and the critique of architectural ideology

Pier Vittorio Aureli

In 1962, the poet and literary critic Franco Fortini published in the journal Il Menabò an essay titled "Astuti come Colombe" (Shrewd as Doves).[1] The title inverts Jesus's famous exhortation to his disciples "to be shrewd as snakes and innocent as doves." With this statement, Fortini presented a critical program for intellectual work vis-à-vis capitalist development. The article critically responded to a previous issue of the journal entirely devoted to the theme of culture in relationship to industrial work. In this issue there were essays written, among others, by Italo Calvino and Umberto Eco. For these "progressive" intellectuals, the factory became in the 1960s the new cultural epicenter of literary and artistic experimental practices. This new sensibility that mixed socialist reformism and artistic experimentation gave impetus to the avant-garde revival in Italy of which Eco's Gruppo 63 became the most important manifestation. Avant-garde techniques such as collage, estrangement, and technological experimentation became the devices through which the members of Gruppo 63 attempted to sublimate the effects of industrialization on social relationships. Fortini directed his critique at this ideological use of cultural experimentation in order to mediate (and mystify) the effects of production both on society and, especially, on intellectual work. The two poles that defined Fortini's critique comprised, on the one hand, an analysis of the political economy of intellectual work and, on the other, an analysis of its aesthetic manifestation. Political economy was used by Fortini as a tool to describe the way capitalist affirmation within society manifested itself through its systematic cultural self-deception. This self-deception was, according to Fortini, achieved often by capitalism's instrumentalization of progressive, utopian and socially committed culture. The use of aesthetics was a way to trust artworks not only as authors' products but also as artifacts that revealed in their concreteness the sensual features of capitalist integration. Drawing on political economy and aesthetics, Fortini constructed a critique that was neither aimed at a rational reform of capitalist development, nor at a romantic resistance against the effects to such development. The main objective of Fortini's critique was to demonstrate how capitalist development was the source of a number of ideological manifestations that were meant to satisfy the good conscience of progressive intellectuals.

According to Fortini, the idea itself of progressiveness, of scientific truth, of social emancipation through the "just" use of technology was responsible for hiding how capital was far more deeply embedded into the cultural management of everyday life than was assumed. Thus, for Fortini it was precisely "progressive thinking" that was the worst enemy of a true political emancipation from capital. Facing the extreme level of cultural mystification implied in the cultural industry in which modernization was reformism and reformism was the new progressive face of capitalist domination, Fortini's approach to being critical involved becoming "shrewd as doves and innocent as snakes." Moreover, for Fortini it was precisely a critical analysis of the seemingly most genuine attempts of social reform advanced by leftist movements and institutions that often revealed the true features of capitalist domination. Fortini's critique, as it was advanced in his essay and later in his book of which "Astuti come Colombe" was the center-piece, can be seen as the harbinger of a new approach to cultural theory that would be practiced by a new generation of intellectuals, artists, writers and architects. Such an approach no longer sided with the official institutions of the left, but on the contrary, often criticized them. Above all, Fortini's "Astuti come Colombe" invoked not a critique of capitalism per se but rather of the way the most advanced forms of capitalistic alienation were embedded within the programs of social amelioration promoted by the welfare state.

\* \* \*

In opposition to previous accounts of Italian architecture in which the work of Manfredo Tafuri, Archizoom and Superstudio has been placed in two different folders—Tafuri within the critical approach of the so-called "Venice School," Archizoom and Superstudio within the movement of the so-called "Radical Architecture"[2]—their extremely different positions share not only a common critique of capitalism as it was embodied by the city and its architecture but also a critique of the reformist and utopian aspirations of "progressive" culture, identified both with late modern architecture and with the neo-avant-gardes of the 1960s. In spite of Tafuri's famous dismissal of their work, both Archizoom and Superstudio were clearly influenced by Tafuri's attempts to construct a critical genealogy of modern architecture and its involvement in capitalist development. As admitted by Andrea Branzi, Archizoom's "No-stop City" (1969–1971), the seminal project for total urbanization of the entire world, was conceived among other things as the attempt to translate into design terms Tafuri's critique of architectural ideology as it was formulated in his famous essay "Per una critica dell'ideolgia architettonica" (For a critique of architectural ideology), published in the Marxist journal *Contropiano* in 1969.[3] What triggered this interest was the fact that both Archizoom and Tafuri were influenced by the theories of Operaismo, a radical Marxist group of communist militants gathered around the theories of Mario Tronti.

Interpreting the work of Tafuri, Archizoom and Superstudio reacted to a very specific kind of capitalist development—the welfare state. Between the 1950s and the 1960s, Italy went through an intense process of modernization that changed the political, social, and cultural geography of the country. What was happening in the US in the 1930s occurred in the northern part of Italy in the 1960s: namely the beginning of a Fordist-Taylorist organization of work and industrial production. This meant the shift from a backyard capitalism based primarily on accumulation to a capitalism based on the politics of "wage labor," technological innovation, and the *reorganization* of the entire spectrum of social relationships. For this reason, many intellectuals in the early 1960s started to understand capitalism not simply as an unjust process of circulation and distribution, but as Mario Tronti has called it, as the hegemonic work of "The Plan of Capital" (a term explicitly appropriated by Tafuri in *Architecture and Utopia*).[4] The most important political effect of this new cycle was the establishment of the first center-left government in Italy in 1963, in which the Italian Socialist Party (PSI) took an active part. The involvement of the left in the government of a country that was part of the Atlantic Pact was seen by many intellectuals and political activists of the left as the sign of capitalism's development as it incorporated the very forces that had opposed it.

In the second half of the 1950s, following the USSR's 1956 invasion of Hungary and the process of de-Stalinization, the Italian Socialist Party started to gradually withdraw from its historical alliance with the Communist Party and simultaneously intensified its political relationship with the Christian Democrats. At the basis of this political shift was the socialists' belief in the possibility to reform capitalism toward a rational and socially sustainable form of economy. According to the Italian Socialists, rationally *planned* capitalist production could have been used as a means for social justice if reformed at the level of workers' welfare. The concept of *economic planning* was, for the socialists, the rational and fair management of industrial production through the vast and comprehensive organization of a welfare program. For this reason the socialists started to abandon the notion of class conflict in favor of the idea of *reform* (in the form of a scientific management of productive forces) of the production system. As reformism was adopted by progressive politics and by the state, it simultaneously attracted many progressive and liberal intellectuals. To modernize not only became a political and intellectual imperative, it also became a diffused cultural mentality. Within the wave of the euphorically rationalist ethos provoked by reformism, strong interest gathered around issues of new regional planning (the legacy of social-democratic urbanism) and the role of design in all aspects of everyday life. The cultural prototype of the new wave of socialist reformism was the affirmation of Adriano Olivetti's "Comunità," an attempt to transform a factory into a cultural campus that elevated production as the possibility of a socially sustainable and culturally articulated community. Olivetti involved not only managers, but also artists, designers, and writers in the work at his plant.[5] The intent of Olivetti was to demonstrate, on the one hand, the intrinsically rational nature of production and, on the other, the possibility of a new social humanism based on industrial development.

The new wave of class conflict that took place in Italy in the 1960s started precisely from the criticism of the reformist ideology that accepted and even idealized production as a scientific and therefore reformable configuration of development. The principal opposition came from a group of leftist militants affiliated with the journal *Quaderni Rossi*, who became known as "the Operaists." One of the main theses of this group, as it was first formulated by one of its leaders, the socialist activist and translator of Marx, Raniero Panzieri, was that workers should not only demand the social reform of the modes of production but also claim political power over them. In an essay fundamental to the beginning of Italian autonomous Marxism, Panzieri called for "workers' control" (*controllo operaio*)[6] to combat the very essence of production. The critique of capitalism was to be directed not only at means of circulation and consumption but also, and most of all, at methods of production itself, at what Panzieri called the "machines," the techno-social apparatus required to extrapolate surplus value from the whole of social relationships.[7] On the one hand, this critique was based on a direct reading of Marx, especially the Marx of the fourth section of the first book of *Capital* where the founder of modern communism describes several passages in the history of industrial production, and of the *Grundrisse*; and on the other, it was based on a renewed use of the critique of ideology, which was aimed against all those institutions preserving the reality of production as an essential form of capitalist sovereignty—the state, the unions, and culture per se.[8] It was precisely the critique of "culture," and especially of progressive leftist culture that became the target of the Operaists critique of ideology, a critique that also attempted to rethink the function of intellectuals within the framework of class struggle.

\* \* \*

Through his intense activity of historicizing the development of architectural modernity from the Renaissance to 1970s neo-avant-garde, Manfredo Tafuri was the first intellectual in the field of architectural history and criticism to advance a critique of architectural ideology. Tafuri's critique was addressed not so much at architecture's complacency with capital, but rather at the reformist impetus of modern architecture since the eighteenth century. As much as the Operaists' critique of ideology was aimed at demystifying the cunning of ideology embedded in the reformist agenda of the progressive left, Tafuri's critique was aimed at demystifying the progressive aspirations of modern architecture, especially the practices of the more socially engaged architects. As Tafuri himself remarked in one of his last interviews:

> For us the critique of ideology was a critique of the left. My own program was to develop a critique of the ideological thought that has pervaded architectural history, art history, and history in general. . . One should always address the critique of ideology towards his or her own ideology, not the ideology of his or her enemy. What needs to be de-ideologicized is precisely the cultural context within which one fights.[9]

Between 1964 and 1965, Tafuri, having gone through a severe process of self-critique as a politically committed architect, abandoned the profession in order to fully concentrate on historical research. A few years before, Tafuri, together with Luigi Piccinato and Vieri Quilici, formed a design and research collective called AUA (Architetti Urbanisti Associati). The goal of AUA was to integrate as one an approach to architectural design, urban planning, and urban research. Apart from participating in important national competitions such as the one for the new Centro Direzionale (business district) in Turin in 1962, the AUA undertook extensive research on new urban formations and proposed a plan for a linear city in the vicinity of Rome.

It is clear that at this time Tafuri was still convinced of the possibility of reforming the urban reality by means of architecture and planning. But it was while writing a monograph of the Roman architect and urban planner Ludovico Quaroni that Tafuri became increasingly skeptical about practicing.[10] More than a monographic survey on Quaroni, the book was a deep analysis of the post-war Italian architectural culture of which Quaroni was one of the most intellectually tormented protagonists. While Quaroni had tried exceptionally hard to develop projects and plans with a reformist agenda, he concluded that these attempts did not simply fail, they revealed a deeper problem in the very social and political administration of the city. (For example, the Italian government, led by the Christian Democrats, boycotted any attempt to draft a comprehensive law on urbanism in order to favor market speculation.) While writing this book, Tafuri came to the conclusion that the only way to overcome the impasse of the reformist agenda was to unearth the impasse of the discipline itself vis-à-vis the development of the city. It became urgent for Tafuri to see historical research as a *critical project* that questioned architecture especially in regard to its relationship with urban form.

Even if Tafuri would explicitly adopt a Marxian perspective on architecture and urban development only in the late 1960s, already at this time he identified the problem of modern architecture with its impossibility to *contain* and *direct* the development of the modern city, and this issue became the starting point for Tafuri's first important book—*Teorie e storia dell'architettura* (Theories and History of Architecture)—in which he put forward a fundamental critique of how modern architectural historiography consistently mystifies the contradictions of architecture by rendering its history as progressive narrative.[11] He demonstrated how such historical perspective systematically masked the very cause of such progress and obscured the cultural crisis provoked by the development of modern culture.

Tafuri first applied this critique of ideology to those traditions within historiography that have deliberately attempted to make modern and contemporary architects confident about the reformist origins of their historical mandate. Tafuri referred especially to what he defined as "Operative History," a kind of history written with the specific and ideological goal to legitimize the tradition of modern architecture.[12] Among the protagonists of operative history, Tafuri placed almost all the major historians of modern architecture, Nikolaus Pevsner, Sigfried Giedion, and Bruno Zevi most notably. The object of Tafuri's critique was not so much (or not only) the historical deformations of these historians, but rather the ideology of reformism implicit in operative history and its pretension to solve the contradictions left open by the past toward a coherent agenda for the future. By editing out these contradictions, operative history had helped to render as almost *natural* the political forces shaping historical processes. Although initially Tafuri's critique of operative history was not a class critique, it was the radical anti-reformism emerging from *Theories and History* that led Operaists intellectuals such as Alberto Asor Rosa and Massimo Cacciari to invite Tafuri to contribute to their journal *Contropiano*.

Tafuri's contribution to *Contropiano* consisted of four essays: "Per una critica dell'ideologia architettonica" (For a critique of architectural ideology) (1969); "Lavoro intellettuale e sviluppo capitalistico" (Intellectual work and capitalist development) (1970–1972); "Social Democrazia e città nella Repubblica di Weimar" (Social democracy and the city during the Weimar Republic) (1971–1972); "Austromarxismo e città: Das Rote Wien" (Austro-Marxism and the city: the Red Vienna) (1971–1972).[13] All four articles can be read as the first attempt to apply the Marxist critique of ideology practiced by the Operaists to the historiography of modern architecture. A year before, the young historian Francesco dal Co had published an essay on the same topic but focused on the architecture of the Modern Movement. With Tafuri, the critique of ideology was extended back in order to address the development of architecture since the eighteenth century. Tafuri's first contribution to *Contropiano*, "For a critique of architectural ideology," can be seen as the blueprint of a research program that the Roman historian would share with a group of young researchers and professors at the school of architecture in Venice where he was invited to teach in 1968. In this essay, Tafuri analyzed the way formal and spatial invention in architecture has often played an ideological role within capitalist development. Tafuri conducted his historical analysis by selecting exemplary case studies, from Marc-Antoine Laugier's theories to Le Corbusier's Plan Obus for Algiers. These cases were analyzed by Tafuri as chapters of a genealogy leading up to twentieth-century avant-garde culture. The novelty of Tafuri's analysis lay in the way in which he understood the parallels between avant-garde practices and the crisis provoked by capitalist development. For Tafuri, the iconoclastic attitude of the early avant-gardes was the product of the most advanced forms of bourgeois culture. If capitalist development destroyed the values of the pre-industrial era, the most advanced forms of bourgeois culture accepted and sublimated this process in order to control it.

In the same issue of *Contropiano* in which Tafuri published his essay, the young philosopher and Operaist militant Massimo Cacciari published a long essay titled "Per una genesi del pensiero negativo" (For a genesis of negative thought).[14] According to Cacciari, thinkers such as Friedrich Nietzsche and Max Weber showed how bourgeois mentality had already accepted the unresolvable value crisis brought on by the development of modernity (and capitalism), and made of such acceptance not a passive position but an effective *will to power* over capitalist development itself. For the editors of *Contropiano*, a reinvention of such a form of power—the negative thought—was necessary for working-class political culture and implied an extreme critique of the leftist progressive "reform" of capitalism that merely provided the capitalists with an effective weapon to dominate the working class.[15] It is precisely within this context that Tafuri constructed his critique of architectural ideology. If Fortini showed Tafuri how to resist the temptation of reformism, the editorial project of *Contropiano* provided him with the terms in which anti-reformism could be translated back into working-class critique. According to Tafuri, modern architecture and especially its avant-garde moments could have been described as ideological prefigurations of the upcoming effects of capitalist development. In so doing, modernist architectural culture had a precise role in *naturalizing* these effects and making them socially and culturally acceptable.[16]

For Tafuri, only two projects had understood in non-ideological terms the way capital directed urban development: Ludwig Hilberseimer's studies on the Metropolis, and Le Corbusier's Plan Obus. In particular, Hilberseimer's approach to the city was for Tafuri the most lucid analysis of how capitalist development affected the planning of the city. In the 1920s Hilberseimer declared that the project of the city had to consist in organically linking the total circulatory system and the single inhabitable cell. Hilberseimer eliminated the building itself as the cornerstone of city planning. For him, the city was no longer a composition of buildings, but a *process of production*, in tune with the economic cycle. As Tafuri wrote:

> Once the true unity of the production cycle has been identified in the city, the only task the architect can have is to organize the cycle. Taking this proposition to its extreme conclusion, Hilberseimer insists on the role of elaborating "organizational models" as the only one that can fully reflect the need for Taylorizing building production, as the new task of the technician, who is now completely integrated into this process. . . For Hilberseimer, the object was not in crisis because it had already disappeared from his spectrum of considerations.[17]

In the second half of the 1960s, Hilberseimer became a cult figure among a new generation of architects, as he was also being rediscovered by Giorgio Grassi, an architect close to Aldo Rossi, who in 1967 edited and introduced the Italian translation of Hilberseimer's late book *Entfaltung einer Planungsidee*.[18] Compared to the picturesque urban utopias of the 1960s, Hilberseimer's *Groszstadt* appeared as a project that fully accepted capitalist control over urban reality while demystifying its pretended representations through the radically didactic, "inhuman" simplicity of its architectonic form. Hilberseimer was attractive for the consistency and rigor of his writing, a style far distant from the more propaganda-like pronouncements of such better-known Modern Movement architects as Le Corbusier. Like young Italian architects of the 1960s, Hilberseimer was a prolific writer and a reluctant builder; like them, he produced a highly sophisticated theory of the city paired with an absolute simplicity of the project.

But if for Rossi and Grassi the obstinate simplicity of Hilberseimer's architecture constituted the reference for a public and civic architecture of the city, for Archizoom and Superstudio, on the contrary, the same formal simplicity inspired a form of city that had no value to represent other than its own use-value as a system to be appropriated by the emerging urban proletariat. Hilberseimer's *Groszstadt* was understood by Archizoom and Superstudio as the representation of a city without architecture. The representational techniques of Branzi and Archizoom clearly appear to have been inherited from Hilberseimer's black and white perspectives of the *Groszstadt* and the repetitive patterns in his projects for the American suburbs. Both Archizoom's and Hilberseimer's cold urban representations paradoxically combine the maximum effort to eliminate any architecturally expressive gesture with an image made only by architectural signs like columns, walls, elevators, and furniture.

\* \* \*

The members of Archizoom and Superstudio met at the school of architecture in Florence in the early 1960s.[19] The formation of these two groups was an act of both emulation and sarcastic parody of the British collective Archigram. Their first joint exhibition in Pistoia in 1966, emblematically titled "Superarchitettura," was an attempt to link architecture, industrial design, and pop-art within a political vision. The exhibition consisted of a series of design objects emphatically addressing pop imagery. For Archizoom and Superstudio, influenced by the Operaist analysis of capitalistic development, Pop Art imagery was assumed to be a "realist approach" to a society no longer driven by the austere ethos of the postwar period.

A fundamental consequence of the advent of the welfare state was the phenomenon of mass-consumerism. While pre-welfare state capitalism was focused on production and profit, welfare state capitalism organically linked production to workers' consumption; increased consumption was understood to increase productivity. In the 1960s, the workers' capacity to consume went beyond the necessity for reproduction and included all the social and cultural spheres from recreation to education. Yet the logic of the welfare state—to keep at balance production and consumption—operated within the overall goal of making workers *work*. In the welfare state, especially in Italy, consumption was used in order to tighten the relationship between the labor force and the need to work.

But at the same time, the abrupt economic development that made Italy an industrial country in the span of a very few years produced a new subjectivity that was far from being "tempered." The Operaists called this emerging subjectivity a "rude razza pagana" (a rude pagan race). Far from the skilled industrial worker and the small artisan, the rude pagan race celebrated by the Operaists had as a key subject the unskilled worker of the assembly line, the mass-worker. The mass-worker had no personal attachment to his or her work—the only interest was the wage—and his or her slogan was *less work and more money*. In this, the resultant detachment between life and work was defined by the Operaists as the "refusal of work," not a strike but the progressive abolition of work as a necessity for living.[20] The goal of the refusal of work was to disengage the workers' income from wages determined by the capitalist to make profit. Within this theoretical framework, uncontrolled hedonism even in the brutal and alienated form of mass-consumption was interpreted by the Operaists as a potential social force that, if exacerbated, would open the gap between the workers' income and capitalist profit, and thus between workers and capital.

It is from this perspective that the premises of Archizoom's and Superstudio's seminal projects, No-stop City and the Continuous Monument, should be understood. Both projects aimed at the exaggeration *per absurdum* of the urban condition by pushing to the extreme its inclusive and totalizing logic.

\* \* \*

The origin of both Archizoom's No-stop City and Superstudio's Continuous Monument can be traced back to an early student collaboration between the members of the two groups. In 1964, for their fourth-year course in architectural design, Andrea Branzi, Cristiano Toraldo di Francia, Gilberto Corretti, Massimo Morozzi, and Ali Navai proposed a project titled "La città estrusa" (the extruded city).[21] The team proposed turning the vast area between Florence and Prato into a gigantic industrial machine and conceived of the city as the all-inclusive extrusion of its productive conditions. As annotated by Gilberto Corretti, future member of Archizoom:

> The concept of Città Estrusa is very banal: it comes from the idea of the city as transmission belt linking the whole urban agglomeration between Prato and Florence. This transmission belt contains all the industrial equipment necessary to production and administration; it can also contain housing. Città Estrusa is the very extrusion of all the urban elements that form the productive apparatus of the region.[22]

The project was clearly inspired by Tronti's seminal text, "La società e la Fabbrica," in which the Roman philosopher emphasized how production was not limited to the space of the factory but involved all aspects of social life.[23] "Città Estrusa" represented the visualization of the all-inclusive logic of welfare state capitalism at a gigantic scale, modeled following the monumental language of Louis Kahn and Villa Adriana. These odd references were a *de facto* critique of the functional sobriety of welfare state architecture and then-trendy Scandinavian architecture and interior design. This critique of the reformist aspirations of modern architecture as embodied in Scandinavian modernism with its functional and elegant design was even more exacerbated in the graduation projects of Branzi, Corretti, Toraldo, and Morozzi. In sarcastic opposition to what at that time were the preferred subjects for graduation in architecture—the "workers village," "the civic center for a small community"—Branzi, Morozzi, Corretti, and Toraldo worked on topics such as shopping malls, amusement parks or touristic resorts, themes taken from the emerging pop and consumerist culture of the 1960s. The crass vulgarity of the rude pagan race was combined with the extreme monumentality of the architectural inventions of Piranesi and Ledoux. The goal was to create a paradoxical architectural language that was no longer reducible to the "standards" and "functions" typical of modern architecture.

It was within this perspective, then, that both the members of Archizoom and Superstudio encountered the work of Aldo Rossi.[24] Rossi's early projects—such as his competition entry for a business district in Turin and his interest in the "Architecture of Reason" (as manifested in his long and enthusiastic review of Emil Kaufmann's From *Ledoux* to *Le Corbusier*)—became a fundamental point of reference for both Superstudio and Archizoom. After their early projects and exhibitions, both groups became increasingly skeptical of the formal excess of pop-imagery, and Rossi's austere forms and precise readings of the city triggered a different mode of interpretation of the urban condition. While the goal for both groups remained the search for models that would signal the total urbanization of the world, the language of these models was no longer imagined through the colorful images of Archigram, but rather through the austere and indifferent rational language of Rossi and the most extreme protagonists of rational architecture, from Durand to Hilberseimer.

Superstudio's Continuous Monument was initially proposed as an entry for the international competition "Architecture and Freedom" launched by *Trigon 69*, an international exhibition of architecture organized in Graz in 1969.[25] In opposition to the pop and formal complexity of their early work, the Continuous Monument was designed as the least complex form imaginable: a viaduct that would gradually absorb within its section the entire urbanization of the world. In early collages representing the project, the Continuous Monument passes through different contexts such as the city of Graz or the American desert without making reference to any local condition. While in the initial drawings the Continuous Monument was designed literally as a viaduct, in later images it took the form of different simple architectural compositions that would eventually frame different urban scenarios.

The architecture of the Continuous Monument was determined by one single logic—the grid—and it was conceived as the most abstract and ultimate architectural form possible. Both the literality of Minimal Art and the severity of Le Corbusier's Plan Obus became important references for the project.[26] Already in his Contropiano essay, Tafuri had addressed the Plan Obus as the most lucid architectural anticipation of welfare state logic in which the city was reduced to one economic and spatial system, that of a linear infrastructural support. Following this observation, Superstudio imagined the city no longer as a composition of objects and spaces, but as one single linear object that would leave the rest of the earth completely free from urbanization. The Continuous Monument was thus a strategy that simultaneously proposed a complete urbanization of the world while it tried to preserve the unbuilt landscape. The city as a composition of different objects is gradually replaced by a continuous architectural system made of the same material: a grid-shaped curtain wall.

The Continuous Monument is both the idealistic projection of an architecture freed from the ideology of the metropolis with its multitude of images and different styles and a sarcastic comment on the emerging post-industrial architecture made of anonymous and abstract curtain-wall buildings. In the same way that Carl Andre's, Donald Judd's, and Robert Smithson's industrially fabricated artworks (admired by the members of Superstudio)[27] echoed the increasingly generic architecture of urban sprawl, the generic formal character of Superstudio's Continuous Monument mirrored the run of corporate office buildings. For Superstudio, the cold and minimal architecture of new office spaces was both the ultimate result of modernism and the beginning of a new hyper-rationalist architecture not so dissimilar from the neo-rationalist language introduced by Rossi and Grassi in the mid-1960s.

In order to push to its logical conclusion the idea of the Continuous Monument, Superstudio decided to develop a series of furniture objects the group called "Istogrammi di Architettura" (Histograms of Architecture).[28] The histograms were bare volumetric compositions with neither scale nor program. Presented in the form of a universal grammar for architecture based on the extrusion of the grid, the histograms aimed at eliminating any further production of industrially manufactured objects. Praised by an enthusiastic young Rem Koolhaas, who in a letter to Natalini referred to the Histograms as "easy architecture," they were conceived as the ultimate destruction of design and thus of any further spatial and formal invention by means of architecture. For this reason the histograms of architecture were alternatively called by Superstudio "tombstones of architecture." As Toraldo admitted, with the histograms, Superstudio proposed a deliberate suicide of architecture in the face of its complete absorption by capital.[29] After such a suicide, for Superstudio the only thing left was "life" itself, life completely liberated from the need of objects.

During the 1970s, Superstudio developed projects in which architecture was replaced first by "fundamental acts"—ceremonies and rituals that were supposed to re-enact an authentic understanding of the relationship between man and his environment—and later by extensive research on extra-urban and peasant culture. With these projects, the activities of the group ended.

This conclusion of their work announces the crucial difference with Archizoom's projects. If Superstudio searched for the ultimate freedom from urbanization, Archizoom proposed the opposite strategy. In their model for total urbanization, they literally imagined the whole inhabitable surface of the globe being gradually covered by an extensive urban system that would spread urban facilities everywhere in the form of continuous indoor space. If, with the Continuous Monument, Superstudio proposed an architecture without the city, with No-stop City, Archizoom proposed a model for a city without architecture.

An early scheme for the project explains No-stop City as a proposal for a "non-figurative architecture" made of urban equipment such as columns, elevators, bathrooms, etc.[30] No-stop City was conceived by Archizoom as the spatial condition that would clearly reveal what Marx in the *Grundrisse* defined as the core of industrial capital: "*labour sans phrase.*"[31] According to Marx, a generic, non-specified labor force is the ultimate result of the organization of industrial labor in which what is exploited is not a particular laboring skill, but the mere human capability to work, to be mentally and physically productive.[32] Following such an understanding of labor, every architectural aspect of the No-stop City was stripped away in order to render the ultimate essence of the metropolis: a gigantic and expanded factory. Archizoom's particular polemical target was Archigram's technophilia and their attempt to translate technological development into a specific and highly figurative architectural language. Imagined as the overlapping of the three fundamental spatial archetypes of the industrial city— the factory, the parking lot and the supermarket—No-stop City expanded the logic of the factory to the entire urban condition, and thus the application of Tronti's thesis that the working-class revolution was possible only where capitalistic development was more advanced. Urbanization's extreme intensification would trigger workers to progressively detach themselves from the logic of wage, dependent as it is on the balance between production and consumption. In the intentions of Archizoom, the exaggerated scenario depicted in No-stop City aimed to bring within capitalistic development "a state of permanent confusion, and therefore a collapse of the entire system."[33] As Branzi has recently admitted, the two fundamental references for the project were precisely the two "city plans" that Tafuri addressed as the most paradigmatic examples of capitalistic urban development: Piranesi's Campo Marzio and Hilberseimer's studies on the architecture of the *Groszstadt.*[34] For Tafuri, Piranesi's Campo Marzio (1762) was the anticipation of an urban form no longer reducible to an overall principle and prefigured the urban condition in which capital would gradually disconnect the organic link between the city and its architecture. Piranesi had effectively demonstrated not only that architecture could not recompose the city into a unitary system, but also that architecture itself as an object could not be designed according to timeless principles. After Campo Marzio, it was clear that architecture as an artifact could only play an ideological role as "representation" of the city.

Following Tafuri's observations, Archizoom developed No-stop City as a city without architecture, merely deploying super-large *apparati* such as the climatic control of large indoor spaces and the even distribution of facilities and urban equipment, and containing super-small elements such as the inhabitable closet that contained all the necessary domestic equipment for living. The occasion for a concrete application of the principles of No-stop City was the competition for the new University of Florence launched in 1970. The program of the competition asked for the design of a vast university campus in the area between Florence and Prato, the same site of the "Città Estrusa." The brief presented the theme of the university as a vast and articulated nexus for the different residential and productive centers that already existed in the area. The competition program was thus suggesting a scenario that confirmed the fundamental hypothesis of No-stop City: the evolution of the city towards a much more integrated condition in which not only material production but also housing and education form a unified system devoid of any boundary. The project proposed by Archizoom consisted of a grid measuring 125 meters by 125 meters that organized the entire flat territory available. The grid would be increasingly filled with programs contained within generic buildings.[35] Designed as generic boxes with no external openings, these buildings were imagined by Archizoom as vast containers that would accommodate any sort of program or activity. The intention of the project was to propose a scheme that would be as anonymous as possible, made of the most generic and simple solutions. In the face of capital's ultimate integration with the city there was no more room for formal invention or stylistic diversity. For Archizoom the competition encouraged a useless parade of "different" interpretations of the brief in which the only job left to the architect was to decorate something he or she could not even understand in its entire spatial and political logic. For this reason, Archizoom decided to break the rule of anonymity for the competition and signed their entry, ironically calling their proposal "I progetti si firmano" (projects must be signed). If anonymity in competitions pushes the participants to radicalize their personal style in order to be more easily recognizable, Archizoom signed their entry in order to be as anonymous as possible.

* * *

Archizoom and Superstudio came to an end in the second half of the 1970s. Ironically their work ended when it started to achieve international recognition and become the model of young practices that would emerge in the following twenty years. However, the reason their work exhausted its energy was above all dependent on the changing cultural and political climate in Italy. The critical and historiographic work of Tafuri and the proposals by Archizoom and Superstudio must be seen in the cultural, political, and temporal context in which they practiced. Their work was not simply a critique of modern architecture but a more general critique of architecture's (and the architect's) political mandate in a capitalist society. Already in the 1970s, the state began to violently retake control. The bombing of Piazza Fontana on December 12, 1969, initially attributed to anarchists, started a long season of state-driven undercover operations to counter revolutionary movements. At the end of the 1970s, the intensity of struggle dramatically decreased and with it the momentum for many intellectuals to connect their work with political militancy. The critical work of Tafuri on modern architecture slowed and the proposals by Archizoom and Superstudio lost their momentum as members withdrew into more conventional (or commercial) ways of practicing architecture. What remains of the work of these groups, beyond the vintage recuperation of their images, is the radical rethinking of architecture as not merely a producer of buildings but as creative and critical activity focused on the spatial and political reality of the city. If the examples of Tafuri, Archizoom, and Superstudio are limited to their time, the challenge to rethink the role of architecture beyond the mere production of "buildings" is still open today.

## Notes

1 Franco Fortini, "Astuti come colombe," in *Verifica dei Poteri* (Turin: Einaudi, 1965), 68–88.

2 "Architettura Radicale" is a term that became popular after Germano Celant's famous essay "Radical Design" in the catalogue of the 1972 exhibition *Italy: The New Domestic Landscape* at the MoMA in New York which featured, among others, the work of Archizoom and Superstudio. See Germano Celant, "Radical Architecture," in *Italy: The New Domestic Landscape: Achievements and Problems of Italian Design*, ed. Emilio Ambasz (New York: The Museum of Modern Art, 1972), 380–387. See also Paola Navone and Bruno Orlandoni, *Architettura "Radicale"* (Milan: Documenti di Casabella, 1974).

3 Andrea Branzi, in discussion with the author, August 17, 2011. See Manfredo Tafuri, "Per una Critica dell'ideologia architettonica," *Contropiano* 1 (1969): 31–79; translated as "Toward a Critique of Architectural Ideology," in *Architecture Theory since 1968*, ed. K. Michael Hays (Cambridge, MA: MIT Press, 1998), 6–35.

4 "Il piano del capitale" was the title of a fundamental essay by Mario Tronti published in 1962 in the journal *Quaderni Rossi*. In this essay, the Roman philosopher who would have a strong influence on Tafuri's political analysis of architectural and urban history attempted to analyze capitalist domination as a vast, integral, almost bio-political project that extended political sovereignty to all aspects of human labor. See Mario Tronti, "Il piano del capitale," *Quaderni Rossi* 3 (1962): 45–71.

5 The Olivetti plant was located at Ivrea, Piedmont, where Olivetti promoted a campus in which the main facilities were designed by Italian modernist architects. The project was pursued as an attempt to reform industrial life toward a communitarian spirit, and for this reason it attracted many leftist progressive intellectuals that were hired by Olivetti as "cultural" producers. For a study on the Olivetti town in Ivrea, see Patrizia Bonifazio, *Olivetti Costruisce: Architettura Moderna a Ivrea* (Milan: Skira Editore, 2006).

6 Raniero Panzieri and Lucio Libertini, "Sette tesi sul controllo operaio," in *Mondo Operaio* (February 1958); republished in *Mondo Operaio: Rassegna Mensile di Politica, Economia e Cultura, Antologia 1952–1964* (Florence: Luciano Landi, 1965), 880–903.

7  Raniero Panzieri, "Sull'uso delle macchine nel Neo-capitalismo," *Quaderni Rossi* 1 (1961): 53–72.

8  For an overview on the development of Operaismo and after, see Stephen Wright, *Storming Heaven: Class Composition in Italian Autonomist Marxism* (London: Pluto Press, 2003). For an overview on the early Operaismo, and especially on its most influential figures—Panzieri and Mario Tronti—see Pier Vittorio Aureli, *The Project of Autonomy: Politics and Architecture Within and Against Capitalism* (New York: Princeton Architectural Press, 2008).

9  Manfredo Tafuri, interview by Luisa Passerini, *La Storia come Progetto* (Los Angles: Oral History Program, University of California, Los Angeles, and the Getty Center for the History of Art and Humanities, 1993), 44.

10 See Manfredo Tafuri, *Ludovico Quaroni e lo sviluppo dell'architettura moderna in Italia* (Milan: Edizioni di Comunità, 1964).

11 Manfredo Tafuri, *Teorie e storia dell'architettura* (Bari: Laterza, 1968).

12 Ibid., 161–194.

13 Manfredo Tafuri, "Lavoro Intellettuale e Sviluppo Capitalistico," *Contropiano* 2, 70 (1970): 241–281; Tafuri, "Social Democrazia e città nella Repubblica di Weimar," *Contropiano* 1, 71 (1971): 257–311; Tafuri, "Austromarxismo e città. Das Rote Wien," *Contropiano* 2, 21 (1971): 257–312.

14 Massimo Cacciari, "Sulla genesi del pensiero negativo," *Contropiano* 1 (1969): 131–201.

15 This negative tradition is in many ways related to the middle passage through nihilism prophesied by Nietzsche en route to a transvaluation of values. But it is also notably negative, and requires its own eventual negation.

16 It is never clear if these "avant-garde" movements are simply appropriated or in fact presage another maneuver by capital on its path of further appropriation and sub-jugation. In terms of technological avant-gardes, it is always a case of the latter. In terms of forms of subjectivization it is not so clear.

17 Manfredo Tafuri, "Towards a Critique of Architectural Ideology," in *Architectural Theory since 1968*, ed. K. Michael Hays, trans. Stephen Sartarelli (Cambridge, MA: MIT Press, 1998), 22.

18 Ludwig Hilberseimer, *Entfaltung einer Planungsidee* (Berlin: Bauwelt Fundamente, 1963); Ludwig Hilberseimer, *Una idea di piano*, introduction and trans. Giorgio Grassi (Padua: Marsilio, 1967). Note that the book was published in the series "Polis" directed by Rossi for the Marsilio publishing house. Hilberseimer is also the most cited architect in Grassi's most important book, *La costruzione logica dell'architettura*, also published by Marsilio in 1967.

19 For an accurate historical account of the beginnings of both Archizoom and Superstudio see Roberto Gargiani, *Dall'onda pop alla superficie neutra. Archizoom Associati 1966–1974* (Milan: Electa, 2008); Roberto Gargiani and Beatrice Lampariello, *Superstudio* (Bari: Laterza, 2010).

20 See the seminal essay by Mario Tronti, "La strategia del rifiuto," in *Operai e Capitale* (Turin: Einaudi, 1966), 364–389.

21 Navone and Orlandoni, *Architettura "Radicale,"* 109.

22 As quoted in Roberto Gargiani, *Archizoom Associati 1966–1974: Dall'onda pop alla superficie neutra* (Milan: Electa, 2007), 11.

23 Mario Tronti, "La fabbrica e la società," *Quaderni Rossi* 2 (1962): 1–31; republished in *Operai e Capitale*, (Turin: Giulio Einaudi editore, 1966), 39–59.

24 Branzi, discussion. Andrea Branzi has admitted the strong influence of Aldo Rossi's theories and projects on his work.

25 Wilfred Skreiner and Horst Gerhard Haberl, *Italien, Jugoslawien, Osterreich dreilanderbiennale Trigon 69. Architektur und Freiheit* (Graz: Kunsterhaus Graz Burging, 1969); see also Superstudio, "Lettera da Graz. Una mostra sul tema: Architettura e Libertà. Trigon 69," *Domus* 481, (December 1969): 49–54.

26 As stated by Cristiano Toraldo di Francia in discussion with the author, October 24, 2010.

27 Toraldo di Francia, discussion.

28 The Histograms of architecture were developed by Superstudio in 1970 as small models, and a few months later some of these models were produced by the Abet Print company which exhibited them in the spring of 1970. Later the collection would be bought by the famous furniture design company Zanotta which mass-produced them. The name "histograms" was suggested by the physicist Edoardo Boncinelli because of their resemblance to tridimensional diagrams used for scientific purposes. See Superstudio, "Dai cataloghi del Superstudio: Istogrammi," *Domus* 497 (April 1971): 497–496. See also Roberto Gargiani and Beatrice Lampariello, *Superstudio*, 41–51.

29 Toraldo di Francia, discussion.

30 This diagram was published only recently in Andrea Branzi, ed., *No-Stop City, Archizoom Associati* (HYX: Orleans, 2006), 5; the project No-Stop City was published in several magazines. The most important publications are: Andrea Branzi, "City, Assembly Line of Social Issues: Ideology and Theory of the Metropolis," *Casabella* 350, 51 (1970): 22–34; Andrea Branzi, "No-stop City: Residential Parkings. Climatic Universal System," *Domus* 496 (1971): 49–54.

31 Karl Marx, *Grundrisse: Outlines of the Critique of Political Economy* (London: Penguin, 1973), 51.

32 As Marx stated,

> Indifference towards specific labors corresponds to a form of society in which individuals can with ease transfer from one labor to another, and where the specific kind is a matter of chance for them, hence of indifference. Not only the category, labor, but labor in reality has here become the means of creating wealth in general, and has ceased to be organically linked with particular individuals in any specific form. Such a state of affairs is at its most developed in the most modern form of existence of bourgeois society—in the United States.
>
> (Marx, *Grundrisse*, 51.)

33 Branzi, "City, Assembly Line of Social Issues," 161.

34 Branzi, discussion.

35 Roberto Gargiani, *Archizoom Associati 1966–1974: Dall'onda pop alla superficie neutra* (Milan: Electa, 2007), 196–197.

# Chapter 8

# Context: 1970–2000

The world inhabited by Rem Koolhaas in the 1990s can't be located nationally. Not only is a significant part of Koolhaas's appeal his political non-identifiability—yes, he is Dutch, but that conjures up nothing specific, and his teaching and professional allegiances are multi-centered—but any practice with traction, architectural or otherwise, must at this point in time be global. The economic conditions that accompany this lack of grounding rotate around the US, but a US that is economically and politically determined by politics and trade agreements not of its own making.

In the 1980s, Reagonomics, with its supply-side bias that cut social programs, eliminated governmental regulations of industry, and increased defense spending, nevertheless expanded the deficit as military spending outweighed domestic savings. The strong hand of the Federal Reserve under Chairman Paul Volker and later Alan Greenspan was required to control inflation. This was not *laissez-faire* economics—it was regulated deregulation. The healthy economy under Bill Clinton in the 1990s, stimulated by a computer hardware and software revolution that transformed the manner in which many industries operated, allowed the government to post its first surplus in many decades. However, as during Reagan's administration, this was achieved by strengthening the market, reducing welfare benefits, and the liberal use of a strong Federal Reserve.

The era from the 1970s–1990s was marked by several important economic and political events: the Iranian hostage crisis, the Intermediate-Range Nuclear Forces Treaty (INF) between the US and the USSR (1987), the collapse of the Berlin Wall (1989), the breakup of Yugoslavia (1991–1995), the Gulf War (1991), the disbanding of the Soviet Union (1991), and the US embargo on China after the suppression of the Tiananmen Square protests (1989). The global economy was affected by the virtual collapse of the OPEC cartel, the American economy was redefined by the neo-liberal North American Free-Trade Agreement (NAFTA), and Europe changed politically with the expansion of NATO to include Hungary, Poland, and the Czech Republic.

The dominance of the American model, which after the collapse of the Soviet Union seemed to stand alone, was challenged by new Asian paradigms. Japan's economy provided an example—both positive and negative—against which the US would come to measure itself. In the 1980s, Japan's highly successful emphasis on long-term planning and strong coordination between corporations, banks, and government indicated that strong government control produced growth more effectively than *laissez-faire* competition. When Japan fell into a prolonged recession in the 1990s, the US felt its less planned, more competitive approach had been justified and confirmed. China's economic reform after Mao's death in 1976 embraced the market, combining a vast domestic distribution network with openness to imports and an unusually high reinvestment rate. This "state capitalism" was never a potential mirror for the US economy—its communist context and enormous access to cheap labor was an impossible comparison—but China's swift entry into the world market changed the game the US economy played, not merely because it became a competing exporter and a new market, but because its access to cheap labor altered labor dynamics in the US as well.

One could say that this era of regulated deregulation is architecturally matched by the domination of personalities with asocial agendas who sought to "popularize" certain architectural styles. A more thorough analysis of the post-modern era, within which sits the specific story of Rem Koolhaas, is made in Mary McLeod's "Architecture and Politics in the Reagan Era: From Post-Modernism to Deconstruction" (*Assemblage* 8, February 1989), an original piece that lingers as a model for this anthology. Here Dunham-Jones shows how Koolhaas's CCTV project is the quintessential example of his efforts to embrace global commercial capitalism while simultaneously standing critically above it. This confusing both/neither approach, representing a surprising rebuke to architecture theory, exposes a retreat of social theory in general at this time.

Peggy Deamer

Chapter 8

# Irrational exuberance: Rem Koolhaas and the 1990s

Ellen Dunham-Jones

## Irrational exuberance

The 1990s saw the end of the cold war, the collapse of the Soviet Union, the opening of China, and the rise of neoliberalism, globalization, the internet, the dot.com boom, and "The New Economy." Capitalism had won, and enthusiasm for its ability to raise standards of living, promote democracy, and advance technology increasingly squelched the remaining 1960s-era critiques of its consequences. Instead, corporate ideology co-opted countercultural revolutionary songs and slogans from the 1960s to cheer on 1990s-style reengineering for the information age, marketing individualism as well as the commodification of dissent.[1] Did architectural discourse similarly morph 1960s radicalism into 1990s icon-making during this period of rising faith in free markets and digital technology? What happened to architectural criticism during a period that saw the end of welfare as we knew it in the US and acceptance of the widening gap between rich and poor as an unfortunate, but necessary, by-product of modernization and a healthy economy? Was it only in the 1990s that Rem Koolhaas could ride this global socio-economic restructuring and emerge as one of architectural design culture's leading avant-gardists while celebrating capitalism?

Equating capitalism with modernization and change, Koolhaas identified early on how global capitalism in the 1990s created dynamic, highly speculative urban conditions that were transforming the contemporary city. As he acerbically pointed out, these forces also destabilized and liberated architectural thinking from staid preconceptions, while providing a market for the kinds of radical, iconic buildings he designs. The powerful combination of 1960s irreverence and 1990s relevance in his work catapulted his star status while revealing

**8.1**
Showing the uneasy but undeniable conjoining of art and commerce, *Content*, the catalog to a 2003 exhibition on the work of Rem Koolhaas and OMA, depicts Alan Greenspan making his point about irrational exuberance. Here it is used to illustrate an article on how museums have been subjected to market-driven privatization—from new forms of corporate franchising to attention-getting expansion of facilities. Photograph by Ellen Dunham-Jones

the contradictory paradoxes involved in trying to marry art and capitalism, radicalism and pragmatism, icon-making and city-making. Nonetheless, over the course of the decade, his writings and designs contributed significantly to the discourse's shift away from critical theory towards post-critical, non-judgmental research, and from autonomy towards engagement, albeit engagement increasingly only with the elite beneficiaries of the New Economy, now often referred to as "the 1%." From a contemporary perspective the question is, what is Koolhaas's legacy vis à vis what is considered progressive practice?

Robert Shiller, author and professor of economics at Yale University, explains that the phrase "irrational exuberance" came to be used to describe a heightened state of speculative fervor.[2] While this aptly applies to Koolhaas himself, the phrase famously originated two years into the dot.com boom in a speech given on December 5, 1996 by then Chairman of the US Federal Reserve, Alan Greenspan. After tracing the history of debates over the bank's power and the varying indicators used by the bank to determine whether to tighten or loosen monetary supply, Greenspan stated, "When industrial product was the centerpiece of the economy during the first two-thirds of this century, our overall price indexes served us well."[3] Then Greenspan asked, "What is the price of a unit of software or a legal opinion?" and "how do we know when irrational exuberance has unduly escalated asset values, which then become subject to unexpected and prolonged contractions as they have in Japan for the past decade?"[4] As Shiller and others have amply pointed out, the impact of that question alone led to an immediate slump in stock markets around the world. The phrase continued to be evoked when the dot.com boom went bust in March 2000, and again when the burst housing bubble and the stock market crash of 2008 triggered the Global Financial Crisis.

Linking Koolhaas to "irrational exuberance" is not intended to implicate him in any of these specific market crises, but it does foreground his success plumbing the intersection of the pragmatic corporate world on the one hand and the "delirious" world of desire, possibility, and volatility on the other. Acutely aware of these and other inherent contradictions tugging at architects, Koolhaas revels in their creative friction. An exceedingly compelling contrarian, he also excels at flipping our expectations. He uses his timely positioning of "bigness," shopping, and "the ¥€$ regime" to promise architecture "a realignment with neutrality"[5] to liberate architects from past socially conscious obligations. Instead of critiquing capitalist society, bolstering the civic and the public, or ministering to the needs of the impoverished, he justifies the idea that architects, even if not especially avant-gardists, are now free to serve the market. Koolhaas is not alone in these endeavors, but his essays and design projects in the 1990s smoothed the way for the wave of iconic "starchitecture" object-buildings that followed. They were also particularly influential in stoking his protégés' speculative fervor and embrace of the post-critical.[6] In both cases, Koolhaas has encouraged the shedding of the crippling shackles of critical theory for a surfboard with which to ride the shock waves of the new economy.[7]

## Koolhaas's counterculture roots

A self-proclaimed *soixante-huitarde*, Koolhaas was a 24-year-old journalist and scriptwriter living in Paris in May, 1968, when student protests and labor strikes brought the economy of the nation to a standstill. He witnessed, but did not participate in, the marches and violent rebellions against the rigidity of French bureaucracy, persistent class discrimination, low wages for the working class, and unequal access to universities. Rather than internalize the lessons of class struggle, Koolhaas developed an acute resistance to the restrictions of planned societies and a commitment to promoting individual freedom. That fall he enrolled at the Architectural Association (AA) in London.

Education at the AA then was a rich anti-establishment mix including the Archigram technopop movement, parodies from Superstudio, and tropical affordable housing. In 1970, Bernard Tschumi joined the faculty fresh from Paris where he too at age 24 observed the 1968 riots. His course, "Politics of Space," introduced the AA to the more politicized French Situationist and post-structuralist critique of architecture's complicity with a corrupt capitalist society. In addition to readings from the avant-garde literary journal *Tel Quel*, his students learned how the post-'68 École de Beaux Arts was transformed by sit-ins and construction classes held in forced occupations of banking offices where discriminatory loan practices were discussed.[8] Design was dismissed as irrelevant to the more important reform of the overly technocratic structure of the state. Modern functionalist planning was allied with bureaucracy, and *à la* Jean-Paul Sartre, deemed alienating. Via the writings of Henri Lefebvre, Jean Baudrillard, and Guy Debord, students were taught to challenge capitalist rationality, the commodification of everyday life, and being lulled into complacency by the society of the spectacle.

Tschumi was fascinated in particular by the 1920s-era anti-establishment writings of George Bataille, a rebellious surrealist. Bataille cited architecture as the source of the repressive order of society, arguing that "great monuments are erected like dikes, opposing the logic and majesty of authority against all disturbing elements: it is in the form of cathedral and palace that Church or State speaks to the multitudes and imposes silence upon them."[9]

For Koolhaas, his defining "Bataille-soaked" moment came towards the end of his studies when he documented and analyzed the Berlin Wall as architecture:

> In the early seventies, it was impossible not to sense an enormous reservoir of resentment *against* architecture, with new evidence of its inadequacies—its cruel and exhausted performance—accumulating daily; *looking at the wall as architecture, it was inevitable to transpose the despair, hatred, frustration it inspired to the field of architecture* . . . Were not division, enclosure (i.e., imprisonment), and exclusion —which defined the wall's performance and explained its efficiency—the essential stratagems of *any* architecture? In comparison, the sixties dream of architecture's liberating potential—in which I had been marinating for years as a student—seemed feeble rhetorical play. It evaporated on the spot.[10]

Bataille's influence led both Tschumi and Koolhaas to seek means to liberate architecture from itself, to destabilize and deconstruct architecture's will to order space and society.[11] In their design work in the 1990s, both give particular attention to ramps, spaces of movement, and sculpted voids as indeterminate, unprogrammed sites for transient events. Both employ montage, text, and abundant translucent materials to de-emphasize formal boundaries. Perhaps most innovatively, both seek means of enabling programmatic instability to counteract architectural rigidity. Tschumi articulated this strategy in terms of cross-programming, trans-programming, and dis-programming.[12] Koolhaas has focused more on contradicting external monolithic forms with interiors populated by highly diversified spaces and activities. Expanding beyond the design of buildings, his practice, OMA, established AMO, their research wing, in 1999. The firm's services now include media, politics, renewable energy, and fashion. For Tschumi, the point has been to create an architecture against architecture.[13] Similarly, Koolhaas has referred to his interest in advancing a "post-architectural modernity,"[14] "after-architecture,"[15] and his "search for 'another' architecture."[16]

## Delirious capital

To find "another" architecture, Koolhaas went to New York City. Instead of the imposing language of church or state silencing the masses, he found a crowd-pleasing, market-based modern architecture unburdened by either the moralizing functionalist rhetoric accompanying Bauhausian dreams of a classless society, or the 1960s critiques of the society of the spectacle. His 1978 book *Delirious New York* documents with delight "Manhattanism"—an entrepreneurial blend of fantasy and pragmatism, a quality that inspires much of his own design work. He shows how the city embodies capitalist rationality through the regularity of the street grid, gridded facades, the integration of elevator technology, and the technical precision of the Rockettes' kick line, while simultaneously responding to the surreal, diverse, often erotic desires of the metropolis's collective unconscious— especially vivid in the fantastical artifice of elite interiors, dramatic skyscrapers, and Salvador Dali's interventions. Manhattan's untheorized, unplanned genius is presented as the resolution of these contradictory dynamics and their inten- sification into a dense, socially liberating "culture of congestion."[17] As the book jacket proclaims, Manhattan, from the beginning, has been devoted to the most rational, efficient, and utilitarian pursuit of the *irrational*.

Through detailed histories and speculative psycho-histories of the architects, designs, and paradoxes presented by the grid, the skyscraper, Coney Island, Rockefeller Center, and the United Nations, Koolhaas lovingly portrays a non-reductivist architecture and urbanism that is simultaneously modern and romantic. He demonstrates how both are results of the market's ability to respond to and elicit desire rather than moralizing top-down dictums. He argues that Manhattan produced "an architecture that is at once ambitious and popular . . . a shameless architecture that has been loved in direct proportion to its defiant lack of self-hatred, has been respected exactly to the degree that it went too far. Manhattan has consistently inspired in its beholders *ecstasy about architecture*."[18] The threat to the ecstatic culture of congestion is presented by the villain in the story: Le Corbusier and his rationalist "towers in the park" proposals. In a nod to his contemporaries, Koolhaas states that Le Corbusier was thwarted by his over- reliance on theory and inadequate attention to the importance of metaphor and the unconscious in Manhattan's development.

Koolhaas argues that the more artificial and surreal the city has become, the greater the role of the unconscious in making sense of it. He offers Salvador Dali's Paranoid-Critical Method (PCM) as a tool for producing a "delirium of interpretation." Described as the propping-up of limp, unprovable conjectures by the crutches of Cartesian rationality, the PCM serves Koolhaas both as a method for resolving market dynamics with the fabrications, grafts, and urban ambitions in his own design work, and as an indirect parody of the 1970s critical theory surrounding him.

With *Delirious New York's* not-so-subtle critiques of the increasingly insular and unpopular world of avant-garde "architecture for architects," Koolhaas differentiated himself from both the high-modern minimalism of 1970s corporate firms and the theoretical gymnastics of the *Oppositions* crowd. The countercultural strategy he has continued to evolve critiques what he calls the "exhausted" purist doctrines of architectural culture. Instead of presenting his work as an autonomous art, by the 1995 publication of his massive monograph S,M,L,XL, he foregrounds the competing realities of client-based practice in a capitalist economy.[19] His point is not simply to shock, although he does, and does again in 2003 with the follow-up catalog-as-tabloid *Content*. Rather, his point is to recognize architecture as the contradictory confluence of art and commerce, fantasy and pragmatism, and pretensions of omnipotence and realities of clients and constraints. And while such a position was radically out of step with the structuralist and post-structuralist discourse of his peers in the 1970s, it set him up beautifully to work with high-profile clients like Prada, the Guggenheim, and Universal Studios in the 1990s.

The trope that holds the contradictory forces together in his design work is another legacy from *Delirious New York*: the metropolis. Teeming with ambition, modernity, and difference, metropolitan culture for Koolhaas is a modernizing force and he consistently seeks out its latest manifestations around the globe. When he and three partners established their firm in 1975, a time when cities were emptying out and postmodernism was ascendant, they went against the grain by establishing the Office of Metropolitan Architecture (OMA). In the spirit of Bataille, OMA's work has continued to reject the rigid, repressive, and divisive order of "architecture" in favor of the fluid, dynamic, and productive disorder of the capitalist, market-driven "metropolis." This is most evident in their characteristic weaving of diverse programs together to induce the culture of congestion, whether in a single building or urban plan. Where they break away from Bataille—and from the culture of critique—is in their embrace of the power of capitalism to drive change.

## The New World Order and the new economy

Ironically, if the Berlin Wall launched Koolhaas's critique of architecture, it was the Wall's demolition in 1989 that amplified the relevance of his ideas. Deng Xiaoping's subsequent opening up of Chinese markets in 1992 with the exhortation "Enrich yourselves!" was another accelerant. Not only had capitalism won, but the spirit of '68 had lost. Marxist critiques and labor unions were swatted away by the neoliberal consensus in favor of free markets. Notions of "the public good" were challenged and increasingly replaced by privatization and an emphasis on "individual responsibility." In the New World Order, issues of social justice and social equity between developed and developing nations were increasingly dominated by discussions of market access and economic liberalization. For those in "the new economy," digital access to information was supposed to lead to infinite growth and the end of business cycles. Markets were deregulated, state-owned enterprises were privatized, free trade agreements flowed, and globalization was heralded as the means to progressively improve standards of living. Thomas Friedman advanced the "Golden Arches Theory of Conflict Prevention," observing that no two countries with a McDonald's franchise had ever gone to war with one another.[20] The World Trade Organization, NAFTA, and the Maastricht Treaty promised to expand peace and prosperity by easing the trade of goods and ideas. In the process, they also expanded the size and power of the cities and corporations that jumped into the fray. Koolhaas was one of the few architects to call attention to the implications of this massive economic and political restructuring on the profession of architecture. His contribution was to theorize the virtues of "Bigness."

## Bigness as a response to economic restructuring

In 1994, as his 800,000-square-meter Euralille project and groundbreaking 1,346-page monograph S,M,L,XL were coming to completion, Koolhaas wrote three essays. Collectively, they excoriate his profession for inadequately coming to grips with the New World Order's massive investments in urbanization, generic cities, and big buildings.[21] But rather than serve as a rallying cry to better direct investment and shape the metropolis, the essays' evidence is used to prove the irrelevance of architecture and urbanism's ambitions to order society. Instead of such "illusions of involvement and control,"[22] Koolhaas proposes variations of "go with the flow" and positions himself as the lead surfer on the post-1989 wave of modernization to build a New Europe.

After several near misses in European design competitions for big buildings in the early 1990s, his first big commission was Euralille. A business center, shopping mall, and convention center built as part of a new high-speed

8.2
Euralille is Koolhaas's test application of the ideas of Bigness, the Generic City, and Lite Urbanism. Detached and independent from the historic urban context, the masterplan integrates multiple iconic buildings into the highway, rail, and subway infrastructure for "endless intensifications"; the section stacks dormitories over a hypermart and office buildings over the rail line to form "unnameable hybrids" while the Congrexpo innovatively employs generic detailing. But while the mash-up of the icons is spectacular, the spaces in between them, such as this view of the railway station from the Congrexpo, fail to produce a desirable "culture of congestion." Photograph: Phillip Jones, 1996

8.3
Koolhaas describes
the heart of Euralille
as this "Piranesian
space" where the
movement systems
of cars, people, and
trains most vividly
collide. More
thrilling in the
original sketches
than it is in real life,
it serves as a built
diagram of the
international space
of flows around
which the project
was conceived. Is
this space where
people and vehicles
pass but never fully
intersect the
architecture of
mobile capital?
Photograph: Phillip
Jones, 1996

train station with international connections, the project straddled the highway and rail lines on the periphery of Lille, France. In addition to describing the project in detail in several publications, Koolhaas wrote "Bigness or the problem of Large" to articulate a theory and public relations campaign for bigness of this scale. Although literally referring to big buildings, Bigness also indirectly includes the big business, big government, big firms, and big money required to make them. In other words, Koolhaas, the hip *soixante-huitarde*, was throwing his chips in with the authoritarian establishment. And although he maintained some of his rebellious street cred by throwing in the phrase "fuck context" and heaping derision on his peers, he suggested that the rest of the profession needed to join him to restore its credibility.[23]

Was this Koolhaas at his most contrarian? Was this a pre-emptive justification? For those of us concerned in the 1990s by the inflated scale and predominance of big box stores, shopping malls, and edge cities, his topic was right on target. But his claims of the benefits of Bigness were surprising, if not unconvincing. Accepting the inevitability of large-scale development, he optimistically extols how Bigness "instigates a regime of complexity," "a promiscuous proliferation of events," leading to "programmatic alchemy" between elements and the creation of new events.[24] Recognizing another "Bataille-soaked" opportunity to undercut the authority of architecture-as-exclusion, he further claims that the "art" of architecture is useless in Bigness and that Bigness competes with and preempts the city, surrendering the field ultimately to a scraped, tabula rasa "after-architecture."

Koolhaas likes the tabula rasa, the identity-less vacant lot, "those nothingnesses of infinite potential."[25] They are emblematic of the bulldozing inherent to modernizing the metropolis and echo the neoliberal reprise of the virtues of capitalism's "creative destruction."[26] Don't stand in the way of progress! Koolhaas continues to defend Bigness even when the "after-architecture" landscape it produces is that of the Generic City. In his second essay from 1994, Koolhaas writes, "The Generic City is all that remains of what used to be the city."[27] Giving emphasis to its unhealthy attributes, he says, "Compared to the classical city the Generic City is *sedated*, usually perceived from a sedentary position . . . The serenity of the Generic City is achieved by the *evacuation* of the public realm . . . Its main attraction is its anomie."[28] He likens the anonymous interchangeability of buildings in the Generic City to mass global immigration and speculates that they are more welcoming to such groups than beautiful medieval city centers with their strict behavioral codes and air of exclusion.[29] Atlanta's sprawl, Disneyfied European historic centers, and most of Asia's new development are all examples of the Generic City. And despite his low opinion of them, he argues that, like Bigness, modernization demands and perpetually reproduces the Generic City. In the world of globalization, everything is accessible, everything is information, everything is generic.[30] Plus, he argues that the ever-expanding metropolis has outgrown the capacity of the center to remain central. Instead of lamenting this loss of identity, he suggests that this expansion liberates the periphery from its second-class status and asks provocatively, "What if we are witnessing a global liberation movement: 'down with character!'"[31]

Having reinforced the uselessness of the "art" of architecture in the market-driven Generic City of Bigness, Koolhaas next dresses down the planning profession. In his third essay, "What Ever Happened to Urbanism?," he scathingly criticizes the sterile efforts and "lost battle" of urbanists to control and plan the unfolding of the metropolis. He is especially dismissive of postmodernists and New Urbanists. "Pervasive urbanization has modified the urban condition itself beyond recognition. 'The' city no longer exists. As the concept of the city is distorted and stretched beyond precedent, each insistence on its primordial condition—in terms of images, rules, fabrication—irrevocably leads via nostalgia to irrelevance."[32]

At issue for Koolhaas is not whether the development patterns of the historic center or the periphery are good or bad.[33] Similarly, he never questions the costs or benefits, winners or losers, of the impacts of modernization and global capitalism. He accepts them as givens and uses them to discredit all prior architectural and urbanistic thinking. He is principally interested in establishing relevance to modernization and the perpetual instability and dynamism that implies. Instead of trying to shape the wave of modernization, he proposes that at best architects can ride it. Instead of trying to fix the damage left by the wake of the wave, he looks to the horizon in search of the next wave. Instead of empowering communities to envision and administer their future, he calls for a "Lite Urbanism,"[34] the equivalent of deregulation. And much like Wall Street's arguments for the deregulation of banking at the time, Koolhaas bathes Lite Urbanism's promises in glowing, liberatory, progressive ambitions, while omitting reference to its risks of abuse by the short-term interests of mobile capital:

> If there is to be a "new urbanism" it will not be based on the twin fantasies of order and omnipotence; it will be the staging of uncertainty; it will no longer be concerned with the arrangement of more or less permanent objects but with the irrigation of territories with potential; it will no longer aim for stable configurations but for the creation of enabling fields that accommodate processes that refuse to be crystallized into definitive form; it will no longer be about meticulous definition, the imposition of limits, but about expanding notions, denying boundaries not about separating and identifying entities, but about discovering unnameable hybrids; it will no longer be obsessed with the city but with the manipulation of infrastructure for endless intensifications and diversifications, shortcuts and redistributions—the reinvention of psychological space.[35]

## Big books and the absorption of theory and criticism into research

In 1996, Koolhaas accepted a tenured position at Harvard University and began a research project on the mutations of the contemporary city called "The Harvard Project on the City." The work of the 1990s was published in three big books from 2001–2002: *Great Leap Forward*, *The Harvard Design School Guide to Shopping*, and *Mutations*. More recent studies have included Roman empire building, Lagos, Moscow, and Beijing. Collectively, the publications intend to fill the "theoretical, critical, and operational impasse" in urbanism by "introducing a number of 'copyrighted' terms, which represent the beginning of a conceptual framework to describe and interpret the contemporary urban condition."[36] More spectacle than substance—like their subjects for the most part—the big books are primarily filled with photographs from the documentary fieldwork of his thesis students as well as graphic displays of data, statistics, maps, timelines, and short historical and analytical essays. Criticism is largely excluded. Less polemical than his earlier

essays and much more reliant on graphic evidence, they corroborate his observations on Bigness, the Generic City, and the seeming invulnerability of global
capital to architectural intentions or critique. The biggest difference is that for
the latter part of the 1990s, Koolhaas shifts his focus from the New Europe to
emerging markets around the globe.

China's Pearl River Delta is his inaugural subject and *The Great Leap
Forward* might have been titled *Delirious Shenzhen*. Documenting the unprecedented
pace of modernization resulting from China's experiments with capitalism along
the Pearl River Delta, the 800-page book chronicles the surreal delights produced
by the new market economy. The format is immersive but hardly comprehensive.
Readers are treated to descriptions of the 500 24-hour golf courses, the world's
longest waterfront promenade, the theme park at the center of the city, and the
parking garage that after six months became inhabited by many different
programs and 26 different types of curtain walls. Contradictions are the *sine qua
non* of urbanism for Koolhaas and the book documents what it calls "the city of
exacerbated differences," focusing more on money and program than on its
sprawling physical pattern.

In lectures presenting the work, Koolhaas is less able to maintain the
tone of journalistic neutrality found in the book. He clearly relishes the seemingly
absurd juxtapositions of activities he finds in China and the dizzying perception
of the city as unauthorized event. Although critical of the repetitive and shoddily
built housing complexes, he finds the dynamism and unpredictability of real
estate development in the socialist market economy "a source of freedom."[37] This
is modernization at an unprecedented speed and scale and he is thrilled by the
chaotic ferment wrought by the sudden infusion of state and foreign capital. Yet
the book is remarkably silent on the conditions of the workers on whom the
capital depends.

This omission is telling given that the Special Economic Zone Koolhaas
studied is based on an economy of export-oriented production similar to the
maquiladoras of Mexico or the Export Production Zones of Indonesia. Reliant
upon vast quantities of cheap, docile, non-unionized labor to produce everything
from bootleg compact disks to electronic components for multinational corporations, it would be a mistake to equate their participation in free trade with
growth in individual freedom. Although workers in Shenzhen have gained greater
rights in the past few years and many have improved their standard of living,
local laws are suspended in Free Trade Zones. Governance and justice are generally
administered by the corporations themselves. While *The Great Leap Forward* celebrates
the freedom of capitalist developers, planners, and architects working at a rapid
pace, the mobility of capital and the mobility of individuals are not the same
thing, especially in Asian sweatshops.

If *The Great Leap Forward* focused on capitalism's impact on real estate,
the second tome in the series, the *Harvard Design School Guide to Shopping*, gets down
to the nitty-gritty. It enjoys taking seriously a subject that architecture's elite has
generally refused to engage in, in the process "disqualify(ing) designers from
participating in the twentieth century's biggest contribution to urbanism."[38] The

frontispiece declares that "shopping is arguably the last remaining form of public activity" and "one of the principal—if only—modes by which we experience the city." The book provides detailed documentation and extensive research into the penetration of retail into all forms of life (including airports, museums, and churches), the explosion of data on retail transactions, branding, the logistics of retail expansion, comparative retail building types, and so on. By and large, the information is presented factually with little questioning of the decisions reported. The proliferation of vacant space is presented as a crisis to the industry but is not accompanied by any critique of over-retailing, the impact of dead malls on communities, or how the design of these buildings hastens either their obsolescence or their reuse. Nor is there any discussion of increasingly consumerist societies or the implications of the book's provocative thesis, that shopping is our last public space. Instead, the status quo is simply presented as inevitable, a *fait accompli* beyond challenge.

With all of this research, is Koolhaas interested in transgressing the logic he exposes? On the one hand, he more or less single-handedly brought the discipline's attention to the burgeoning urban landscapes produced by the evolving global economy of the late twentieth and early twenty-first century: Atlanta's consumerist sprawl-scape, the rapid urbanization of the Pearl River Delta, the informal economies of Lagos, and the penetration of spaces for shopping everywhere. While most architectural publications, school lecture series, and museum exhibitions remained focused on individual building designs or theories produced by individual architects, Koolhaas injected the discourse with high-profile, too-big-to-ignore spreads on the larger globalizing world outside. Koolhaas's books have provided valuable and compelling documentation of the impact of mobile capital on the new economically linked, but physically segregated, landscapes of consumption and production.[39]

Koolhaas has also gone much further than most architects in framing his work in terms of a global, social, political, and economic context. *Content*, the catalog to a 2003 exhibition, parodies his celebrity status by imitating the format of a tabloid magazine with sensational articles. The cover depicts President George W. Bush wearing a hat of McDonald's Freedom Fries, Supreme Leader Kim Jong Il as part cyborg, and President Saddam Hussein as Rambo. They are in front of, and set the context for, OMA's design for the CCTV tower in Beijing. The mock story headlines include "Perverted Architecture," "Sweatshop Demographics," "Big Brother Skyscrapers," and "Homicidal Engineering." Inside, stories on OMA's projects since S,M,L,XL are interspersed with numerous advertisements for Prada—one of OMA's repeat clients—as well as Gucci, eBay, and several others, some but not all of which appear to be fake. A timeline of the "¥€$ Regime 1989–2003" tracks the performance of the Dow Jones Index, the rise and fall of political revolutions, and the production of architectural icons. The story's introduction cynically notes, "Architecture contributed a surprising sequence of masterpieces to this drunken party . . . "[40] The saturated format bombards the reader with the graphics of commercial advertising, while the "content" speaks to issues of art and culture.

Architecture has always been both an art and a business, and instead of privileging one over the other, as most architects do, Koolhaas embraces the creative contamination of both worlds. Whether the results are subversive or ambivalent can be debated, but has any other contemporary architect so forcefully had their finger on the pulse of global development patterns and called attention to the role of capital in directing design?[41]

On the other hand, for all of the full-bleed photographs, charts, and individual essays, his research, especially in "The Harvard Project on the City," contains remarkably little assessment or analysis of the findings. His refusal to criticize goes beyond a reactionary response to critical theory or his legacy of disinterested journalistic reporting. Rather than bringing the insular architecture elite's attention to the larger world outside, is it possible that the books have been written more to bring architecture to the attention of the larger world? Perhaps inspired by Dali's PCM, the former scriptwriter is betting that the best way to get the larger world's attention is to show it a mirror. Rather than talking about esoteric architectural ideas in a language that only other architects understand (an occupational hazard), Koolhaas focuses the lens on what's happening in the world outside of architecture. He doesn't paint a flattering picture, but he doesn't alienate or criticize his subject either. In so doing he emerges as well positioned to assist the subject in becoming more appealing. In fact, he emerges as the only architect willing to take that risk since, as his writings repeatedly tell us, architecture and urbanism have failed to address the dynamic needs of the larger world. But, like a mirror, the reflection that Koolhaas's buildings portray is more *au present* than *avant-garde*.

The logics that Koolhaas is interested in transgressing are not those of the larger social, economic, and political world. In fact, he argues that most such utopian efforts by architects to make the world a better place have been disastrous.[42] Rather, the logics he's interested in transgressing are those internal to architectural and urban discourse. Instead of avant-garde aspirations of leading society towards prescribed future outcomes, Koolhaas insists that at best architecture can mirror the flux of the larger world in unprecedented designs and processes intended to defy predictable societal relationships. His architecture holds out the possibility that new, social configurations might emerge but also the possibility that they won't. Heavily reliant on new technologies and forms, his architecture provides the New World Order with the appearance of progressive change without the need for real commitment. Justifying the need for such a new role, Koolhaas has said, "I see 'Architecture' as an endangered brand, and I'm trying to reposition it."[43] His buildings, like his books, rebrand avant-garde architecture as spectacle.

## From the 1990s to now: rebranding the avant-garde

What are we to make of Koolhaas's endorsement of commercialism? He wasn't the only 1960s radical to become a 1990s capitalist. Thomas Frank, the *Harper's Magazine* and former *Wall Street Journal* cultural critic, sums up the 1990s by telling the story of Deadheads in Davos or how former counterculture folks and business leaders found they shared beliefs in markets as organic connections between people and in governments as fundamentally illegitimate.[44] New Yorker writer John Seabrook's 2001 book, *Nobrow: The Culture of Marketing, the Marketing of Culture*, tells similar stories of the merging in the 1990s of highbrow art and literary culture with lowbrow commerce and money. In 1994, Tschumi began calling on architects to "accelerate capitalism."[45] Both he and Koolhaas were by this time safely ensconced in tenured positions at Ivy League schools. Both had been exhibited at the Museum of Modern Art in New York with prestigious one-man shows, big fat monographs, and were inevitably referred to as "avant-garde." One might interpret their enthusiasm for capitalism as a disingenuous tactic by two counterculture heroes to suddenly justify the mainstream system they found themselves comfortably within. Alternatively, it might reflect their discovery in the 1990s that destabilization—one of the great legacies of the counterculture— turns out to be best accomplished by venture capitalists, big business, and mobile money markets.

In either case, Koolhaas has positioned himself (much more overtly than Tschumi) to spin the interdependencies between architecture and the New World Order. And his success at eviscerating conventional notions of avant- gardism has been remarkable. In theory circles, as the 1990s ticked to a close, a new generation followed Koolhaas's lead to declare the end of the critical project and the virtues of being post-critical.[46] Michael Speaks described the shift as moving away from theory's concerns for truth towards intelligence's concerns for doing and action.[47] This has manifested in various not particularly coordinated ways. These include a revived general interest in pragmatism, the notion of pro- jective practices, digital design and fabrication, diagramming and/or datascapes as the basis of design, as well as landscape urbanism's focus on evolving processes. Koolhaas's influence trickles through all of them in the de-emphasis on theory and formalism and heightened interest in research, experimentation, perfor- mance, and ambitions that are, ironically, internally focused on disciplinary advances rather than externally focused on what is happening in the larger world, let alone on leading societal change.

In the profession, the more conspicuous legacy of Koolhaas's rebrand- ing is in the proliferation of large, avant-garde icon buildings declaring their owner's participation in the New World Order and their designer's participation in the global economy. The trophies of globalization have evolved from high-design corporate banks by high-profile corporate design firms—notably Sir Norman Foster's HSBC Bank Headquarters in Hong Kong from 1979–1985— to edgy, cultural facilities such as Frank Gehry's Guggenheim Museum at Bilbao designed from 1991–1997, to a daring state-owned media company like Koolhaas's CCTV Headquarters in Beijing from 2002–2012. In the competitive global game of calling attention to one's progressive cachet, each new entrant tries to raise the bar, and the budget.

This is far removed from the 1980s when "critical architecture" was expected to incorporate some aspect of resistance to capitalist totalization, compromised though such resistance might be.[48] Today, avant-garde architecture,

**8.4**
CCTV's enigmatic form appears well schooled in lessons from *Delirious New York*. It uses the PCM—an improbable gesture supported by the crutches of Cartesian rationalism—to reinvent the skyscraper as a shape-shifting loop. However, walking around the very large superblock it sits on, seeing the residential settlements it directly abuts, two of which are shown here, one can't help but wonder why Koolhaas didn't connect the tower to Beijing's grid and internal block structure as he learned worked so well in Manhattan. Photograph: Phillip Jones, 2012

big capital, and authoritarian states have found ways to support each other very cozily. At the global scale, the buildings of such couplings have successfully signaled the emergence of new players in the global economy. But at the local level, instead of challenging the class structure or economic power of the status quo, high design increasingly serves to distinguish its elite patron class from the man in the street.

OMA's design for CCTV's 10,000 employees and thousands of daily visitors exemplifies the complexities and contradictions of avant-gardism's embrace of Bigness and spectacle. In a district of skyscrapers, CCTV calls attention to itself by rejecting both the tower and the corporate campus typologies. The main headquarters building is twisted into an asymmetrical upside-down U-shape while the Television Cultural Center is L-shaped. Both sit on a 20-hectare, four-block cleared site in Beijing's expanding Central Business District, not-so-centrally located on the Third Ring Road. Remnants of the residential hutongs that used to occupy the site are still visible (see Figure 8.4) but will soon be replaced by SOM's award-winning network of walkable green boulevards, expanded transit ways, and numerous new sites for commercial high-rises. Plans call for the plinth of the CCTV buildings to connect to the CBD's forthcoming boulevards and have direct escalator access to the subway station and to a route for public tours. However, as the headquarters and production facilities for China's state-run television, with capacity to broadcast 250 channels, the buildings are also heavily secured. The main building sits behind guard booths and security fences along the two primary streets. Bermed gardens for employees—designed to resemble Piranesi's *Campo Marzio dell'Antica Roma* from the public observation deck above— further distance the building from the streets and local context. Part witty allusion to the role of empires as collectors of foreign architectures, the gardens also read as fenced-off suburban office park landscape buffers. As such they manage to make walking around the building not only unwelcoming, but surprisingly boring. The buildings' shape-shifting forms and daunting 75-meter, 13-storey cantilever make for stunning views from within and from a distance, but are least engaging from the sidewalk.

This is surprising coming from the author of *Delirious New York* and a scholar of cities. He taught us to appreciate the richness of the culture of congestion's tight interlocking of the public life in the street with the private life of the skyscraper interior. Instead, at CCTV he trades Manhattan's duo of "the schism and the lobotomy" for the internalized programmatic promiscuity of

**8.5**
In accordance with Koolhaas's theory of Bigness, the CCTV Tower not only operates independent of context, it meets the main avenue with a security fence and landscape berms. Photograph: Phillip Jones, 2012

Bigness and the once-villainous city-killing model of the Corbusian "towers in the park."[49] In a self-fulfilling prophecy, he argues against addressing the street since the political life that it once supported no longer exists.[50] He treats the existing street as "residue" and conceives of CCTV not as in the city, but *as* a city, perhaps the greatest flaw of Bigness. Bigness not only re-establishes architecture as an agent of exclusion, it negates any possibility of fostering inclusive congruency.

In the end, CCTV is a spectacular object that is simultaneously rational and irrational, exuberant and withdrawn, monumental and unstable. But, sadly, the one contradiction it doesn't resolve is the choice between icon-making and city-making. It ends up rebranding architecture and avant-gardism in service to the society of the spectacle rather than to the culture of congestion.

Is the larger legacy of Koolhaas and the 1990s the rebranding of architecture not as the source of authority and order but as the accommodating mirror to the authority and disorder of the market? In 2011 Koolhaas said, "neoliberalism has turned architecture into a 'cherry on the cake' affair . . . I'm not saying that neoliberalism has destroyed architecture. But it has assigned it a new role and limited its range."[51] Is the role of the avant-garde to cozy up with big capital to produce architecturally daring and socially unambitious icon buildings whose collective impact is more "architectural petting zoo" than urbanism?[52] In the emerging markets that Koolhaas targets, this may well be the case. However, where capital is scarce and markets are suffering from the bursting of irrationally exuberant bubbles, architects and urbanists are finding other highly creative means to advance agendas overlooked by the starchitects, including proactive improvements to the city. This may be one of the contradictions of capitalism.

## Notes

1  See Thomas Frank and Matt Weiland, eds., *Commodify Your Dissent: Salvos from The Baffler* (New York: W.W. Norton & Co., 1997).

2  Robert Shiller, "Origin of the Term," Definition of Irrational Exuberance, accessed August 28, 2012, http://www.irrationalexuberance.com/definition.htm.

3  Alan Greenspan, "The Challenge of Central Banking in a Democratic Society," The Federal Reserve Board, accessed August 28, 2012, http://www.federalreserve.gov/boarddocs/speeches/1996/19961205.htm.

4  Ibid.

5  Rem Koolhaas, "Bigness or the Problem of Large," in *S,M,L,XL: Office of Metropolitan Architecture*, ed. Jennifer Sigler (New York: The Monacelli Press, 1995), 514.

6  For more detail see Henry Francis Mallgrave and David Goodman, "Chapter 10: Pragmatism and Post-Criticality," in *An Introduction to Architectural Theory: 1968 to the Present* (West Sussex, UK: Wiley-Blackwell, 2011), 177–193.

7  In 1985, summarizing his findings on Manhattan in the context of OMA's ambitions Koolhaas wrote, "This architecture relates to the forces of the *Groszstadt* like a surfer to the waves," and contrasted it to the fantasies of control that architects "wallowed" in during the 1970s. "Elegy for the Vacant Lot," *S,M,L,XL*, 937.

8  See Martin Pawley and Bernard Tschumi, "The Beaux Arts Since '68," *Architectural Design* 41 (September, 1971): 533–566. See also Louis Martin, "Transpositions: On the Intellectual Origins of Tschumi's Architectural Theory," *Assemblage* 11 (April 1990): 23–35.

9  George Bataille, "Architecture," *Documents* 2 (May, 1929), trans. Betsy Wing in *Against Architecture, The Writings of George Bataille*, Denis Hollier (Cambridge, MA: MIT Press, 1989), 47.

10  Koolhaas, "Field Trip, A(A) MEMOIR (First and Last . . .)," in S,M,L,XL, 226.

11  I have argued this in more detail in Ellen Dunham-Jones, "The Generation of '68–Today: Bernard Tschumi, Rem Koolhaas and the Institutionalization of Critique," *Proceedings of the 86th ACSA Annual Meeting and Technology Conference: Constructing Identity "Souped-up" and "Unplugged"* (Washington DC: Association of Collegiate Schools of Architecture, 1998), 527–533.

12  See Bernard Tschumi, "Abstract Mediation and Strategy," *Architecture and Disjunction* (Cambridge, MA: The MIT Press, 1994), 205.

13  Bernard Tschumi, *Cinegramme Folie* (New York: Princeton Architectural Press, 1987), vii.

14  Rem Koolhaas, "Sixteen Years of OMA," in *OMA-Rem Koolhaas Architecture 1970–1990*, ed. Jacques Lucan (New York: Princeton Architectural Press, 1991), 163.

15  Koolhaas, "Bigness or the Problem of Large," in S,M,L,XL, 516.

16  Koolhaas, "Introduction," in S,M,L,XL, xix.

17  Perhaps the most concise definition of this term is "Manhattan represents the apotheosis of the ideal of density per se, both of population and of infrastructure; its architecture promises a state of congestion on all possible levels, and exploits this congestion to inspire and support particular forms of social intercourse that together form a unique *culture of congestion*." Rem Koolhaas, "'Life in the Metropolis' or 'The Culture of Congestion,'" *Architectural Design* 47, 5 (August 1977): 319–325.

18  Rem Koolhaas, *Delirious New York* (New York: Oxford University Press, 1978), 7.

19  See "Introduction," and the opening endpapers documenting the firm's income and expenditures, employee turnover, and travel, S,M,L,XL, i–xiii, xix.

20  Thomas Friedman, *The Lexus and the Olive Tree* (New York: Anchor Books, 2000), 239–264.

21  Architectural discourse at the time was focused on either "dismantlement or disappearance," terms Koolhaas used to describe the theory of deconstruction's attack on the Whole and the theories of digital/virtual media's attack on the Real. Koolhaas chastises the profession for missing out on the historic opportunity, writing, "Paradoxically, the Whole and the Real ceased to exist as possible enterprises for the architect exactly at the moment where the approaching end of the second millennium saw an all-out rush to reorganization, consolidation, expansion, a clamoring for megascale. Otherwise engaged, an entire profession was incapable, finally, of exploiting dramatic social and economic events that, if confronted, could restore its credibility." Koolhaas, "Bigness or the Problem of Large," in S,M,L,XL, 508–509.

22  Koolhaas, "What Ever Happened to Urbanism?" in S,M,L,XL, 965.

23  Koolhaas, "Bigness or the Problem of Large," in S,M,L,XL, 495–516.

24  Ibid., 497–512.

25  In reference to the site for the Parc de la Villette design competition in Paris. See Koolhaas, "Elegy for a Vacant Lot," in S,M,L,XL, 937.

26  Joseph Schumpeter coined the term in his 1942 book *Capitalism, Socialism and Democracy* based on Karl Marx's observations about capitalism's need to destroy and reconfigure existing economic orders so as to create new wealth.

27  Koolhaas, "The Generic City," in S,M,L,XL, 1252.

28  Ibid., 1250–1251.

29  "Interview with Star Architect Rem Koolhaas: We're Building Assembly Line Cities and Buildings," *Spiegel Online*, December 16, 2011, accessed August 28, 2012, http://www.spiegel.de/international/zeitgeist/interview-with-star-architect-rem-koolhaas-we-re-building-assembly-line-cities-and-buildings-a-803798.html.

30  Rem Koolhaas, "Harvard GSD Lecture" (lecture, Harvard Graduate School of Design, Cambridge, MA, April 22, 1998).

31  Koolhaas, "The Generic City," in S,M,L,XL, 1248.

32  Koolhaas, "What Ever Happened to Urbanism?," in S,M,L,XL, 963.

33  In fact he has voiced different opinions. After studying Atlanta, Singapore and the peripheries around Paris in the late 1980s, he described the work as part of "a retro-active manifesto for the yet to be recognized beauty of the late twentieth-century urban landscape." Rem Koolhaas, "Postscript: Introduction For New Research 'The Contemporary City,'" in *Theorizing a New Agenda for Architecture: An Anthology of Architectural Theory 1965–1995*, ed. Kate Nesbitt (New York: Princeton Architecture Press, 1995), 325. In 2001 he scathingly described similar landscapes as "junkspace." Rem Koolhaas, "Junkspace," in *Harvard Design School Guide to Shopping*, ed. Chuihua Judy Chang, Jeffrey Inaba, Rem Koolhaas, and Sze Tsung Leung (Koln: Taschen, 2001), 408–421.

34  Koolhaas, "What Ever Happened to Urbanism?," in S,M,L,XL, 971.

35  Ibid., 969.

36  Chuihua Judy Chang, Jeffrey Inaba, Rem Koolhaas, and Sze Tsung Leung, eds., *The Great Leap Forward* (Koln: Taschen, 2001), 27–28.

37  Rem Koolhaas, public lecture, Columbia University Graduate School of Architecture, Planning and Preservation, New York, NY, March 26, 1996).

38  Daniel Herman, "High Architecture," in *Harvard Design School Guide to Shopping*, 391.

39  For further discussion of the interrelations between sprawl, Free Trade Zones, and Global Cities, see Ellen Dunham-Jones, "Economic Sustainability in the Post-Industrial Landscape," in *The Green Braid, Towards an Architecture of Ecology, Economy, and Equity*, ed. Kim Tanzer and Rafael Longoria (Abingdon, Oxon: Routledge, 2007), 44–59.

40  Theo Deutinger, Maja Borchers, Matthew Murphy, Nanne de Ru, Max Schwitalla, and Sebastian Thomas, "¥€$ Regime: 1989–2003," in *Content*, ed. Rem Koolhaas (Koln: Taschen, 2004), 240–251.

41  In fact, I have argued—and would continue to argue—that Andres Duany and the new urbanists have also focused considerably on the role of capital in shaping the built environment. However, until recently, most of their focus has been limited to development patterns in the US. See Ellen Dunham-Jones, "Real Radicalism: Duany and Koolhaas," *Harvard Design Magazine* 1 (Winter/Spring 1997): 51.

42  Koolhaas, "Utopia Station," in *Content*, 393.

43  Cited in Hal Foster, "Bigness," *London Review of Books* 23, 23 (November 29, 2001): 16.

44  Thomas Frank, *One Market Under God: Extreme Capitalism, Market Populism, and the End of Economic Democracy* (New York; Anchor Books, 2000), xii.

45  Tschumi concluded a public lecture on his work at Columbia University's School of Architecture, Planning and Preservation in April, 1994, challenging students to "accelerate capitalism." He expanded on his intentions in "Urban Pleasures and the Moral Good," in *Assemblage* 25 (Cambridge, MA: MIT Press, December 1994), 6–13.

46  See R.E. Somol and Sarah Whiting, "Notes Around The Doppler Effect and other Moods of Modernism," in *Perspecta* 33 *"Mining Autonomy": The Yale Architecture Journal*, ed. Michael Osman et al. (Cambridge, MA: The MIT Press, 2002), 72–77.

47  Michael Speaks, "Intelligence After Theory," in Perspecta 38, "Architecture After All": *The Yale Architecture Journal*, ed. Marcus Carter et al. (Cambridge, MA: The MIT Press, 2006): 103–106.

48  Manfredo Tafuri and Benjamin Buchloh are two of the better-known critics of the co-optation of art and architecture by commerce.

49  Despite a lack of apparent follow-through, on August 5, 2003, at Tsinghua University in Beijing, Koolhaas presented CCTV as "embedded in a project for prospective preservation and a competition for a low-rise CBD, revealing an interlocking hypothesis for Beijing's future land use . . . the beginnings of a 'Beijing Manifesto.'" See *Content*, 487.

50  "The exterior of the city is no longer a collective theater where 'it' happens; there's no collective 'it' left. The street has become residue, organizational device, mere segment of the continuous metropolitan plane where the remnants of the past face the equipments of the new in an uneasy standoff." Koolhaas, "Bigness," in S,M,L,XL, 514.

51  "Interview," *Speigel Online*, December 16, 2011, accessed August 28, 2012, http://www.spiegel.de/international/zeitgeist/interview-with-star-architect-rem-koolhaas-we-re-building-assembly-line-cities-and-buildings-a-803798-3.html.

52  Koolhaas has been associated with this description of the Arts District in Dallas. See Blair Kamin, "A Work Still in Progress," *Chicago Tribune*, March 18, 2011.

# Chapter 9

# Context: 1990–2010

The globalized economy in evidence over the last twenty years has, at the small scale, affected mobile architectural practices, and, at the large scale, changed the scope of subjects to which architects paid attention. With the Guggenheim Museum Bilbao on the one hand and new showcase developments in Asia on the other, the architectural community—and cultural observers in general—began to pay attention to the monetary mechanisms in which architecture participated, not just the objects produced. Indeed, this is precisely what Dunham-Jones in the previous chapter identifies as Koolhaas's Clinton-era revelation: it's the money, stupid.

The economic success that Frank Gehry's Guggenheim Museum brought to Bilbao not only garnered unprecedented attention to an architect now rightfully deemed a "star," but to a marginal city that needed and received revitalization. In Asian regions thought to be equally marginal, iconic super-tall skyscrapers began to appear: Shun Hing Square in Shenzhen (1996); CITIC Plaza in Guangzhou (1997); Petronas Twin Towers in Kuala Lumpur (1997). And while these towers initially received attention for the local revitalization they both symbolized and hoped to produce, the more interesting story has proven to be the financial mechanisms that enabled them, particularly those in nominally anti-capitalist China. In fact, the first two aforementioned projects were each the result of China's implementation of Special Economic Zones (SEZs), areas of exception that permit businesses to operate independently of the state's embedded financial and political system—essentially to exist outside the law. While not invented by the Chinese, China was the first to use them to effect significant economic modernization. SEZs were introduced to China by Deng Xiaoping in 1979 to test ways of opening the country to foreign investment and development, Guangdong province and Shenzhen being first among such experiments.

The SEZ has since become a favored mechanism, allowing many Asian countries to escape the centralized and development-inhibiting economic policies of Socialism and Communism. Included under the SEZ umbrella are Free Trade Zones (FTZs) and Export Processing Zones (EPZs); each uses customs and tax exemptions to attract foreign capital, create jobs, and develop infrastructure. India is distinct not because it lacks a socialist context—indeed, after liberation in 1947 it became highly centralized, following a Soviet model until reforms "liberalized" the economy—but because its three-tier federal, state, and local government system fails to deliver public services and is riddled with corruption. Functioning from the bottom up, it contrasts with top-down Chinese governance. As Nathan Rich indicates, the consequence in terms of the Indian built environment is less coherent and less iconic if nevertheless attention grabbing given its size, audacity, and ability to capitalize on tropes of modernity.

After economic reforms driven by the IMF bailout of India in 1991, which included deregulation, privatization, tax reforms, controls on inflation, and opening its markets to international trade, India's economy grew rapidly, becoming by 2007 the second fastest growing economy after China. Central to this growth is India's large service industry, which accounts for 57.2 percent of its GDP and 34 percent of its labor force. This in turn has been fueled by global dominance in offshore outsourcing due to India's cheap labor and English-speaking, British-trained middleclass. Still, India's favored investment-baiting lure is the SEZ, with 143 such zones currently active and 643 more approved as of June 2012.

Vis-à-vis the world economy, India and its BRIC(S) colleagues (Brazil, Russia, India, China—and, since 2010, South Africa) operate on the thesis that China will soon become the dominant global supplier of manufactured goods, India of services, and Brazil and Russia of raw materials. While neither a political alliance nor a formal trade association, BRICS is considered to be an attack on the Western-dominated IMF and World Bank. It is anticipated that the BRICS economies will overtake the G7 by 2027. By then, Western tropes of modern-ization will no longer be tropes; they will be the new real thing.

Peggy Deamer

Chapter 9

# Globally integrated/ locally fractured: the extraordinary development of Gurgaon, India

## Nathan Rich

Globalization can't happen anywhere. The work of global production, trade, and finance is only possible in specific types of space—space with access to particular labor forces and highly specialized infrastructures that can neutralize the difficulties brought on by long distances, global communication, and the transfer of goods and information.

The past two decades have witnessed enormous growth in countries like India and China that offered the right labor pools but lacked modern infrastructure and the complex systems necessary to do global work. As a result, highly concentrated zones have emerged where physical and technical infrastructures are established to make global transmissions and communication possible. In some cases these zones are corporate parks and shipping logistics centers, in others they are entirely new cities.

One such place, on the outskirts of Delhi, is the gleaming new city of Gurgaon. In the past 20 years, Gurgaon has grown from a patchwork of small farms to one of India's most important financial centers and a hub for global outsourcing. Since 2001 the population has increased by nearly 75 percent, with over 1.5 million people reported in the 2011 census.[1] It is home to over one hundred international corporate offices, more than half of which are US-based companies, and has quickly become India's third wealthiest city by per capita income. Planners and policy-makers have been incapable of keeping up with the incredible rate of growth. As a result, private developers have been almost

**9.1**
In less than 20 years, private developers have transformed Gurgaon from a patchwork of small farms to a hub for global outsourcing. Photo by Kathryn Stutts

entirely responsible for the construction of this city, roughly the size of Philadelphia. Within this context, a new type of urban condition has emerged: an archipelago of private zones, with little public fabric holding them together. Glassy skyscrapers grow from dirt roads. Private companies provide basic services like water and electricity. Militarized fences and gates protect favored users from poorer outsiders. Simply put, Gurgaon's story is one of privatization. It represents the front line of a nation that is increasingly reliant on private companies to provide public services. It is the manifestation of a development-driven, deregulated economic power free to build a city, and its ongoing success ensures that Gurgaon will serve as a development model for elsewhere in India and the world.

## History

Gurgaon was a small farming village ten miles southwest of Delhi until India began its efforts toward economic liberalization. In terms of municipal boundaries, it is difficult to delineate the dynamic shape of the Delhi metropolis, except by a series of ever larger and less regulated development zones. The city Delhi is located in the city-sized state of Delhi, surrounded by the states of Uttar Pradesh to the east and Haryana to the west. The state is divided into two *tahsils*, and the urban core—the Delhi Urban Area (DUA)—into five Community Development Blocks. The surrounding mix of agriculture and suburb is located within the Delhi Metropolitan Area (DMA). The newer urban fringe cities in Uttar Pradesh: Noida and Ghaziabad, and Haryana: Faridabad, Rewari, Rohtak, Sonipat, and Gurgaon, fall within the outer ring of the National Capital Region (NCR). Despite urban oases like Gurgaon, the NCR is primarily rural in character.[2]

The first wave of massive expansion in Delhi and the NCR followed India's independence and partition from Pakistan in 1947, swelling the population of this once-regional city by 90 percent.[3] Population growth continued by 50 percent each decade, quickly outstripping local infrastructure services. In the 1950s and 1960s, the municipal government sought private industry to employ this new population, and eased industry's path toward growth. Not until in the 1980s—partially in anticipation of the 1982 Asian Games—did Delhi seek to enforce restrictions on land use, relocating noxious factories outside of the city center to the DMA.[4]

In 1991, the Indian government began to open their economy to international trade and investment as part of a transition from socialism to capitalism. New policies favored the acquisition and development of agricultural sites away from the city center, where oversight was minimal.[5] Along with these changes, much of Gurgaon—among several hundred other sites—was given the status of Special Economic Zone (SEZ), which, through a series of legal exemptions, allowed multinational corporations the freedom to establish tax-free, customs-free facilities for a range of functions from manufacturing to management to housing.[6] SEZs in the NCR helped investors avoid overlapping networks of control that confused the regulation and enforcement of land policy, since as many as 120 public bodies might work in the same territory.[7] Around the same time, India's largest real estate development company, Delhi Land & Finance (DLF), began buying plots of land within SEZs at extremely low cost. The Development Act of 1957 banned real estate speculation in Delhi, but Gurgaon fell outside the law's territory.

In this deregulated context, DLF had free reign. They owned much of the land surrounding the single very wide highway connecting Gurgaon to Delhi and to the Indira Gandhi International Airport, allowing direct, unimpeded connections for travel and telecommunication infrastructures. At first it seemed Gurgaon would be another of India's famed "technopolis" cities like Noida, Hyderabad, Chennai, and Bangalore, but DLF envisioned something very different. Beginning in the mid-1990s, through heavy marketing and financial incentives, DLF pursued tenants that would bring different, non-technology-driven markets to Gurgaon. The shift began in 1994 when the group completed its first commercial project, "The Corporate Park." This was the first international-class office building in the area and among the first to lease space in it were PepsiCo, GE Capital, Compaq, Mobil, and Fluor Daniel.[8] Other Fortune 500 companies quickly followed and brought with them demand for a new kind of lifestyle. Upscale residential complexes were built, many by DLF, to house this new international middle-class workforce.

Because much of Gurgaon began as a deregulated SEZ, nothing was planned in advance. There were no public services, no transportation plans, and no basic infrastructure. Despite the fact that all new buildings were wired for seamless global communication (many were, after all, call-in centers), most of the glassy high-rises had independent septic systems and electrical generators. This meant that Gurgaon had at once a strong global connection—teleconferencing rooms were ubiquitous—and a visceral disconnection from greater Delhi. Gurgaon was more "plugged in" to the global network than it was to Delhi's local infrastructure.

As more and more people left the cramped city to seek Gurgaon's open space, private complexes emerged that provided reliable infrastructure services. Land bankers assembled enormous development plots by cobbling together obscure deeds and titles from local farmers, effectively creating a now-common Indian expression on land ownership, *you don't own it until you sell it*. According to one developer, "100-acre plots could be a collection of 200 different claims, some signed with a farmer's thumbprint."[9]

At first, development on sites like these was limited to less than 12 acres. Even so, planners and policy-makers could not keep up with the rapid pace of development, and supporting infrastructure was not built quickly enough to meet demand. This led to a 2002 deregulation creating the designation, "integrated townships." Integrated townships permit additional development square-footage of at least 100 acres in exchange for the developer provision of services such as water, electricity, schools, and hospitals. More services supplied equaled further reduction in government taxes. Section 2, line vii of the Integrated Township law states, "The Developer will retain the lands for community services such as (i) schools (ii) shopping complex (iii) community centres (iv) ration shop (v) hospital/dispensary. These services will be developed by (the) developer (sic) himself and shall be made operational before the houses are occupied."[10] Although the townships were a welcome alternative to chaotic plot-by-plot developments, they accelerated the already existing trend toward the privatization of resources. The private sector's need for infrastructure outpaced the government's ability to provide it, and the government, in turn, had passed this responsibility back to developers. With the Integrated Township law, privatized water, electricity, hospitals, and schools transformed from economic trend to government policy.

Integrated townships can be legally financed by 100 percent foreign direct investment.[11] This fact, combined with the freedoms afforded by SEZs, quickly made integrated townships a clear and direct mechanism for bringing foreign money into the otherwise murky Indian market. By 2007, nearly two dozen US firms were invested in the Indian real estate market, including heavy hitters like The Blackstone Group, Hines Development, and Goldman Sachs.[12]

## Cars, malls, and the public realm

Private developers, many from abroad, were officially responsible for building the city. With little incentive to build public space or infrastructure, they utilized integrated townships to create enormous private enclaves. Many of these enclaves do in fact have town centers and parks. Shalini Vig Wadhwa, General Manager for Corporate Communications at DLF, describes one such DLF plan: "[It is a] walk-to-work concept, a shoppers [sic] delight with a variety of malls and small arcades for regular daily needs, the best schools, hospitals, entertainment via clubs and cine complexes all add to the integrated township [sic]."[13] Another design brief echoed the principles of human scale, walkability, and architectural diversity professed by New Urbanists in the United States:

> Public spaces shall create intrinsic value themselves, as the public realm is rare, yet severely needed, in today's Indian cities. These public spaces shall be filled with numerous plants, trees, ponds, and natural elements, and include zones for pedestrian and other recreational activities. The variety of residential, commercial, retail and civic components of the project will be linked together by walk-able distances. The scheme will be further composed of a mixture of different types and sizes of streets, spaces and buildings. This intelligently-conceived urban environment will provide both diversity and definition to individual localities within the township.[14]

Despite these efforts, the capacity for integrated townships to provide a diversity of public space is limited by perimeter walls. Because there is no public realm outside the townships, most township streets simply end abruptly at property boundaries. For many township residents this means their lives are contained within the boundaries of private property. One Gurgaon father explains:

> My daughters are certainly in private property when they go from their bedroom to their school. Leave their bedroom, go out of their door, catch the lift downstairs . . . and the school gate opens out onto our complex. So they don't have to cross any roads or anything like that. That was initially one of the important reasons why we chose to live here. From the bedroom to their school is about a five minute walk.[15]

Outside these boundary walls, there is no public realm, only empty plots waiting to be developed.

It goes without saying that navigating the landscape outside township walls requires a car. Between 1981 and 2001, the population of all six major cities in India—Delhi, Mumbai, Kolkata, Chennai, Bangalore, and Hyderabad—doubled, while vehicle use rose eight times.[16] This type of urban fragmentation is common to large cities worldwide, where private complexes "can be of sufficient size and complexity to act as mini-cities in themselves, and usually are poorly

**9.2**
There is little
public realm or
infrastructure
outside the
boundaries of the
large, private
integrated township
developments.
Photo by Leo
Stevens

connected and car-dependent."[17] Cars are not only the single means by which workers can move from their residences in one enclave to their offices in another, they have also become an extension of the privacy and security that Gurgaon residents have come to expect. Within the next 20 years, India is expected to grow from being the eleventh largest car market in the world to the third largest. Sprawling archipelago cities like Gurgaon encourage that trend. Already, car ownership in greater Delhi, including Gurgaon, is seven times what it is elsewhere in India.[18]

The expansion of auto travel has nurtured a new kind of lifestyle. The busy, exuberant street life that proliferates in most Indian cities is virtually absent from Gurgaon. The energy and commerce of traditional cities has been harnessed in a new kind of space—retail malls. Gurgaon is currently home to 43 malls, most built since 2007. Among these is the nation's largest, The Mall of India, which boasts 4.5 million square feet of shopping. With names like "Ambience Shopping Center" and "The Sahara Mall," these spaces are clearly not just for retail consumption, but represent a private oasis for a wealthy self-selecting group looking for close interaction with similar people. The malls are a simulacra of the public environment traditionally found in cities—a place where public activities can be planned and controlled.

The architecture of Gurgaon has likewise been transfigured into something new: a patchwork of styles and historical references. It feels like a place

built by a people without history or tradition, and as such represents a dramatic departure from older Indian cities. Office towers are designed in a glassy, space-age older style that signifies an abstract technological future. Stuccoed, Spanish-revival housing complexes named "Palm Springs" and "The Santa Barbara Towers" have blue pools and green lawns, recalling gated communities in Florida and California. Nearby, high modern condominium towers face the blistering Gurgaon sun, boasting floor to ceiling glass. Prices for these homes start at the equivalent of $200,000, or roughly 270 times the average Indian income. Conspicuously absent are the *chawls*, temples, and other native building types integral to most Indian cities.

Despite continued growth, Gurgaon is beginning to come up against the limits of its meteoric rise. Resources are ever more stretched and the contingencies necessary for maintaining Gurgaon's culture and comforts are ever more numerous and extreme. Flashy renderings of new buildings promise a lifestyle that markets won't support and that builders can't deliver.

## Infrastructure and scarcity of resources

In the spring of 2008, I visited Gurgaon with a group of architects. We were hosted by a local real estate developer who walked us through future development sites. One was beside a dirt road on the northern tip of development Sector 33, one kilometer from its closest neighbor, a sparkling new retail mall.

**9.3**
Private shopping malls have replaced the busy public environments traditionally found in Indian cities. Photo by Leo Stevens

The farmers who once worked there still lived nearby in sheet metal shacks; they watched our group skeptically as we toured their former home. Many subsequently started working as security guards in the neighboring mall, their farm long ago dried up.

As early as 2008, Gurgaon's water table was nearly depleted, so most parts of the city received intermittent supply from a 65 km drain, including this part of Sector 33 which had no tap and no functioning well.[19] The surrounding farms were, however, known to be periodically flooded by raw sewage. Today, because Gurgaon continues to lack an integrated sewer system, new buildings typically use individual, overstretched septic tanks that leach into surrounding empty sites.

This scene is in striking contrast to the buildings planned for the site. "Spaze Privy" will be a luxury residential complex, "nestled in a green and serene backdrop."[20] According to its website, "the swanky apartments at Spaze Privy are designed to complement the fine lifestyle that you have always dreamt about." Residents will enjoy modular kitchens, air conditioning, a health club, a swimming pool, high-end bath fittings and jogging tracks. Spaze Privy has presold its 3300-square-foot, million-dollar penthouse units boasting five bedrooms and five baths, and a private indoor lap pool. The website promises to protect residents from Gurgaon's scarce resources: drinking water is provided by onsite tankers and cisterns, independent diesel generators ensure 100 percent electricity back-up, and 24/7 security is maintained by an entry checkpoint and a private onsite security team. The complex will have its own school and its own grocery store. Most units will have servant quarters and rules ensuring that maids and servants follow strict security protocols. The story on the website is clear: Spaze Privy offers protection and respite from the scarcity and dangers of the city—a private oasis for an exceptional few.

This type of disconnection is everywhere in Gurgaon. Such exclusive communities are not unique, but have popped up across the developing world, emphasizing barriers. As the urban planner Peter Marcuse explains "We would expect to see a substantial expansion of these kinds of enclaves, housing many of those most directly benefitting from processes of globalization . . ."[21]

Gated communities and secure office complexes protect a wealthy upper class from the extreme poverty that surrounds them. Militarized borders and surveillance systems organize the relationship between these sites and "the outside." Sociologist Saskia Sassen describes sites like these as "'Elements of a new socio-spatial order' . . . [that have] had devastating effects on large sectors of the urban economy."[22] "New, highly polarized urban landscapes are emerging where 'premium' infrastructure networks . . . selectively connect together the most favoured users and places, both within and between cities."[23] Extreme infrastructural and logistical contingencies make this polarization possible. Because Gurgaon has no functioning public infrastructure, resources are rerouted, protected, and hoarded to serve a select few. Those who are lucky enough to live inside the fortified walls get pools and high-speed internet. Those outside lack even running water. For every rich enclave, there are many poor ones. The slum population in upwardly mobile urban Delhi is 18.7 percent relative to entire population; yet in Faridabad, the next strut over from Gurgaon, it is 46.5 percent.[24] In Gurgaon, these extremes are all the more dramatic because of Gurgaon's highly limited resources. In the pursuit of rapid growth and profit, and in the service of global interests, entrenched local problems have been summarily cast aside, allowing a bloated market to keep growing.

Water is Gurgaon's most pressing problem. At the current rate of consumption Gurgaon is projected to run out of water completely by 2040.[25] Studies by the Indian Central Ground Water Board show that Gurgaon's groundwater supply has dropped roughly six meters in the past two years. This crisis peaked in March 2008, when 70 percent of Gurgaon residents were without running water for four straight days. During that time, water was primarily supplied by private contractors who charged landowners for access to water tankers.[26] To counteract the depletion of groundwater supplies, the state government recently enacted a complete ban on new drilling for wells. As a result, as many as 40–45 percent of Gurgaon residents now pay up to 1000 rupees per month to have their water trucked in by private companies.[27]

Electricity is in equally short supply. The government provides power to Gurgaon, but it isn't remotely adequate and daily blackouts are common. The lights go off, the city is in a silent dark, and then one by one the diesel generators kick in, filling the air with exhaust. Residents say this happens so often they no longer keep track of when they are using government power and when not.[28] Residents who moved to Gurgaon years ago were promised that the noisy generators outside their windows would be temporary, but they are still in near constant use.

Legal and financial systems in Gurgaon similarly favor the growth of the private sector at a cost to public resources. The SEZs allow developers and multinational corporations to build in completely tax-free areas, which comprise much of the city. The bribery and corruption behind the financing for these projects is well documented, and is the subject of public controversy. The urban fringe continues to be developed with local government consent despite its lack of infrastructure in part because local government officials can expect personal windfalls in return for their cooperation.[29] In January, 2011, the Haryana State Industrial and Infrastructural Development Corporation (HSIIDC)—a government body overseeing public works in Gurgaon—was caught selling land it had acquired for public infrastructure use to a private developer.

Today, Gurgaon is littered with stalled construction sites. Nonetheless, ground continues to be broken on new projects promising the same luxuries. These projects are floated by bank loans that might never be paid back. Such loans are artificially easy to get, which allows an already bloated market to keep growing. There are echoes here of the recent US mortgage crisis. In Gurgaon, however, there is no complex system of derivatives and credit default swaps hiding a corrupt trail. Bankers are simply bribed outright. The "Bribes for Loans" scandal, which broke in November 2010, exposed a group of Indian developers, many working in Gurgaon, who simply paid bankers sums of cash in exchange for guaranteed construction loans.[30]

Propping up luxury with the expense of water shortages, electrical blackouts, and financial corruption hits poorest populations the hardest. As a result, violent clashes between poor residents, Gurgaon developers, and municipal authorities have become commonplace. In September, 2010, a large group of service class workers stormed the Municipal Commissioner's office, demanding infrastructure improvements. Ratan Singh, chairman of the Joint Action Forum of Residents Association, declared, "The roads are full of ditches, the sewage water is seeping into houses, and there is garbage strewn all over the place. They are only looting the people. There is no accountability of funds and nobody seems to have an idea where the money is going."[31]

Increasingly, these problems also extend to Gurgaon's wealthier residents. Many people pre-pay for luxury homes that are never finished. Others move into expensive condominiums only to find that they barely stand. Latika Thukral bought property in the World Spa complex, and when the project was delayed, she and several other residents started the World Spa Action Group. "There are no regulations for the real estate business. We bought these apartments six years ago. They were supposed to be delivered three or four years back . . . half a million to a million US dollars per apartment . . . They should have that money to deliver these apartments. They have already been paid for 90–100 percent. It means they have diverted those funds somewhere else."[32]

## A broken model and a new middle class

Capitalism, by its very nature, undermined local autonomy as well as local self-sufficiency, and it introduced an element of instability, indeed of active corrosion into existing cities. In its emphasis on speculation, not security, upon profit-making innovations, rather than on value conserving traditions and continuities, capitalism tended to dismantle the whole structure of urban life and place it upon a new impersonal basis: money and profit.[33]

In 2009 the Haryana State Government announced The Gurgaon Masterplan for 2025, a bold plan for addressing the city's many problems. The masterplan maps show a new 37,500 acre site immediately south of Gurgaon currently being prepared for what will be called "Manesar," or more commonly, "New Gurgaon." According to Bhupinder Singh Hooda, the Chief Minister of Haryana, New Gurgaon will be built on a purely Public Private Partnership (PPP) model, meaning that the government and the developers will have an equal financial stake in its construction. "There will be adequate parking space, greenery, commercial space, and open areas. The new city will be developed in the next 5–10 years. When you build a new city, you can actually plan for everything from sewage disposal and water, to roads."[34] The plan provides for an estimated 200 percent population increase—3,000,000 people—over the next 15 years, and offers many logical improvements over old Gurgaon. For example, all roads

in the planned sectors will be interconnected, unlike existing roads that end abruptly. The plan also calls for a metro connecting New Gurgaon to Delhi, providing relief to the congested Delhi–Gurgaon Expressway. Real estate investment websites are exuberant about its potential. According to Propertynice.com, "New Gurgaon . . . has all the ingredients of being the next commercial hub with better infrastructure facilities . . . and is developing as a favored investment location and new growth center as these localities satisfy the necessary requirements of accessibility, business facilities and affordability."[35]

The ease with which public officials are able to abandon Gurgaon for an altogether new dream underlines just how fractured Gurgaon has become. Private, unregulated forces built a house of cards, and as it continues to collapse they just move on to an entirely new venture. While the introduction of the Public Private Partnership as an organizing principle in the development of New Gurgaon may provide the sheen of government oversight, it should be viewed with skepticism. Policy-makers have been quick to praise the PPP model without any evidence of its effectiveness.[36] Other Indian PPPs have represented a fundamental rewiring of the relationship between the state and the market, with benefits typically skewed toward the latter. For example, in 2002 the Delhi–Gurgaon Expressway was hailed as a successful model for Public Private Partnership, but

**9.4**
A striking disconnection between old and new is everywhere in Gurgaon. Photo by Kathryn Stutts

ten years after the project's inception, the government ended up paying the private operator, Jaypee-DSC Ventures Ltd (JVL), three times the original fee on account of delays and poor planning.[37] Despite these overruns, the agreement between public authorities and JVL stipulated that the private company reserved the right to 20 years of toll collection on the expressway, and, most egregiously, included a non-compete clause stating that the government could not in the future build a competing road. The PPP therefore enabled a *private* monopoly: the worst of both worlds, neither competition nor government regulation ensure acceptable quality or basic standards.

Gurgaon is a highly intensified example of the displacement of public infrastructure recently seen in cities, nations, and economies across the globe. Austerity throughout Europe is leading to massive cuts in infrastructure spending. The congressional majority in the US is waging a war on "big government," while New Deal-era roads and bridges crumble. The author and social activist Naomi Klein writes about this trend, calling places like Gurgaon "fast forward versions of what 'free market' forces are doing to our societies."[38] She warns of a world where governments fall short and private industry picks up the slack. "We lurch into a radically segregated future where some of us will fall off the map and others ascend to a parallel privatized state, one equipped with well-paved highways and skyways, safe bridges, boutique charter schools, fast-lane airport terminals, and deluxe subways."[39] Champions of privatized infrastructure hail the efficiencies and profits of privatized public services. The lesson of Gurgaon is, left to their own devices, private markets will never produce good urbanism or places that are sustainable in the long term.

Much has been made about the "flatness" of the globalized world and the neutralization of distance and place. These arguments are built around the power of macro-processes like global travel and digital communications, which dominate the rhetoric around globalization, but take for granted the localized conditions where the work of globalization gets done. Gurgaon emerged hastily and without central planning. Public agents sped up the process with laws that deregulated the scale of construction projects, and the means by which they were financed. While these are global phenomena seen in other growing global cities, each manifestation of them is particular, and in Gurgaon's case—with a government that is almost unique in its inability to provide services—is particularly striking.

But despite corruption and the major shortcomings outlined above, Gurgaon signals an unmistakable widening of horizons for middle-class Indians. India's economy is growing at a rate of 7 to 9 percent annually, and the number of people in the middle class is rapidly expanding. For many of them, Gurgaon's privatized infrastructures, however stretched, are far more reliable than the public ones they were accustomed to in older cities. These developments represent the actualization of upward mobility for a new class of hardworking, educated Indians.

Ironically, Gurgaon's many problems have become a rallying point for these newly empowered citizens. Community groups have begun forming that advocate on behalf of citizens, provide a platform for public grievances, and take action working on the street. One example is "I am Gurgaon," an initiative aimed at "awakening a responsible, aware and vigilant populace in order to make our city a better place to live in."[40] Among its many projects are a water conservation and recycling program, a drive to plant trees throughout the city, and an effort to teach school children environmental awareness. "I am Gurgaon" is a coalition of people from diverse backgrounds. Although it formed out of hardship, it signals the emergence of an active society in Gurgaon.

The near total collapse of top-down forces in Gurgaon offers an opportunity for citizens' groups to play a more active role there and elsewhere in India than they ever have before. Empowered by money and education, these groups understand that neither government nor private development will attend to their basic needs, and they are therefore taking shape as new third category of stakeholder. As ground-up organizations who would be the primary beneficiaries of a better functioning, more equitable, more sustainable city, they may be the most important factor determining the fate of Gurgaon.

## Notes

1 "73.9 percent Increase in Gurgaon's Population," *Times of India*, April 6, 2011, accessed August, 2012, http://articles.timesofindia.indiatimes.com/2011-04-06/gurgaon/29387845_1_literacy-rate-female-population-census-officials.

2 Baleshaw Thakur, "The Structure and Dynamics of the Urban Fringe of Delhi," in *The Urban Fringe of Indian Cities*, ed. Jutta K. Dikshit (Rawat Publications: New Delhi, 2011), 176.

3 Vinod Tewari, ed., *The Role of Urban and Peri-Urban Agriculture in Metropolitan City Management in the Developing Countries: A Case Study of Delhi*, Research Study Series Number 74 (National Institute of Urban Affairs, New Delhi, 2000), 91. This was also the moment when Delhi was declared the new national capitol.

4 Ibid., 92.

5 Siddharth Raja, "Investing in India," *Urban Land* 61, 10 (October, 2002): 100.

6 Tax-exempt zones of intensive industrial activity were created in India as early as the 1990s as a mechanism to encourage foreign investment and sidestep government regulation. The term "Special Economic Zone" became widely used to describe these zones after the Special Economic Zone Policy was enacted by the Indian Department of Commerce in the year 2000.

7 I. Milbert, "Law, Urban Policies and the Role of Intermediaries in Delhi," in *New Forms of Urban Governance in India*, ed. I.A.S. Baud and J. De Wit (Sage Publications, New Delhi, 2008), 181.

8 Government of India, Ministry of Commerce and Industry, Guidelines for FDI in development of integrated township including housing and building material, Section 2.vii.

9 Anonymous Gurgaon developer, in discussion with the author, January, 2011.

10 Ministry of Commerce and Industry, Department of Industrial Policy and Promotion, SIA(FC Division), accessed August, 2012, http://siadipp.nic.in/policy/changes/press3_02.htm.

11  "Trendy Townships in Delhi," *Delhi Capital*, accessed August, 2012, http://www.delhicapital.com/real-estate-delhi/news/trendy-township-in-delhi.html.

12  Marjie Meeman, *I am Gurgaon. The New Urban India*, Video, VPRO 2009.

13  "India to be the World's Third Largest Car Market," *Express India*, December 1, 2005, accessed August, 2012, http://www.expressindia.com/news/fullstory.php?newsid=59286.

14  Excerpt from a confidential design brief.

15  Aravind Adiga, "India's Mania for Malls," *Time Magazine*, September 13, 2004, accessed August, 2012, http://www.time.com/time/magazine/article/0,9171,695915,00.html.

16  M. Ramachandran and Sameer Kochhar, eds. *Urban Renewal: Policy and Response* (Academic Foundation, New Delhi, 2009), 67.

17  Mike Jencks et al., "World Cities and Urban Form," in *World Cities and Urban Form: Fragmented, Polycentric, Sustainable?*, ed. Mike Jencks, Daniel Kozak and Pattaranan Takkanon (Routledge, London and New York, 2008), 5.

18  "Spaze Privy," accessed August, 2012, http://www.spaze.in/spaze-privy.aspx.

19  "India," accessed August, 2012, http://cee45q.stanford.edu/2003/briefing_book/india.html.

20  "Spaze Privy."

21  Peter Marcuse, "Globalization and the Forms of Cities," in *World Cities and Urban Form: Polycentric, Sustainable?*, ed. Mike Jencks, Daniel Kozak and Pattaranan Takkanon (Routeledge: London and New York, 2008), 32.

22  Saskia Sassen, "The Global City: Strategic Site, New Frontier," *American Studies* 41, 2–3 (Summer/Fall, 2000): 83.

23  Stephen Graham and Simon Marvin, "Networked Infrastructures, Technological Mobilities and the Urban Condition," *Psychology Press* (July, 2001): 15.

24  Vijay Neekhra, Takashi Onishi and Tetsuo Kidokoro, "The Inner Truth of Slums in Mega Cities," in *World Cities and Urban Form: Fragmented, Polycentric, Sustainable?* ed. Mike Jencks, Daniel Kozak and Pattaranan Takkanon (Routledge, London and New York, 2008), 343. From the Census of India, 2001.

25  1000 rupees is equal to roughly $25. An average software developer in Gurgaon makes $7500 per year. An average security guard in Gurgaon makes $500 per year.

26  "Gurgaon SEZ Developers Run Into Water Hurdle," *Business Standard*, January 20, 2011, accessed August, 2012, http://www.business-standard.com/india/news/gurgaon-sez-developers-run-into-water-hurdle/422369/.

27  Meeman, 2009.

28  Ibid.

29  D. N. Dhanagare, "On Encounter between Urban Fringe and Neoliberal Capitalism," in *The Urban Fringe of Indian Cities*, ed. Jutta K. Dikshit (Rawat Publications, New Delhi, 2011), 27.

30  Meeman, 2009.

31  Lewis Mumford, *The City in History* (Houghton Mifflin Harcourt, New York, 1968), 416.

32  "I am Gurgaon," accessed August, 2012, http://iamgurgaon.org/About.htm.

33  Mumford, 416.

34  Klein, 48.

35  "Projects in New Gurgaon," Propertynice.com, written February 5, 2011, accessed August, 2012, http://blog.propertynice.com/projects-in-new-gurgaon/.

36  Lynn B. Sagalyn, "Public–Private Partnerships and Urban Governance: Coordinates and Policy Issues," in *Global Urbanization*, ed. Eugenie L. Birch and Susan M. Wachter (University of Pennsylvania Press, Philadelphia, 2011), 192.

37  Nivedita Mukherjee, "Life is a Two-Way Street," Outlookindia.com, April 2008, accessed August, 2012.

38  Naomi Klein, "Disaster Capitalism: The Economy of Catastrophe," *Harper's Magazine* (October, 2007): 54.

39  Ibid.

40  "Canon Tree Plantation Drive for a Greener Tomorrow," *The Telegraph*, April 23, 2012, accessed August, 2012, http://www.business-standard.com/india/news/gurgaon-sez-developers-run-into-water-hurdle/422369/.

# Chapter 10

# Context: 2000

In this final (chronological chapter), returning to England where the book began, and to the Expo program pivotal to the debate binding Cole and Ruskin, is oddly appropriate; the more things change, the more they stay the same.

Of course things have changed hugely. The world and the global economy in 2000 are no longer centered in England or Europe; the dominant economies are no longer based on manufacturing; and they no longer adhere to particular nation-states. Major trends facing the global economy—the growth of the internet, cross-border mergers, business process outsourcing (BPO), and the multiplication of businesses whose business is business-management—attest to capitalism's migration of location and substance. Multinational corporations like Walmart, Starbucks, Sony Red Bull, Pfizer, Nike, ING Group Boeing, and Apple fanned out and incorporated globally. Transnational corporations like Vodafone, Phillips Electronics, Volvo, Nokia, and BP make international agreements designed by the World Trade Organization more important than those of any state government. Outsourcing, making countries like India economic players, has forced corporations to distinguish between core and non-core processes in order to concentrate on their essential strengths, shifting employment and limiting the power of labor unions. Internet growth, originally centered in America, has, since 1999, been located outside the US with Latin American growth four times that of the rest of the world.

But for all the differences between economic life in 1845 and 2000, certain similarities remain. Europe and America (if not England per se) still dominate use of the internet, for all its growth elsewhere; Europe and America still dominate—with GE, AT&T, Disney, Time Warner, News Corporation, Viacom & Seagrams, and Bertelsman—global media; the division between haves and have-nots, between the 1 percent and the 99 percent, is intact and ever more distinct; those in a position of power are still white and male; technological advances still threaten employment; the economy is just as unstable and volatile as ever—only now this affects the entire world population.

What this means for architecture is represented, as Simon Sadler indicates, by the Millennium Dome: a star architect—the profession's 1 percent—designing a bombastically unbombastic building that, despite its size, addresses no one in particular.

Peggy Deamer

Chapter 10

# Spectacular failure: the architecture of late capitalism at the Millennium Dome[1]

Simon Sadler

> Architecture immortalizes and glorifies something. Hence there can be no
> architecture where there is nothing to glorify.
>
> Ludwig Wittgenstein[2]

There are ways in which the UK's Millennium Dome of 2000, built near London
to contain a national and international celebration of life in the first year of the
new millennium, could be claimed as a success. With 6.5 million visitors, it
matched its historic forebears, the 1851 Great Exhibition and 1951 Festival of
Britain, whose respective 150th and 50th anniversaries it commemorated a year
early. The Dome affirmed a continuing role for the state in the cultural definition
of its people and its times, and this role was inclusive, liberal, multicultural. The
Dome channeled investment into an area of urban deprivation and provided a
sampling of turn-of-the-century biomorphic, surrealistic, and deconstructivist
architectural taste. Given the size of the gamble, it was a credit to the Dome's
organizers that the show opened on time and with exhibits in it. Its hemorrhaging
of money only followed a grand tradition established by the New York World's
Fairs of 1939–40 and 1964–65, for example, and by New Orleans in 1984, and
by the 1992 Columbus projects in Genoa and Seville.[3]

But fretful polls taken at the Dome in 2000 showed that while most
visitors were enjoying their day,[4] nothing indicated that they were *overwhelmed* by
the Millennium Experience. It is recalled as a debacle, especially in comparison

to the success of the Great Exhibition and the Festival of Britain. Distinct from 1851 and 1951, it is fair to say, the Dome fell short *experientially* and as a *spectacle*. This "spectacular failure," more than a cruel pun by which to title this chapter, paradoxically confirms the Millennium Dome's relevance to cultural, economic, and architectural history, because some $1.3 billion (£850 million) was unable to purchase a satisfactory spectacle. Debate over the Dome's perceived failure revolved at the time around commonplace and interrelated matters such as location, management, and content. Yet the Dome's lack of appeal was ultimately attributable to something less tangible and much harder to pin onto individual actors. On the one hand, the malfunction in the Dome's content programming is attributable to its fraught relationship with free market capitalism; on the other hand, the malfunction in the Dome's formal program is attributable to its exemplification of a mode of British design that welcomed the age of flows as though "flow" and "formlessness" are analogous. The coalescence of the two problems of form and content was nothing less than phenomenological.

Christopher Frayling, Provost of the Royal College of Art and a member of the watchdog group monitoring the quality of the Millennium Dome's contents, responded to the question of what was at stake at the Millennium Dome by joking, "The possibility of a coherent international celebration in the age of postmodernism."[5] Frayling's quip acknowledged that the organizers were presented with a potentially fascinating and exhilarating curatorial challenge—one

10.1
Richard Rogers
Partnership,
Millennium Dome,
Deptford, London,
1999, general view.
Author photo

which British designers had long wanted, intrigued as they had been since the 1960s with post-industrialization and the formation of identity. So the Dome's problem wasn't postmodernism *per se*, but the conflation of postmodernism with neo-liberalism—of confusing liquid identities with liquid markets. The Dome's visitors were offered neither a nostalgic affirmation of their British nationhood nor a futuristic vision of a reordered world. The Dome's putative general theme of Time suspended its visitors in a present threatened by change, without bearings in work, place, or belief. The Millennium Experience failed to direct its visitors' attention toward anything; it failed to structure consciousness because it was embarrassed by a tacit ideological program of "reskilling" devised to satisfy its sponsors' demand for flexible labor and the state's unease about the loss of traditional industries.

If capitalism's best-known structuration of experience is the phenomenon of the "spectacle," in which capital is condensed into an image mediating social relations and disguising structural inequality, we might expect that the acceleration of capital flows in late capitalism would produce a more *intense* spectacle. But at the Dome, it did not. In this, the Millennium Dome is a parable in the story of architecture and capitalism. At one level, it illustrates the folly of the state's attempt to script a meaningful national political program around late capitalism. At another level, it illustrates that state and capitalism alike have lost their 1851-like ability to induce wonder.[6] If the political economy scoring the Millennium Experience was late capitalism, then it follows that the Dome is a case study in the phenomenological failure of late capitalism.

Late capitalism, we could therefore speculate, is *beyond* representation, beyond spectacle, beyond even the so-called postmodern sublime—that pleasurable terror induced by the vast and unimaginable networks of capital, change, and communications that undergird it. What is intriguing about the Dome is that it attempted to induce the sublime through its size and cost, and that this effort proved comic in comparison to the *actual* postmodern sublime, which is contrarily sensed at an *everyday* level. The disconnect of scales that exemplified postmodern life circa 2000—micro and macro, desktop and network, industrial park and transnationalism—was more profoundly experienced in British daily life than at the Millennium Dome. If deterritorialization was already domesticated in visitors' own lives, it was all the more dispiriting to find deterritorialization being domesticated at the Dome's various "zones": the Dome's Talk zone, for example (designed by the Imagination Group and sponsored by British Telecom) presented "the chance to send an email and surf the net"[7]—as though that same experience was not readily available through the desktop computers invading workplaces, schools, libraries, and homes across the UK.

## Zoned out: the inscrutability of late capitalism

The phenomenological confusion induced by the Millennium Dome can be traced to an ambiguous program that evolved over several years between governments (Conservative, then New Labour), the civil service, consultants, and sponsors. The Dome was of a place (Deptford), at the putative center of a nation (in Greater

London), and at the putative center of time (near Greenwich), marked by that sacrosanct typology of a dome. A Millennium Show, performed several times a day, was accompanied by an exhibition with three general sub-themes containing a total of 14 zones: Who We Are (Faith, Body, Mind, and Self Portrait, the latter a depiction of British people), What We Do (Work, Learning, Rest, Play, Talk, Money, Journey), and Where We Live (Shared Ground, Living Island, Home Planet). But this deterritorialized zoning mirrored the deterritorializing sponsorship of the Dome by transnational corporations and signaled a squeamishness about place, nation, and belief.

Though it is the nature of expositions to enforce a consensus, the Millennium Dome, perhaps uniquely in exposition history, purported to show a consensus by eschewing its right to invent the world. "What you see shaped in the Dome was shaped by the opinions and wishes of thousands of people across the UK who told researchers what they wanted in their Millennium celebrations," the Millennium Experience Guide claimed. "People wanted the Dome to address the challenges and opportunities we face at the beginning of the new Millennium," it went on, adding, "These are issues common to people in all countries."[8]

The Dome's theme of Time had the potential to corral something akin to a transcendent popular metaphysics. Sometime Dome creative director Stephen Bayley suggested a wish-list of bold "scriptwriters" for the Dome like Elaine Scarry, Cabot Professor of Aesthetics and the General Theory of Value at Harvard.[9] A stymied Bayley resigned, and as the Dome's management rapidly turned over in the years and months leading up to the Dome's opening, the Dome's management strove to make the theme of Time more accessible. For instance, Coggs and Sprinx, the cartoon characters hastily conceived in 1999 by Dome consultants wanting to capture the imaginations of younger patrons, asked visitors "to help them keep the time machine going by filling it with bits of time—in the shape of foam balls."[10]

One challenge, surely, was that historic moments in time are made historic by events, whereas the millennium could not be historic, at least in the ostensibly secular terms demanded by the Dome, since the millennium marked no event. Britain in 1000CE or 1CE or 1000BCE brought no images or ideas to mind, and the Dome offered none. All nations are subject to the 24 hour clock measured from the Dome's site at Greenwich, but only two-thirds of the world recognized the second millennium. The only legitimate claim to the millennium's historic significance, then, was Christian, and forewords to the Dome's Guide written by the Queen and the Reverend Dr. Richard A. Burridge furnished a certain religious intonation, lightly underscored by the sacred connotations of the dome typology itself. But the decision to make one of the Dome's fourteen zones address Faith (including a History of Christianity exhibition) was controversial, with architecture by Eva Jirinca Architects and an installation by James Turrell bringing a muted, nonrepresentational, New Age religiosity to the exhibition.

According to Michael Hardt and Antonio Negri's Empire—perhaps the most-read political treatise to appear in the year of the Millennium Dome—

the epoch-defining phenomenon common to people in all countries was neither time nor faith but the ascent of a global and information-based economy, coalesced into a single capitalist "Empire" subsuming the sovereignty of nation-states and universalizing identity through (unequal) economic relations. Whether or not one accepts the details of Hardt and Negri's Marxist argument, it was hard not to be struck by the ways in which the Dome avoided all explicit reference to geopolitics, even where one of the zones (Mind, designed by the Office of Zaha Hadid) was sponsored by defense, security and aerospace manufacturers (British Aerospace and Marconi Electronic Systems). While "modern" imperialism was based around nation-states, the new "postmodern" imperialism of Empire was based on tacit transnational client relations established by ruling powers, led by the United States. Accordingly, the Dome was, as it were, flagless, without the stars of the European Union, without the crossed stripes of the UK's Union flag, and without the stars-and-stripes of the US-based multinational corporations which were the Dome's sole overseas sponsors.[11] The Millennium Dome was British, then, only to the extent that explicitly overseas exhibits were neither invited nor received.

This elaborately facile allegory of the experience of late capitalism, by turns too literal and too inscrutable, was shared across the Dome's zones. In the Money zone, visitors would understand that an economy can overheat, because the space in which they stood was hot, and the zone's "pipes buckle and bend with the heat."[12] The Work zone (designed by the studio coincidentally named WORK) exalted re-skilling, availing visitors of job opportunities available through display monitors, and supporting, philosophically and structurally, the Learning zone built above it (also by WORK) and connected to it by escalator. Play itself was instrumentalized as a technologically driven re-skilling exercise at the Dome's Play zone (designed by Land Design Studio)—"It allows us to challenge ourselves, express our creativity and discover things we did not know we could do."[13] The Play zone contained the world's largest table-football game, provided so that visitors could experience teamwork, while 5,000 Post-It notes on a wall in the Work zone reminded visitors of the synchronous challenge posed by multi-tasking and "hot-desking." At the Mind zone, the intelligence of the human learner was illustrated by "a real-life colony of South American Leaf Cutter Ants" and "a 3D mapping of the internet."[14] Likewise, Act 1 of the centerpiece acrobatic and musical Millennium Show (circled by the zones like radiating chapels) depicted an Edenic natural harmony as a multitude of balancing acts being shattered by industrialization; Act 2 recalled the "era of technology and greed" "symbolized by the construction of a giant iron tower," which collapsed to be supplanted in Act 3 "as a beautiful tree drives its way upwards from the ruins, a symbol of new life reaching into an uncertain yet hopeful future."[15] This ahistorical, uncritical parable of change without agency was surely only possible in the near-absence of charitable, educational, and labor movement sponsors. In fact, the interface with the Dome's labor was made through the US-headquartered contracting and training company, Manpower, which was extensively involved with the contracting of Dome employees ("Hosts") and sponsorship of the Work zone.

We know Fredric Jameson's famous dictum that postmodernism is the cultural logic of late capitalism, and we know that the accelerated flows of capital in the late twentieth century run through multinational corporations, globalized markets, reorganized labor, and mass consumption.[16] But the Dome could not acknowledge its liaison with late capitalism explicitly, and reciprocally late capitalism was hamstrung at the Dome by its shotgun marriage with discourses of state, identity, aspiration, and faith.[17] Here, the Dome's inability to articulate its claimed theme of Time recalls that neo-Marxist thinkers such as Walter Benjamin and Guy Debord once warned that capitalism cannot represent the portentousness of Time because capitalism dwells in a perpetual, history-denying present. As Debord put it in thesis 154 of *The Society of the Spectacle*, in a thought which is appropriate to the Dome:

> The epoch which displays its time to itself as essentially the sudden return of multiple festivals is also an epoch without festivals . . . When its vulgarized pseudo-festivals . . . incite a surplus of economic expenditure, they lead only to deception always compensated by the promise of a new deception. In the spectacle, the lower the use value of modern survival-time, the more highly it is exalted. The reality of time has been replaced by the *advertisement* of time.[18]

## The circus in the cathedral: British design and the end of aura

In addition to this critique of the Dome as a still-born effort to present the postmodern, the Dome was something of a terminal moment for the "Sixties" ethos of postwar British design as well. It was an ethos that had long accepted, welcomed even, the flattening of a centralized, hierarchical British political, cultural, and national identity in favor of one more amorphous, youthful, enterprising, popular. The Millennium Dome was to have been the apotheosis of this tendency.

The challenge of designing for an emerging postindustrial "space of flows," in which the ur-forms of modernity are not the factory, radio, silo, liner, and worker rally (as they were for, say, the Bauhaus) but the leisure center, computer network, logistics depot, airport, and music festival, became central to advanced British design. In the 1960s, Harold Wilson's Labour government, whose fascination with modernization is sometimes considered a precursor to that of the New Labour administration that presided over the Dome, addressed what it described in 1963 as the "White Heat of technological revolution" making Britain "no place for restrictive practices or for outdated measures on either side of industry." The design philosophies of Richard Rogers (since 1981 a Labour Peer) and longtime colleague Mike Davies, the chief architect and lead architect respectively of the Millennium Dome structure and of the Rest zone within, were formed by White Heat, their early years as progressive architects in the 1960s showing a fascination with technological, physical, and social mobility. White Heat was apparent, too, in the theoretical and visionary speculations of fellow travelers like the Archigram group, under whose members the Millennium Show's designer, Mark Fisher, had once trained. With barely a degree of separation, in fact, key designers at the Dome were related through training and influence by this genealogy of British, "postindustrial," White Heat design education spanning from the 1960s to the 1980s.

Signal to this movement was the importance of immaterial personal interaction, entertainment, data, consumption, and representation, with Britain sailing forth into the age of the "weightless economy."[19] The pastoral vision of White Heat imagined Britain freed by the automation of repetitive labor so that masses of Britons could take part in creative leisure and an information-driven economy, the landscape dotted with appearing and disappearing events like so many fairs and circuses. The Dome presented no history of older industrial skills, communities, or unions about which to feel nostalgic: "the supposedly 'good old days' of a job for life," the Dome's Work zone cautioned, "often led to a lifetime of boredom."[20] Richard Rogers, it is reported, initially imagined the Dome as a sublime void[21] (in his notorious 1977 essay on Piano + Rogers's Pompidou Centre, Jean Baudrillard suggested with some vitriol that emptiness would have been the Pompidou Centre's ideal content).[22] When complete, Rogers's shallow saucer stood watch over the Dome's knolls of screens—the partial realization of Archigram's Instant City projects of the late 1960s—and the vortex of Mark Fisher's appearing and disappearing Millennium Show. The training of the cast and technicians, some of whom had no previous experience in performance, "positioned the UK firmly at the forefront of contemporary circus" (a possible if unlikely emergent area of Britain's national and economic life) and would "be a valuable legacy from the Dome to the entertainment industry."[23]

A type of taste reigned at the Dome that might be described as avant-garde middlebrow or, as it was named early in the New Labour administration, a "Cool Britannia." Cool Britannia attempted to recapture, update, and re-thermostat for the 1990s the White Heat creative energy of the British 1960s. Cool Britannia's intellectual property would, it was hoped, fill the vacuum left by the large-scale departure for Asia of the UK's manufacturing base, rendering the Millennium Dome, in turn, Britain's first post-industrial great exhibition. The Department of Trade and Industry's 1998 exhibition *powerhouse::uk* [sic], positioned at London's venerable Horse Guards parade ground, served as a tiny, low-cost, high-style prototype of the Dome, its inflatable housing engineered by Buro Happold (engineers of the Dome structure) and designed by Nigel Coates (designer of the Dome's Body zone). Similar to the "Britain Can Make It" initiatives of 1946 (precursors to the 1951 Festival of Britain), *powerhouse::uk* conveyed the belief that it was possible for design to avert the crisis of UK economic restructuring. Britain's surviving competitive advantage, it was argued, was to be found in its postindustrial goods—creativity, research, finance, tourism, communications—and its global client base.

The Dome seemingly offered the triumphal moment of an architecture of images. Images are the mainstay of the spectacle, and the Millennium Dome had many images, arrayed through montages and electronic displays. But they

10.2
Nigel Coates and
Buro Happold,
powerhouse::uk
pavilion, Horse
Guards, London,
1998. Author photo

could not fill the largest enclosed space on earth, and they were mostly of a style seen in popular media, offering little in the way of a window onto an alternative reality. By contrast, the material contents of the Festival of Britain, as slight as they were, gave visitors glimpses of technologies and industries rarely-, or not-yet-seen: the world's largest sheet of plate glass; a Post Office railway; a display of new British Railways locomotives; a 74-inch reflecting telescope; historic aircraft; rear portions of an oil tanker, passenger liner, and factory ship protruded from the Sea and Ships pavilion.[24] In the great tradition of fairs that had previously showcased electrification and telephones, the Festival of Britain was a chance for visitors to learn something about the startling, new, publicly funded sciences—the atom, the radio telescope, hemoglobin. The most popular exhibit at the Dome, Nigel Coates's abstract walk-through human body in the Body zone, curiously prioritized a funhouse atmosphere over scientific insight. The chief breakthrough technology at the time of the Millennium Dome, the exponentially expanding internet, was immaterial and invisible, and the most interesting products of the Dome's sponsors were generally cloaked by business secrecy. How much more absorbing would the Mind zone have been, one study has speculated, had it revealed the defense products of its sponsor rather than the dissimulated metaphor of an ant colony?[25]

The scarcity of uniquely meaningful or rare objects at the Dome contributed to the sense that it lacked charisma; it had no *aura*. It was this want that so struck a German reviewer visiting the Dome on behalf of the magazine *Bauen und Wohnen*.[26] The lack of aura mattered because the Dome's ultimate ancestry, via the great exhibitions, was in the medieval pilgrimage destination and fair,[27] and without an aura the Dome could expect few pilgrims (to turn to thesis 20 of Debord's *Society of the Spectacle*: "The spectacle is the material reconstruction of the religious illusion").[28] The Dome declared itself a consumer product and was perceived as nothing better. And while the Dome's structure was praised as a feat of engineering, it nonetheless bore a responsibility for the project's phenomenological failure to generate a sense of event or place. It was too knowable, its plan centralized and perceived in the round, whereas the great world exhibitions were essentially impossible to visit in their entirety. The Dome was literal: this structure was how one covered a big space quickly and, oddly, it did not look particularly big from the outside. During daylight hours, its filtered interior light was lifeless, almost claustrophobic, diffused by the membrane rather than directed in the manner of, say, the oculus of the Roman Pantheon. The most dramatic moment of luminescence, which occurred after dark, was perceptible only from the outside as the Dome lit up from within. The huge interior space had no sense of scale, except at the end of the Millennium Show when the vast height was momentarily exploited by the ascending "tree of life"—and even then, it was at the expense of rendering the central space dead the rest of the time, obscured from the outer circuit of pavilions.

At a symbolic 365 meters in diameter and rising to a height of 50 meters, this largest single-roofed structure in the world was certainly iconic, and like the basilica form of the Crystal Palace, the domic form at Deptford referred to a great lineage in architectural history—the Pantheon, Hagia Sophia, the Florence Basilica, St Paul's.[29] But it was frequently observed that the Dome was not, in fact, a dome as such, but a canopy[30]—an apparently pedantic structural fact which may nonetheless have been of significance in visitors' perceptions of the Dome, which inspired the awe not of a dome (even of great domed sports stadia or the massive geodesics of Montreal in 1967 and Osaka in 1970) but of a marquee. It communicated, then, the idea not of "great architecture," but of the circus, a connotation confirmed by the 160 acrobats at its center. Yes, it recalled the spontaneist cultures of the sixties, when radical architects had imagined deploying mobile architecture to *defeat* the tyranny of monumentality and the hegemonic forces it represented—but now the spontaneist culture represented hegemony. The expo-visiting public, moreover, has historically been impressed by the *appearance* of monumentality produced instantly (as at the Chicago Worlds Fair of 1893, for instance) rather than by stalwart largeness.

The Dome was no place of pilgrimage, nor did it, by way of compensation, succeed as a fun-fair. The Dome offered weak visceral rewards. It had only one "ride" (Home Planet), and the body was rarely lifted, so that the Dome lacked vistas. The provision of sensory reward was meanwhile repaid richly at three of London's other Millennium projects. These drew on a tried-and-trusted nineteenth-century sense of spectacle, successfully feigning innocence of overt sponsorship or ideological programs. The London Eye reinvented the Chicago Worlds Fair device of the Ferris wheel, furnishing the double spectacle of the great wheeled structure and the city laid out before it; how well this had worked, too, at the Eiffel Tower of 1889. The Millennium Bridge, by Rogers's old colleague Norman Foster and former engineering collaborator Ove Arup, offered startling views (and in its initial accidental lack of structural integrity, a bodily sensation, making it an enormous crowd pleaser). The Millennium Bridge connected the opposite bank of the River Thames to the new Tate Modern gallery at Bankside, London's third major "millennial" project. Indeed, the overwhelming success of the Tate Modern is instructive by comparison to the Dome.[31] Designed by Herzog and de Meuron at the disused Bankside power station, the Tate Modern combined absence and spatial excess with a vertical circulation that wended its way up through the cathedral-like multi-storey void of its emptied turbine hall. It contained unique and valuable objects. It dispensed with household corporate names courted by the Dome. It arrogantly offered aesthetic redemption in the stead of consensus.

Compounding the ambiguity of architectural cues was the Dome's nostalgia, almost ironic, in its reference to the Festival of Britain's Dome of Discovery. Instead of being totally iconic—of itself—the Dome referred to that past icon, long lost but still dear to the generation of Rogers. Whether or not these subtleties of modern architectural history were appreciated by lay visitors, a certain retro-futurism probably was apparent, the Dome looking like what the future used to look like (i.e., a flying saucer). This was quite different to, say, the recently opened Guggenheim Museum Bilbao, which had sensationally introduced the visiting public to then-forward-looking trends in deconstructivism and to long-forgotten expressionist fantasies.

10.3
Richard Rogers Partnership, Millennium Dome, Deptford, London, 1999, interior view with the Millennium exhibits under demolition. Photo: Simon Bradley

To some extent the Millennium Experience was a distant extrusion of the "spindly" and "brief" apparition of 1951,[32] and the Dome, like the Festival of Britain, claimed to be a small town.[33] Critically, however, the Dome failed to adopt the Festival's attentiveness to clearly presented civic space—as though spatial planning, in the era of free-market economics, had been set aside with economic planning. Most commentary about the Festival of Britain found that what mattered about being there was just being there, out in the convivial throngs, illuminated nights and breezy days, whereas the Dome had no overall planner, the atmosphere of a hub airport, and only a plastic sky.

According to Martin Heidegger, the modernized world will resort, in its efforts to overwhelm its subjects, to pure extensio.[34] This was the Dome's final desperate appeal to visitors, employing anachronistic referents to scale to boast (somewhat inaccurately) that the Dome could swallow the Eiffel Tower on its side, Trafalgar Square, 94 African elephants in a straight line or 18,000 double-decker buses.[35] Had the organizers brought those real things to the Dome, they would indeed have created a spectacle—if still no mandate, with none of the revolutionary political glue that laid the ground for the Festival of Britain (the Education Act, National Health, the New Towns Act, the Town and Country Planning Act, and the nationalization program of the 1940s).[36] What the Festival of Britain and the "old" Labour Party realized is that, to be harnessed for the good of community, to carve out a public sphere, intervention into the economic has to be focused. The hemispherical shape of the Millennium Dome inevitably recalled that receding liberal-democratic dream of the "public sphere," and projected a neo-liberal dream, something we might call a "public-private sphere." The Dome's spectacular failure underscored that in an age of "flows," design cannot flow too, but must intervene decisively, damming up the flows long enough to create a state of grace apart from pure economic exchange.

## Notes

1  This chapter is based on papers I presented in 2001: "The Festival of Britain and the Millennium Dome," at The Twentieth Century Society conference "The Festival at Fifty," Royal Festival Hall, London; "Spectacular Failures," for the session "Altered Zones," The Association of Art Historians' Annual Conference, Oxford Brookes University. My thanks to the respective convenors.

2  Ludwig Wittgenstein, Culture and Value, ed. G.H. von Wright (Oxford: Blackwell, 1980), 69, quoted in Adrian Forty, "Versailles—a political theme park?," in Architecture and the Sites of History, ed. Iain Borden and David Dunster (Oxford: Butterworth, 1995), 53.

3  See John E. Findling, "Fair Legacies: Expo 92 and Cartuja 93," in Fair Representations: World's Fairs and the Modern World, ed. Robert W. Rydell and Nancy E. Gwinn (Amsterdam: VU University Press, 1994), 184.

4  See Vanessa Thorpe, "Some gems of Dome data," The Observer, Sunday, December 31, 2000, http://www.guardianunlimited.co.uk/dome/article/. When asked if they were having a fun day, 8.9 percent had "No Opinion," 3.6 percent said "No," and 87.6 percent said "Yes" in a BBC poll in August. MORI found similar results.

5  Deborah Cameron and Colin MacCabe, "Interview with Christopher Frayling," *Critical Quarterly* 41, 4 (December 1999): 48.

6  See too Mark Dorrian, "'The Way the World Sees London': Thoughts on a Millennial Urban Spectacle," in *Architecture between Spectacle and Use*, ed. Anthony Vidler (New Haven and London: Yale University Press, 2008), 41–57.

7  Anon., "Talk," *Millennium Experience: The Guide* (London: New Millennium Experience Company, 1999), 49.

8  Anon., "Introduction," *Millennium Experience: The Guide*, 8.

9  See Stephen Bayley, "A Doomed Dome," *Times Literary Supplement*, November 3, 2000, 18.

10  Anon., "Money," *Millennium Experience: The Guide*, 70.

11  The majority of the Dome's sponsors were multinational corporations whose products were percolating the globalized economy or driving it via electronics, media, and transportation. Four had earlier dropped the territorially specific moniker "British" from their names—BT (the formerly nationalized telecommunications industry of the UK); Sky television (once known as British Sky Broadcasting, and owned overseas by the world's most powerful media conglomerate); BAA Airports (the formerly nationalized airport network); and BAE Systems (a previously nationalized aerospace industry). Admittedly, the Dome numbered some quintessentially "British" sponsors, including the high street names of the stores Boots, Marks & Spencer, and Tesco, though they were shadowed by US-headquartered multinationals such as Ford, MacDonald's and Manpower. Among the Official Suppliers to the Dome were nearly as many American as British corporations. Almost all of the Dome's sponsors were based in the service sector rather than heavy industry.

12  Anon., "Money," *Millennium Experience: The Guide*, 52.

13  Ibid.

14  Anon., "Mind," *Millennium Experience*, 22–23.

15  Anon., "The Millennium Show," *Millennium Experience*, 12.

16  See Fredric Jameson, *Postmodernism, or, The Cultural Logic of Late Capitalism* (Durham: Duke University Press, 1991). See also Ernest Mandel, *Late Capitalism* (London: Humanities Press), 1975.

17  On the Dome's connection to neo-liberalism, see Jim McGuigan and Abigail Gilmore, "The Millennium Dome: Sponsoring, Meaning and Visiting," *International Journal of Cultural Policy* 8 (2002): 7, and Jim McGuigan, "The Social Construction of a Cultural Disaster: New Labour's Millennium Experience," *Cultural Studies* 17 (2003): 669–690.

18  Guy Debord, *La société du spectacle*, 1967, trans. *The Society of the Spectacle*, 1970, revised 1977 (London: Rebel Press, 1987), n.p.

19  A phrase used in McGuigan and Gilmore, "The Millennium Dome," 7.

20  Anon., "Work," *Millennium Experience*, 34.

21  See Geoff Lightfoot and Simon Lilley, "Moments, Monuments and Explication: The Standing of the Millennium Dome," *Culture and Organization* 8, 3 (2002): 244.

22  See Jean Baudrillard, "The Beaubourg-Effect: Imposion and Deterrence," trans. R. Krauss and A. Michelson, *October* 20 (1982): 3–13.

23  Anon., "The Millennium Show," *Millennium Experience*, 13.

24 See, for instance, William Feaver, "Festival Star," in *A Tonic to the Nation*, ed. Mary Banham and Bevis Hillier (London: Thames and Hudson, 1976), 52. My thanks, too, to Simon Bradley for information.

25 See McGuigan and Gilmore, "The Millennium Dome," 11.

26 See Oliver J. Domeisen, "Monuments to a Nation: Palaces, Domes, Cathedrals and Other Attempts to Entertain the British Public," *Werk, Bauen und Wohnen* 9 (2000): 28–42.

27 See, too, James Gilbert, "World's Fairs as Historical Events," in Rydell and Gwinn, "Fair Representation," 23.

28 See Debord, *Society*, n.p.

29 On the Dome's construction and symbolism see, for instance, Colin Davies, "There's No Place Like Dome," *World Architecture* 77 (1999): 50–55; Thomas A. Markus, "What do Domes Mean?," *Critical Quarterly* 41, 4 (December 1999): 4–11.

30 A point made, for instance, by Stephen Bayley, "A Doomed Dome."

31 For detailed comparison between the Dome and Tate Modern, see Domeisen, "Monuments to a Nation," 42.

32 On "Festival Style," see Banham and Hillier, "Festival Star."

33 Anon., "Introduction," *Millennium Experience*, 8.

34 Martin Heidegger, "Building, Dwelling, Thinking," in *Poetry, Language, Thought* (New York: Harper and Row, 1971), 143–161.

35 See Anon., "Dome Facts," *Millennium Experience*, 120–121.

36 See, for instance, Adrian Forty, "Festival Politics," in Banham and Hillier, "Festival Star," 30f.

# Coda: liberal

## Keller Easterling

The cast of *Beyond the Fringe* discussing "Home thoughts from abroad":

*Jonathan Miller*: Of course they have inherited our two party system.
*Dudley Moore*: Oh yes. How does that work?
JM: Well, let's see, you have the Republican Party, you see, which is the equivalent
of our Conservative party. And then you have the Democratic Party
which is the equivalent of our Conservative Party. And then, of course,
there are the liberals in the shape of people like . . .
*All*: [thinking and muttering] Yes, yes, yes . . .
DM: Are the liberals Democrat or Republican?
*Alan Bennett*: Yes. As is convenient for them.[1]

* * *

Market activities often escape theories of capital. Yet for Marxist adherents, the
market continues to behave according to predicted logics. Other scholars and
theorists, recognizing discrepancies, define market logic in terms of familiar
theories of capital that only need to be updated to reflect new aggregations or
new modes of organizing and concentrating assets. Still others, who say that
theoretical capital no longer exists, reify it by creating terms like "post-capital."
Despite a broad and fleeting consensus about what constitutes capitalism—
privately owned assets and trade based on exchange value—this chapter resists
adherence to any overarching theory. Theoretical capital *never* existed. While there
is a desire to create an omnibus theoretical platform, there might be more
instrumentality in admitting that the so-called logics of the free market or
the hegemonic politics of capital can only be willfully mapped onto market
phenomenon. Marxist theories of capital exclude important evidence to make
the world fit a theoretical template. Theories, and the language we use to construct them, sometimes harbor conundrums as well as deliberate manipulations
of meaning. The contradictory details and the fictions and fairy tales on the

ground that also associate with the market are as valuable as any broad consensus about it.

Infrastructure building is often cast as the mascot of theoretical capital and the spearhead of its unstoppable march. For instance, as historian Marc Linder notes, the development of heavy industries like rail "approximately mirrored the geographic penetration of capital . . ."[2] The constellation of scripts that accrete around the heavy industries frequently describe the need for lubrication and freedom so that the collective self-interest of the free market—the invisible hand—may proceed unimpeded as a natural force. At the same time, the large organizations of infrastructures themselves generate significant administrative and bureaucratic structures to rival the state and its military. They also engineer their own subsidies from elected government.

Infrastructure is then a pawn in the longstanding conundrums between laissez-faire and regulation. It is a character in the myth of an unmanipulated free market that must be manipulated to optimize its freedom—an instrument of both the invisible and the visible hand. Moreover, as the scripts of liberalism in their various incarnations from classical liberalism, to New Deal liberalism, to neo-liberalism agitate for the freedom of divergent actors in the market, they pull the story of infrastructure building toward diametrically opposed political positions. In these contradictory scripts—as they double and mimic each other, as they are manipulated by political persuasion—the spatial manifest of infrastructure is caught in a powerful but often absurd ideological vortex. This chapter looks beyond what-ever value lies in attempts at pure and comprehensive logics and asks instead, what is the instrumentality of the impure doubles and fictions that accompany liberalism?

\* \* \*

## The "liberal label"

Simply locating the various strains of liberal thought in philosophical, political, or economic realms should be sufficient to demonstrate that its diverse usage disqualifies it from the banner of any absolute campaign. Speaking of the broader philosophical tradition, political philosopher John Gray has written, "It is a basic error to search for the essence of something as heterogeneous and discontinuous as the liberal tradition. Liberalism is not the kind of thing that has an essence."[3] In political philosophy, liberal thought that interrogates the relationship of the individual to a regime of governance percolates through traditions of different cultures (e.g., French and Anglo-Saxon) with many antecedents and ongoing branches of inquiry. While these inquiries share "family resemblances," as Gray has suggested, the very spirit of the tradition is at odds with a prescription about polity or "a partisan claim for the universal authority of a particular morality." Rather, it is about "the search for terms of coexistence between different moralities."[4]

Yet the liberal label has, of course, been affiliated with very specific party politics. Ronald D. Rotunda's careful study of its usage in the British political context from the nineteenth to the early twentieth century, as well as its migration to the Hoover and FDR administrations, outlines multiple countervailing usages.

When attached to a political platform, the label became more specifically defined, and yet occasionally it also had to bend to respond to political events and fortunes. When, in the early nineteenth-century British Parliament, the Whigs adopted the term liberal, it was massaged as adherents to the party moved between opposition to, and occasional adoption of, Tory principles. As the Tory party adopted the label "Conservative," "Liberal" would settle in as the opposing party. Rotunda tracks shifts in England over the course of the century from "classical" liberalism to new liberalism. New liberalism tolerated notions of welfare while still being opposed to socialism. It advocated for freedom from the tyrannies of big business that shaped the market to its own advantage. Its philosophical sentiments migrated from Jeremy Bentham toward John Stuart Mill. The economic sentiments in Adam Smith's philosophy began to include those curbs on the freedom of *homo economicus* that would secure more freedoms for more people.[5] In 1908, Churchill defended new liberalism against claims of socialism by saying, among other things, "Socialism exalts the rule; Liberalism exalts the man. Socialism attacks capital; Liberalism attacks monopoly."[6] By the 1920s and 1930s, John Maynard Keynes was one of many who adopted the liberal party as the party that might moderate between fascism and socialism. Rotunda writes:

> Old classical liberalism was poured out of the bottle and welfare liberalism was poured in; but although the contents were new, the label "liberalism" was not changed. Since welfare liberalism grew out of basic elements of classical liberalism, it seemed reasonable to many that the same label would be used to describe both philosophies.[7]

During the 1930s in the United States, the liberal label was undergoing similar transformations, even oscillations, in meaning. "Liberal" did not become an important word in American politics until the New Deal, and while President Herbert Hoover would use the word to signal economic liberalism or laissez-faire, Franklin Delano Roosevelt would adopt the word to signal something closer to social liberalism or progressive capitalism that would attract Republican party support for his Democratic policies.[8] Rexford Guy Tugwell, who advised FDR on policy and served as the director of the Resettlement Administration, recalled once talking to Roosevelt about the origin of his use of "liberal," but Roosevelt, well understanding the political power of discrepancy in the script, did not answer him, but rather "laughed and asked if it mattered."[9]

Alan Brinkley, a historian of the US depression era, returns to the same British roots of the liberal label in *Liberalism and its Discontents* (1998), arguing that

> late nineteenth-century (or "classical") liberalism, epitomized in the ideas of the Liberal Republicans of the 1870s and 1880s, rested securely on the individualistic, antistatist assumptions of John Stuart Mill and the Manchester liberals of England. What came to be known as "liberalism" in mid and late twentieth century America has emerged to a significant extent out of a conscious repudiation of the antistatist

elements of that classical tradition. Modern liberalism has been, instead, an effort to build the case for a more active and powerful state (even if one in which ideas of individual rights play an important, often central role). The antistatist liberal tradition of nineteenth-century America has, therefore, increasingly become the property of those who in the twentieth century are generally known as conservatives (or, as some of them prefer, libertarians).[10]

Like Rotunda, Brinkley locates this doubling of the term "liberal" in the New Deal era, reporting the exasperation of conservatives like Herbert Hoover who saw their philosophy lifted for another use. Hoover would characterize the New Deal as the opposite of what he regarded as authentic liberalism, as a loss of individual freedom that was closer to "fascism or communism."[11] In the US post-New Deal period, "liberal" and "conservative" have been used in opposition. The liberal label in contemporary US politics is associated with the left, and linked by opponents to a tradition of "big government" and support for social programs.

Meanwhile, a strain of thought from two Austrian émigrés, Ludwig von Mises and Frederick Hayek, would amplify sentiments about a so-called "true liberalism" standing in contrast to fascism which would go on to be influential in the late twentieth century. Von Mises's 1927 book, *Liberalism*, when translated into English in 1962, was titled *Free and Prosperous Commonwealth: An Exposition of the Ideas of Classical Liberalism* to avoid confusion over the ideological migration of the term in the post-war period.[12] Later editions would work to establish a proper lineage of thought and track the use of the label, which for von Mises meant simply "private ownership of the means of production."[13] Inspired by von Mises, and coming on the heels of a world war over totalitarianism, Hayek would publish *The Road to Serfdom* in 1944, which similarly argued against central government control but nevertheless outlined a role for government in economic planning. Keynes read the book on the way to the Bretton Woods Conference and wrote to Hayek to compliment him on "a grand book," although it was not clear to him precisely how the degree of government planning would be advocated or how it would be assessed.[14]

Those who look for the origins of so-called neoliberalism in a contemporary context, like Marxist geographer David Harvey, return to a moment just on the heels of FDR's presidency when the liberal label would be adopted for a position that swings back through its geographical and ideological migrations. In 1947, the Mont Pelerin Society, a group that included economist and philosopher Friedrich Hayek, Milton Friedman, and Ludwig Von Mises adopted this label.[15] Dealing selectively with the larger philosophical tradition as well as the history of party politics, the Society attempted to reconstruct a true, proper tradition of "classical" liberalism. Hayek traced a lineage of Anglo-Saxon thought from John Locke to Adam Smith to fashion a defense against Keynesianism, regulation, and state intervention of any kind. Harvey argues that while analysts questioned the rigor of the argument, it garnered political support among private wealth, think-tanks, and corporate organizations. It gained academic legitimacy when Hayek and Friedman were awarded the Nobel prize in 1974 and 1976 respectively. Years later, Hayek would be a touchstone for Margaret Thatcher and Ronald Reagan in their global sea change in monetary policy. The triumph of Reaganomics, coinciding with the sympathetic policies of Thatcherism, propelled these ideas in a global context and engendered polarized positions domestically. The neoliberal state that Harvey constructs is one with widening class separations, deregulation, concentrations of wealth, susceptibility to financial crisis, uneven global development as directed by the "Washington Consensus" of the International Monetary Fund (IMF) and the World Bank, and a new association between private global actors and nationalist sentiment. While liberalism, in most of its incarnations, has been put forward as a bulwark against either socialism or fascism, Harvey finds in neoliberal policies a new kind of authoritarianism.[16]

Yet it is not only those on the left, like Harvey, who see in the liberal tradition the dangers of authoritarianism. Indeed, the most formidable critic of the philosophical tradition of liberalism, Carl Schmitt, theorized fascism as its inevitable outcome. Political scientist and Carl Schmitt scholar Joseph P. McCormick draws "clear lines of succession back to Schmitt in all of the major components of contemporary American conservatism," especially those strains associated with Hayek.[17] McCormick discusses fascism as a "radicalization of liberalism." McCormick claims that there is even "a certain fluidity between liberalism, with its apparently insurmountable categorical contradictions, on the one hand, and the phenomenon of fascism, on the other which may not be an altogether distinct alternative to liberalism, but which itself appears to be a product of and solution to, liberalism's theoretical-practical impasses."[18]

Neoliberalism in the US is synonymous with neoconservative positions and a reaction against the political liberalism of the "nanny state" that impinges on the freedom of the individual. The Tea Party movement, emerging during the 2008 election season and flourishing during the first years of the Obama presidency, rediscovered Hayek. Conservative broadcasters like Glenn Beck cite Hayek's The Road to Serfdom and Constitution of Liberty as foundational theory cautioning against the potential despotism that can result from big government.[19] Additional strains of contemporary liberal thought, such as those associated with libertarianism or anarchism, swing between the left and the right and between radical and conservative camps.

For anthropologist Aihwa Ong, the neoliberal state does not create a single monolithic enemy. She challenges characterization of "neoliberalism as a tidal wave of market-driven phenomena that sweeps from dominant countries to smaller ones" and wants to see how "Homo economicus . . . becomes translated, technologized and operationalized in diverse, contemporary situations." In an altered landscape of neoliberal governance populated by new institutions (NGOs and IGOs), and by states that have given up some of their power to proxies, she finds both new dangers and new opportunities for, for instance, tracking the treatment of labor and leveraging needs beyond those related to the citizenship and suffrage offered by the state.[20]

Liberalism in the political science formulations of liberal internationalists or neoliberal institutionalism is an international relations response to realist politics. In texts such as *Power and Independence* or *After Hegemony: Cooperation and Discord in the World Political Economy*, Robert O. Keohane and Joseph S. Nye counter realist global politics with theories about cooperation and international interdependence as orchestrated by international institutions. As in realist formulations, nation states are still the primary actors, although the problems being managed are more directly related to market issues rather than security problems, and they are frequently managed with the technical tools of game theory.[21] This kind of "soft power" or a more recent variant "smart power" remains influential in US foreign policy as the grand strategy of internationalism that John Arquilla and David Ronfeldt identify in their theories of noopolitik.[22] International relations scholar Stephen D. Krasner endorses the apparatus of neoliberal institutionalism in his assessments of the compound forms of sovereignty that any nation juggles, analyzing situations in which various global players in both economic and political situations face multiple, overlapping, and often contradictory logics, laws, and jurisdictions. For Krasner, neoliberal institutionalism is only the most appropriate framework for deploying his technical analysis that must attempt to model stakes within decoupled and hypocritical sovereignty.[23]

Constructing new authorities in an international sphere of global regulation and governance, world society theorists reference the larger philosophical tradition of liberalism to address the individual as an increasingly important subject. Yet they must repeatedly make the distinction between the liberal tradition they claim and, as John W. Meyer has written, the "'neo-liberal' with its raw economistic meanings."[24] Even though the distinction between economic and social liberalism does not produce a durable clarification or separation, the separation is attempted again thusly:

> In many analyses (particularly those focused on the extremes of a revanchist neo-liberalism), the liberal system is about markets, markets are about exploitation, and the subjective freedom of market participants is reactive false consciousness. In the view put forward here, global liberalism has spread as a political, cultural, legal and quasi-religious model of collective action and organization.[25]

As they observe activist organizations in a similar international sphere of influence, political scientists Margaret E. Keck and Kathryn Sikkink see an uneven network rather than an even global diffusion of liberal thought. They argue that activist networks are not "conveyor belts" of liberal politics. Political action lies elsewhere, although it may find opportunity to demand accountability for existing inequalities in this uneven development. They conclude that liberalism alone "lacks the tools to understand how individuals and groups, through their interactions, might constitute new actors and transform understandings of interests and identities."[26]

Despite the longstanding oscillations of the liberal label as well as its refractions through various disciplines, it continues to attract hopeful attention and utopian energies from those who, knowing its scatter of associations, might shrewdly use the script to either alter the terms of a discussion or attach to a long-standing discourse that may even benefit from the label's oscillations and multiple meanings.

In their book *The Science of Passionate Interests: An Introduction to Gabriel Tarde's Economic Anthropology*, Bruno Latour and co-author Vincent Antonin Lépinay consider the work of sociologist Gabriel Tarde. Tarde questioned the terms of economics itself, the existence of *homo economicus*, the visible or invisible hand, and the assumed "providence" that accompanied these beliefs. Concerning the notion of liberalism Tarde wrote, "I am well aware that the liberal school of economists advocates the non-intervention of the state, but advising the state to withdraw when its presence is indiscreet and harmful to its own ends is nonetheless speaking as a statesman and positing rules for an intelligent policy."[27] As a science, Tarde suggested that economics was measuring the wrong indicators, and he chose instead to observe the values and passionate interests generated in social networks, marked by irrational exchanges and contagions that spread through culture. Latour and Antonin Lépinay quote Tarde: "There is no manager more powerful than consumption, nor, as a result, any factor more powerful—albeit indirect—in production than the chatter of individuals in their idle hours."[28] They remind us that Tarde's work was prescient of the viral social networks that are currently central to our economy. Yet in the midst of clearing expectations about cultural scripts they invoke a discussion of liberalism:

> If we agreed once and for all to apply this idea of immanence without any transcendence, could we not once again engage in politics? This politics that the sectarians of Mammon, God of Providence and of automatic Harmony, and that those of the State have been forbidding us from practicing for so long—yes, a politics of liberty. Liberalism then? Why should we be afraid to use the word, as long as we remember that its opposite can only be the term "Providentialism"?[29]

In another example, network theorist Yochai Benkler adopts the term "liberal" to recapture some potentially redemptive qualities of digital peer production on the web. Like Tarde or Latour, he celebrates social engines of economy. While the economic and social aspects of liberalism are often considered separately, Benkler theorizes forms of freedom stemming from a new economic platform—the non-market production of information in shareable networked resources. "Their value is purely derivative from their importance to the actual human beings that inhabit them and are structured—for better or worse—by them."[30] As Benkler considers the possibilities of the new digital platform, he proposes to go beyond the notions of property or market that often appear in liberal thought to consider other human agencies of exchange and production that produce freedom through cooperation rather than self-interest.

Assembling a number of incarnations of liberal thought is perhaps sufficient to provide, while not a comprehensive survey, a sampling of the volatility in the term—volatility consistent with the paradox built into the tradition. As historian Jerrold Seigel has written, "Liberal politics thus vacillates between exalting the state and defending against it, while simultaneously alternating between idealized and demonized visions of society and human nature."[31]

\* \* \*

## Infrastructure and the liberal label

Infrastructure development, as an occasional mascot of liberalism or a utopian liberal state, is a potent subject of investigation. As counterpoint to his fellow Viennese émigrés Hayek and von Mises, economic historian Karl Polanyi considered the funding of heavy industries and large infrastructure projects in *The Great Transformation*. Polanyi writes about the ways in which these projects prompted the creation of what he describes as "*haute* finance"—an "undisclosed social instrumentality at work in the new setting, which could play the role of dynasties and episcopacies under the old . . ."[32] Polanyi considers the "Hundred Years' Peace" and its aftermath. The Hundred Years' Peace, he suggests, might be the name given to the period between 1815 and 1914, a time filled with many small wars, civil wars, and colonial aggression but no sustained general war. The Hundred Years' Peace is coincident with growth in large private civilian organizations, the largest of which were often associated with infrastructure building. The independence of these businesses sponsored the central beliefs of at least one version of economic liberalism.

Polanyi was suggesting that something had shifted, and this was a peace that "rested upon economic organization" that had little to do with war.[33] Indeed many financiers, like the Rothschilds, gambled with war and used it like a valve that could be turned on and off to create currency differentials and their related profits. Piecemeal or "isolated" disturbances could be profitable while sustained war between the major powers would be disastrous.

> Powers got a strangle hold on backward regions, in order to invest in railways, public utilities, ports and other permanent establishments on which their heavy industries made profits. Actually, business and finance were responsible for many colonial wars, but also for the fact that a general conflagration was avoided . . . For every one interest that was furthered by war, there were a dozen that would be adversely affected . . . Every war, almost, was organized by financiers; but peace also was organized by them.[34]

The entrepreneurs and financiers behind heavy industries such as submarine cable, rail, construction, or extraction companies, although they may be publicly owned at some moment in their history, were building large global organizations—organizations so vast that they claimed parity with the state. A nation may conceive of a national highway system, a regional hydroelectric network, or a public national broadcast system, and the infrastructure may be designed to support military or commercial needs in which the state has some stake. Still, some of the most common infrastructures of transportation and communication were initially developed not as public works but as private international enterprises that necessarily developed a management apparatus to administer large numbers of people, and a treasury comparable to that of its host states. The heavy industries were not just waiting to attend to the home state as its contractor of public works or military logistics, but were, rather, working for one of many different national clients. Infrastructures were an economic engine that required legislation, created the need for the banks and stock exchanges of *haute* finance, and established values worth defending militarily. Nineteenth-century British construction firms like Brassy and Peto, after having completed a number of projects at home, began to expand abroad until they were themselves considered to be a "European power" of sorts. Business historian Alfred D. Chandler Jr. has noted of such corollary American organizations that the "visible hand of management replaced what Adam Smith referred to as the invisible hand of market forces."[35]

By the end of the nineteenth century, the US had laid over 200,000 miles of railroad across its continent. Chandler writes, "For several decades the consolidated railroad systems (U.S.) remained the largest business enterprise in the world."[36] Chandler famously used the US railroad to make a case about the supremacy of private enterprises over public enterprises—including the military—to provide "administrative training" and to develop managerial paradigms for emerging multinational enterprises.[37] While the mid-century rail deployed military models of management, the scale of operations by the end of the century required another degree of innovation that no longer involved the military. Rail was the Wal-Mart of the late nineteenth century. Chandler writes as much in a passage worth quoting in full:

> No public enterprise, either, came close to the railroad in size and com-
> plexity of operation. In the 1890s a single railroad system managed
> more men and handled more funds and transactions and used more
> capital than the most complex of American governmental or military
> organizations. In 1891 the Pennsylvania Railroad employed over
> 110,000 workers. In the same year the total number of soldiers, sailors,
> and marines in the United States armed services was 39,492. The
> permanent managerial staff . . . [of the Post Office] . . . was smaller
> than that of the major railroad system. Two years later when the expen-
> ditures of the federal government were 387.5 million and its receipts
> 385.8 million, those of the Pennsylvania Railroad were 96.5 million
> and 135.1 million. That year the total gross national debt of 997 million
> was only 155 million more than the Pennsylvania's capitalization of
> 842 million. In the United States, the railroad, not the government or
> the military, provided training in modern large-scale administration.[38]

The conjunction between railroads and construction forged another link to international finance. Banks often molded financial instruments against the needs of heavy industries involved in extraction, construction, railroads, and telegraph. Their scale was in direct proportion to the scale of the construction endeavor and the amount of money that needed to be amassed to accomplish it. Linder notes that between 1840 and 1870, a "handful of bankers and contractors controlled nearly all railway building in the world, outside the U.S.A."[39] Chandler notes that "the nation's first railroad boom provided a basic impetus to the rise of the large-scale construction firm and the modern investment banking house."[40]

Heavy industries delivering infrastructure and technical capacity shared not only a global financial market but also a need for international technical coordination. They not only generated powerful administrations to rival the state, they developed independent, international organizations of cooperation and peace. On May 17, 1865, in the context of Polanyi's Hundred Years' Peace, the International Telegraph Union (ITU) held its inaugural conference to discuss coordination among telegraph users. The chairman, M. Drouyn de Lhuys, likened the proceedings to a "Peace Conference" to prevent the misunderstandings that are often the result of war. Telecommunications historian Anton Huurdeman has noted that it "was the first international agreement concerning most of Europe since the Peace of Westphalia in 1648."[41] At the signing, delegates of the member nations posed for a group photograph that, unlike the Peace of Westphalia, would not be the subject of commemorative history painting.

The creation of the International Telegraph Union, one of the earliest international organizations, marked the advent of a new form of international sovereignty quite different from Westphalian sovereignty, which was chiefly concerned with the balance of power among nation states. The ITU members had come together not as diplomats to a peace treaty, but as delegates sorting out a number of expediencies that, however much a matter of tedium, would have long-term effects on the formatting of global communications. The International Electrotechnical Commission (EIC) was founded in 1906 to set standards for electrical equipment. The groups simply resumed contact between and after the world wars, establishing common standards for radio use as an "open source" network of sorts, allocating frequencies or coordinating to repair destruction. As a relatively independent public/private parliament convening both private companies and national representatives, it was similar to countless other extra-state organizations, the growth of which was concurrent with the growth of multinational or transnational business enterprises towards the end of the nineteenth century. The influence and power embedded in international infrastructures and the organizations that control them have a broad effect upon the everyday lives of most people on the planet.

Even though the hierarchical administration of business developed its own governance or its own heavy visible hand, this structured authority paradoxically also fueled the notion of *homo economicus*, laissez-faire, and the utopian liberal state, as well as the myth of the market as free, natural, self-balancing, and necessarily independent of state regulation. Polanyi argues that management and cooperation between business entities and between public and private admin-istrations such as ITU coordinating the activities of independent entrepreneurs were *manipulations* demonstrating the impossibility of its magical freedom. Moreover, either cartels on one end of the spectrum or trade unions on the other may fight to increase their freedom from regulation. While he rejected the authoritarianism of Communism, he wished to point out the role that regulation had played in creating the so-called "free market"—an oxymoronic term in Polanyi's formulations. The so-called "free market" has never, Polanyi argued, been free. He wrote, "Laissez-faire was planned; planning was not."[42] Polanyi continues to question who is liberated in this liberal world:

> With the liberal the idea of freedom thus degenerates into a mere advocacy of free enterprise—which is today reduced to a fiction by the hard reality of giant trusts and princely monopolies. This means the fullness of freedom for those whose income, leisure, and security need no enhancing and a mere pittance of liberty for the people, who may in vain attempt to make use of their democratic rights to gain shelter from the power of the owners of property. [43]

Finally, Polanyi's position is that "liberal philosophy . . . leaves no alternative but either to remain faithful to an illusionary idea of freedom and deny the reality of society, or to accept that reality and reject the idea of freedom. The first is the liberal's conclusion; the latter the fascist's."[44]

The end of the Hundred Years' Peace is, of course, marked by global conflicts in which the balances of power are disrupted and nations deputize infrastructure for world wars. In the post-World War II years, prefaces for new editions of von Mises and Hayek that appeared in the 1960s worked to disentangle the notion of liberalism from their Keynesian chapters. International organizations like ITU, GATT (later WTO), IMF or the World Bank, who had been the instru-ments of planning as directed by groups of states, began to develop policies encouraging liberalization of utilities and free market trade. IMF, the World Bank and GATT—the international financial institutions of Pax Americana—espouse free market deregulation while retaining post-World War II, Keynesian-era, global financial regulatory administrations. The institutions are themselves instruments of market manipulation. They set up policies that encourage the free-market, free trade globalism, and liberalization of state run institutions like banks and utilities while also monitoring currencies, interest rates, and trading policies. The infrastructures of trade and telecommunications reflect this shift, yet the policies brought with them all of the paradoxes that haunt the notion of liberalism.

For instance, in arenas of global trade, the "free zone,"—which, prior to the last few decades, was usually a fenced enclave for duty-free warehousing and manufacturing—has recently become a formula for urbanism, a formula that is itself an infrastructural technology. In the 1960s and 1970s, propelled by scripts about nation-building and free trade, promoted by intergovernmental organi-zations like UNIDO or the World Bank, and touted among economists and global financial consultants, the Export Processing Zone (EPZ) was designed to be one means by which developing countries might enter the global marketplace and attract foreign direct investment. Operating under authorities independent from the domestic civil law, the zone offered a space of exemption with everything from tax holidays to relaxed regulation of labor and environmental laws. The EPZ, as an initial, and purportedly temporary, experiment evolved over the ensuing decades to be a broadly disseminated permanent form, while it was increasingly becoming the vessel of free market rhetoric in China and the Middle East. As EPZs multiplied, they also upgraded, breeding with other increasingly prevalent urban forms like the campus, technopole, or office park. These hybrids incorporated a full complement of residential, resort, education, and administration programs designed to benefit from streamlined logistics and legal exemptions. Yet the zone was and often remains the Maquiladora, host to sweatshops and the perfect vessel of corporate externalizing. While the zone has proven to be a suboptimal economic instrument for many countries, global business has become addicted to incentivized urbanism with its lubricated exchanges, cheap labor and legal exemptions. Previously backstage, the zone has taken a position center stage to become a primary organ of global urbanism and a world city paradigm. The zone is extolled by industry boosters as a generous instrument of free market advantage. Yet, since it trades state bureaucracy for potentially even more complex layers of parastate governance, it is itself an instrument of market manipulation and a perverse tool of economic liberalism. Echoing Polyani, "Laissez-faire was planned."

The so-called "liberalization" of utilities like those for telecommunication has been similarly caught between philosophical contradictions. The ITU was just one of a thickening cloud of international organizations, intergovernmental organizations, non-governmental organizations, and global financial institutions (like the World Bank) which, beginning in the 1980s, were pressing for liberalization or privatization of monopoly telecoms like those throughout Africa. In the last 150 years, the ocean floor has received hundreds of strands of submarine cable of all types for telegraph, telephone, and fiber-optic infrastructure. Submarine cabling was one of the heavy industries of the late nineteenth century (among shipping, rail, construction, and mining) that necessitated the development of multinational enterprises, stock markets, and international organizations. East African shores, for instance, first received telegraph cables to connect to their European colonizers. Yet until recently, despite being one of the most populous areas of the world, it remained in a broadband shadow with no fiber-optic submarine cable link and less than 1 percent of the world's broadband capacity. While telecommunications in Africa has recently been distinguished by deprivation, it is now often heralded for its explosive growth. The expansion of new infrastructure capacities into densely populated developing countries has sponsored new models for governance and business. Broadband is written into the platforms of national governments and into the development goals of international organizations like the World Bank and the United Nations. Access to mobile telephony—what the World Bank has called "the world's largest distribution platform"—is treated as a right akin to the right to water or food.

An East African country like Kenya is a good place to sample the political and economic consequences of multiple strains of liberalism as well as new layers of extra-state governance. In play are scripts of, for instance, the laissez-faire liberalism of nineteenth-century telegraph cable contractors, the liberalizing free market of "Washington consensus," and the new liberalism sometimes associated with the digital collective commons. From the vantage point of East Africa, one can measure the difference between a late nineteenth-century world, with a handful of extra-state organizations operating in the margins of national power, and one in which a thick constellation of international organizations, intergovernmental institutions (e.g., the East African Community (EAC) or the New Partnership for Africa's Development (NEPAD)), multinational enterprises, international financial institutions (e.g., the IMF, the World Bank, or the African Development Bank) and non-governmental organizations are advising, funding, researching, investing or alternatively, withholding any of this attention. As the story of Kenya's eventual cable system unfolds, policies of liberalization frequently become policies of regulation, even when these various regulatory frameworks can be used, ironically, to force competition. The new invocations of liberalism associated with the creative commons also encounter paradox as the global entrepreneurs of mobile telephony borrow crowd-sourcing techniques for sharing collective knowledge as a means of creating a customer base for product marketing.

Against all reason, the power of the liberal label seems to increase as its contradictory meanings proliferate on a continuum that spans between opposites. It finds neither pure ally nor enemy in the complex matrix space of infrastructure, and yet it undergirds policy as it is enacted in the newest consortia of global governance. In any one construction of the script, one must continually inquire about whose freedom is celebrated. Moreover, another assessment of its organizational and political disposition is necessary to provide any meaningful sense of how it actually works in culture. What is the organization enacting? What does it privilege or deny?

While architects may be focused on the object forms created by their discipline, a training in reading the active forms that create political disposition in organizations like infrastructure space will provide a very different set of instruments with which to operate on and adjust markets, cultures and polities.

## Notes

1  Alan Bennett, Peter Cook, Dudley Moore, and Jonathan Miller, *Beyond the Fringe*, directed by Duncan Wood (1963; London: Acorn Media, 2005), DVD.

2  Marc Linder, *Projecting Capitalism: A History of the Internationalization of the Construction Industry* (London: Greenwood Press, 1994), 75.

3  John Gray, *The Two Faces of Liberalism* (Cambridge: Polity, 2000).

4  Ibid., 27, 138.

5  Ronald D. Rotunda, *The Politics of Language: Liberalism as Word and Symbol* (Iowa City: University of Iowa Press, 1986).

6  Ibid., 29.

7  Ibid., 27.

8  Ibid., 18-31, 32, 52–63.

9  Ibid., 59.

10  Alan Brinkely, *Liberalism and its Discontents* (Cambridge, MA: Harvard University Press, 1998), 282–284.

11  Ibid.

12  Bettina Bien Greaves, preface to *Liberalism: A Socio-Economic Exposition* (San Francisco: Cobden Press, and Irvington-on-Hudson, NY: The Foundation for Economic Education, Inc., 1985) in Ludwig von Mises, *Liberalism: the Classical Tradition* (Indianapolis: The Liberty Fund, 2006), ix.

13  Ibid., 158.

14  F. A. Hayek, *The Road to Serfdom: Text and Documents, The Definitive Edition*, ed. Bruce Caldwell (Chicago: University of Chicago Press, 2007), xxxvi.

15  David Harvey, *A Brief History of Neoliberalism* (Oxford; New York: Oxford University Press, 2005).

16  Gray, *The Two Faces of Liberalism*; Harvey, *A Brief History of Neoliberalism*.

17  John P. McCormick, *Carl Schmitt's Critique of Liberalism: Against Politics as Technology, Modern European Philosophy* (Cambridge; New York: Cambridge University Press, 1997).

18  Ibid., 13–14.

19  "Glenn Beck does Hayek's _The Road to Serfdom_«Taking Hayek Seriously," accessed July 31, 2012, http://hayekcenter.org/?p=2719; Justin Lahart, "The Glenn Beck Effect: Hayek has a Hit," *Wall Street Journal*, June 17, 2010, accessed July 31, 2012, http://blogs.wsj.com/economics/2010/06/17/the-glenn-beck-effect-hayek-has-a-hit/.

20  Aihwa Ong, *Neoliberalism as Exception: Mutations in Citizenship and Sovereignty* (Durham, NC: Duke University Press, 2006), 12–13.

21  Robert O. Keohane and Joseph S. Nye, *Power and Interdependence: World Politics in Transition* (Boston; Toronto: Little, Brown and Company, 1977); Robert O. Keohane, *After Hegemony: Cooperation and Discord in the World Political Economy* (Princeton, NJ: Princeton University Press, 1984); Stephen D. Krasner, *Sovereignty: Organized Hypocrisy* (Princeton, NJ: Princeton University Press, 1999).

22  John Arquilla and David Ronfeldt, *The Emergence of Noopolitik: Toward an American Information Strategy* (Santa Monica, CA: Rand Corporation, 1999), 27–28.

23  Stephen D. Krasner, *Sovereignty: Organized Hypocrisy* (Princeton, NJ: Princeton University Press, 1999), 60–61.

24  John W. Meyer, "World Society, the Welfare State, and the Life Course: An Institutionalist Perspective" in *World Society: The Writings of John W. Meyer*, ed. Georg Krücken and Gili S. Dori (London: Oxford University Press, 2010), 280–295.

25  Ibid., 292.

26  Margaret E. Keck and Kathryn Sikkink, *Activists Beyond Borders: Advocacy Networks in International Politics* (Ithaca, NY: Cornell University Press, 1998).

27  Gabriel Tarde, *Gabriel Tarde: On Communication and Social Influence, Selected Papers*, ed. Terry N. Clark (Chicago: University of Chicago Press, 1969).

28  Bruno Latour and Vincent Antonin Lépinay, *The Science of Passionate Interests: An Introduction*

to *Gabriel Tarde's Economic Anthropology* (Chicago: Prickly Paradigm Press, distributed by the University of Chicago Press, 2009).

29  Ibid., 5.

30  Yochai Benkler, *The Wealth of Networks: How Social Production Transforms Markets and Freedom* (New Haven: Yale University Press, 2006), 7–16, 19–20, 278–285.

31  Jerrold E. Seigel, foreword to *An Intellectual History of Liberalism, New French Thought* (Princeton, NJ: Princeton University Press, 1994).

32  Karl Polanyi, *The Great Transformation: The Political and Economic Origins of Our Time* (1944; Boston: Beacon Press, 1957), 10.

33  Ibid., 10,18.

34  Ibid., 16.

35  Alfred D. Chandler, Jr., *The Visible Hand: The Managerial Revolution in American Business* (Cambridge, MA: Harvard University Press, 1977), 1.

36  Ibid., 88.

37  Charles F O'Connell, Jr., "The Corps of Engineers and the Rise of Modern Management 1827–1856" in *Military Enterprise and Technological Change*, ed. M. R. Smith (Cambridge, MA: MIT Press, 1985), 90, 116; Robert G. Angevine, *The Railroad and the State: War, Politics and Technology in Nineteenth Century America* (Stanford: Stanford University Press, 2004), xvii.

38  Chandler, Jr., *The Visible Hand*, 204–205.

39  Marc Linder, *Projecting Capitalism: A History of the Internationalization of the Construction Industry* (London: Greenwood Press, 1994), 15.

40  Chandler, Jr. *The Visible Hand*, 94.

41  Anton A. Huurdeman, *The Worldwide History of Telecommunications* (Hoboken, NJ: John Wiley & Sons, 2003), 219.

42  Polanyi, *The Great Transformation*, 147.

43  Ibid., 265.

44  Ibid., 264–265.

# Afterword: architecture without capitalism

## Michael Sorkin

Crammed into Zucotti Park last year, Occupy Wall Street tried to imagine an architecture without capitalism, even in spite of it; the possibility of standing *outside* the system. It proved difficult. The insurgent little city, founded in equity, vamped the real one all around—and simultaneously acted as an inverted special free trade zone for decommodified speech—but eventually it got cold and the cops came. That community, however short-lived, was indelible and its message received: how you choose to assail the system is a product of how you understand it. Occupy understood it at once precisely and diffusely. As the slogan evolved into *We Are The 99%*, though, the critique of capital became articulate and the struggle was quantified, secured to the primal political tether: distribution.

All architecture distributes: mass, space, materials, privilege, access, meaning, shelter, rights. The inevitable nexus of architecture and capital is one of its core fascinations, one of the reasons it can be so efficiently and abundantly *read*. That the legibility of the ostentation all around Zucotti Park—and the deployment of every conceivable police technology to assure Wall Street's perquisites remained unassailed—is only the zillionth instance of architecture's insistence on making its role perfectly clear. In the main, architecture only abets the transparency of capital's inequities. Even the most robust architectural revolutionaries seldom do more than currency conversion, exchanging the material for the symbolic.

What is to be done? Can architecture live without capitalism? Possible approaches:

1.  The old-timey vulgarity of simply looking at architecture as reflexive superstructure on the economic base yields nothing practical. The Man's capacity to co-opt races ahead of our ability to invent, and we, enamored of invention, buy a ticket to ride. Architectural form has completely lost its power to be

dangerous and only its absence—or its violent destruction—threatens anyone. This lesson is not lost on a variety of both state and non-state combatants, including those who created Occupy's reciprocating other across the street at Ground Zero. As ever, though, the question is: who will be left out in the cold? Connoisseurship is not exactly the enemy but its promiscuity can be, especially when seduced by the sublimities of extent. Just because we can understand, and/or deconstruct, any taste culture doesn't mean we must approve of it. The semiotics of evil isn't the same as those in *Graphic Standards*, which embodies a central predicate of resistance, in this case to gravity.

2. Or, the occupation could actually proceed down its own implicit highway and—instead of throwing up encampments on the real estate surplus designated "public" space—move into the trading rooms and live there. Why acquiesce to the ossified production relations inscribed so vividly in the city made by the market? A progressive politics is irrelevant without the courage to demand redistribution. However you parse capital in its historic formation, whether this is the era of Late Capital, Global Capital or Bain Capital, the descriptor is merely convenience. All economies are distribution engines and we vet their moral adequacy via the ethics of appropriation and sharing. What's wrong with the Park Avenue apartment or the Aspen condo is not a matter of the crown molding or the wainscoting, it's the unequal aggrandizement of space, convenience, and privilege embodied and represented. This is obvious, less so what to do about it. In the classic articulation in *The Housing Question*, Engels suggests that the solution is not the meager compensation of meanly built workers' terraces at the blighted end of town, but moving into the surplus space on Central Park West, a highly economical solution.

3. We might test the pathways of renunciation, the sustainable, Gandhian austerities of simply refusing to play ball with consumption, ceasing to be the Strasbourg geese of capital. Indeed, the exponential rise in American obesity threatens to turn each of us into architecture, big as a house. We've certainly been down this path before but there are those, Amish and anarchists and ashram-dwellers, who make these alternatives work, who do (more or less) opt out. Localism is worth thinking about if it can offer a riposte to the "have it your way" co-optations of the multi-nats. In its modern incarnation via our "Enlightenment," politics originated in some state of nature, whether mean and brutish or paradisaical where everyone emerged blinking from their pre-capitalist primitive hut. No coincidence that the ubiquity of this figure—whether Semper's, Laugier's, or those recorded in the intrepid sketchbooks of the explorers in the great age of European colonial expansion—was part of this great era of historicism and linearity, the necessary origin point for someone's foregone conclusion. It's an act that keeps getting repeated, as in the twentieth-century discourse of the *existenzminimum*, the primitive hut of modernity, with its redolent distributive and tectonic simplicities, establishes both an origin point and a zero degree. Back to the trees?

4. We might truly look into the nature of informality, in its perpetual state of negotiation and push-back with the law, as the medium of permanent resistance. Recent thinking has demonstrated that informal operations in the urban realm are not simply a "state of exception" in which the marginal ply their alternative spatial methods while scrounging for a droplet of trickle-down. Rather, as Ananya Roy and others have argued, informality is an "idiom" that is practiced at every level in places like India or Brazil, a form of planning that uses legal hermeneutics, evasion, passivity, and violence to continuously remake the landscape of both construction and rights. This idea of a spatial tractability that is the subject of continuous contention offers both a promising situation, one in which the disenfranchised can continuously find strategic openings for the inscription of their desires and rights, and one in which needs can be modeled at more and more levels, wrested from the terrains of marginality and brought to the center of town. On the other hand, the inbuilt insecurities of such a field of operations give scope for no end of "creative destruction" as strong powers arrogate—via shifty legalism or outright expulsion—the territories they wish to infuse with surplus value.

5. We assert another formula for our rights: the right to the city, the best axis available nowadays. If this means, first, that we demand that property retreat before our demands of access and assembly, then we find a vital tractability, a space of *occupation*. If it means that capital reconfigure itself to accede to our dreams of other ways of living, other relations, other cities, other fantasies, we will have so interrupted and bedazzled its prospects that we can restart the engine of history and ride it down the line. The relevance of utopia is always in its ephemerality: you can learn a lot from dreams.

6. Is there an insurgent style of assimilating/encountering/being in the city? Modernity, as a mode-of-life, and the city have emerged as an intertwined articulation, and the city has spun itself around the variety of perceptual apparatuses that have allowed us to love it, consume it, know it. We've been *flaneurs*, cruising the boulevards with ostentatious purposelessness. Shoppers, liberated from our private confines to mingle with spectacle and otherness unguarded. Drivers, with that fast seriatim view of a space of radical elongation. Film-makers, with our recombinant synthesis of spaces that both are and never were. *Derivistes*, with our blithely deliberate detachment trying our best to experience an aleatory authentic, to chart the unconscious, that space of nearly no accidents. Stoned. Kidnapped. Caught in a shower. Is there a perceptual appliance that turns the capitalist city into its other, flips it, a real *detournement*? Let's keep looking, bumping into strangers, conducing random events. Success will always be evanescent (attempts *are* the outcomes) but failure is always completely clear: if every route across town brings you to McDonald's, the apparatus is defective.

7. OK, then, we *really* celebrate our visionaries. This category is defined by the *present impossibility* of what it alerts us to. It is, of course, necessary to be critical about the condition of impossibility and to be clear about the necessity for limits. A vision that does not include our bodies is ruled out as

not-architecture. We fight capital's big plans by defending our own corporeal construction. There's certainly a conspiracy to make habitation and haberdashery commutative and we must take care not to let the Man camouflage us from ourselves by dappling us with art-for-art bromides and celebrity, studding our skulls with diamonds. Nor should we surrender to our own side's dour, paternalist theories (so often produced between sips of Sancerre as if the way we live our lives is just incidental) and simply assume that all iconoclasm is just another strategy of bourgeois repression. Call it negation if you insist. We cross the bridge of irony or cynicism at some risk: who wants a joyless revolution? Why overvalue Archizoom at Archigram's expense? Why the preference for silence over laughter? A decisive hammer blow is unlikely, but death from a thousand jokes stands a chance.

8.  We wait for the contradictions of that vaunted creative destruction to prove exactly how uncreative it actually is. If the system seduces and abandons its every subject, enslaves us each to a mortgage and leaves every house underwater, everyone will have to move to higher ground, which means saying "fuck it." Marx dreamed of just this kind of collapse. What happens to building when capitalist relations of production are subtracted? Let's find out! Socialism in one dorm room? Crash pad? *Werkbund*? Neighborhood? Town? City? Country? Planet? To find out we must continue to confront a dilemma scarcely unique to liberalism: how much state is enough? I know this much: a welfare state beats a warfare state.

9.  We enter the communism of disembodiment, download our entire capacity onto silicon or its successor and, becoming pure mind, defeat the very palpability of property. Well, maybe this is a step too far: mental architecture is just a metaphor. Let's leave it at that.

# Index